VOTERS' CHOICE

VARIETIES OF AMERICAN ELECTORAL BEHAVIOR

Gerald M. Pomper
Rutgers University

VOTERS'
CHOICE

VARIETIES
OF AMERICAN
ELECTORAL
BEHAVIOR

Dodd, Mead & Company
New York   1975

Copyright © 1975 by Dodd, Mead & Company, Inc.
All rights reserved
No part of this book may be reproduced in any form
without permission in writing from the publisher
Printed in the United States of America

Library of Congress Cataloging in Publication Data

Pomper, Gerald M.
   Voters' choice.

   Includes bibliographical references and index.
   1. Elections—United States. 2. Voting
—United States. 3. United States—Politics and
government—1945-   I. Title.
JK1976.P66   324'.2   75-679
ISBN 0-396-07199-6

To those who have taught me

    public citizenship and family love—

Celia Pomper
Moe Pomper
Isidor Pomper
Lillian Michels
Emanuel Michels
Lorraine Cohen
Sol Cohen

CONTENTS

FIGURES

TABLES

PREFACE

No politically conscious adult today needs to be convinced that in recent years great changes have occurred in American politics. Abroad, the cold war has melted into détente, while Vietnam has forced reevaluation of the nation's mission. Domestically, the black revolution has challenged the conscience of the United States, while American complacency has been disrupted further by economic and social insecurity. Within government, the proud office of the presidency has been besmirched by corruption, near impeachment, and forced resignation.

Further evidence of national metamorphosis is available in the limited area of electoral politics. From 1960 to 1972, presidential contests showed astonishing variability. Close elections were followed by landslides, and Republican victories succeeded Democratic triumphs. Virtually all of the accepted truths of political science came into question during these years, from the solid Democratic character of the South to the inherent Republican character of the expanding suburbs. Along with questions about the stability of the nation, doubts appeared about the persistence of its voting patterns.

Given these changes in circumstances and behavior, analysis of the American electorate must also change. Two decades ago, an intellectual breakthrough was achieved in the discipline of political science. This movement, the "behavioral revolution," advanced the profession toward the goal of scientific rigor, established new methods of analysis, and promoted the development of empirical theory. Perhaps the most notable achievements of this period came in studies of electoral behavior. Led by researchers of the University of Michigan, scholars refined the techniques of survey analysis, challenged many accepted but untested assumptions, and established a body of findings and hypotheses that remain basic to the work of any present or future investigators.

These achievements, however, did not result in final and definitive truths, which are foreign to any true science. In new circumstances, new findings and new theories are required. This necessity is all the greater when we research questions of voting behavior, for these questions are relevant to the basic nature of democracy itself. Elections remain the primary means for popular control of government. Any conclusions about the character of the electorate inevitably go beyond purely descriptive statements and take on the nature of normative evaluations. It is therefore vital both that these statements be as accurate as possible and that we acknowledge their limited applicability to new situations.

Previous findings on voting have often been distorted to denigrate the American electorate. Without malicious intent, but still with real consequences, the voters have been portrayed as limited in their capacity to understand political events and issues, and as subject to devious manipulation. The danger of such statements is not only that they may be false—or true only in some circumstances—but that they may be believed. A notable political scientist, V.O. Key, warned that political reality might then be changed for the worse to conform to these dismal portrayals.

My own evaluation of the electorate is more optimistic. My earliest political memories are of family discussions about presidential elections. The older persons in my unrepresentative world were all partisan Democrats, and they voted without exception for Franklin Roosevelt and usually for all other Democrats. Yet, even now, I cannot dismiss their ballot choices as reflections of pure partisanship, inherited tradition, or sociological reflex. They chose, after considerable discussion, because of their positions on issues and their evaluations of the capabilities of candidates. I believe that similarly serious thought has been devoted to politics in many other American homes, past and present.

Stimulated by these memories and beliefs, I have undertaken this book. In contemporary America, I find considerable evidence that voters are indeed responsive to the real political choices presented to them. Admittedly, some electors' behavior and some elections defy reason and analysis, but much that occurs in American politics is, I believe, both comprehending and comprehensible. To some extent, voters have always displayed basically sound sense in their judgments, but this thoughtful element has been underestimated. To some additional extent, the capacity of voters has increased significantly in recent years. For both reasons, the national electorate deserves detailed examination through a scientific analysis of voting behavior based on the evidence presently available. Such an analysis should be an accurate and contemporary portrait of the American voter, with particular attention to his evolution during a tumultuous period. This is the goal I have sought to realize.

In this endeavor, I have three audiences in mind. First, I hope these chapters will speak to the profession of political science, both those who are sampling it as students and those who have made it their lifework. Second, and perhaps even more important, is the larger public, including members of the electorate. Clearly there is a lack of confidence today in American political institutions. The import of this book, however, is that these failings should not be attributed to the nation's citizens, who are ready to respond to the electoral challenges presented to them. Rather, the primary responsibility is that of the country's political leadership, the third potential audience for this book. A constant theme of the book is that of the critical role of parties and candidates in presenting vital issues to voters for their judgment. If my book has any readers among political elites, I hope they will use it in challenging the nation to overcome its problems and to restore its promise.

A variety of sources and methods are used in this volume. Wherever possible, I have employed quantitative data to support my presentation; statistics can provide a precision and a standard of accuracy that are difficult to attain in prose alone. To relieve any problems in understanding, I have also tried to present verbal arguments and to provide nontechnical explanations of the statistics. Thus, if readers find it necessary to pass over the quantitative material, I remain hopeful that they will follow the verbal discussion. To make the subject manageable, I have confined the research largely to presidential elections from 1960 to 1972, and to the most vital factors. I readily admit that much remains to be done.

As I present these arguments, and their supporting analyses, I am gratified by the help I have received, and discomforted by the burdens I have imposed on others. My debts are greatest to those, largely my colleagues at Livingston College and Rutgers University, who read and commented on chapter drafts: Emmet Hughes, Judson L. James, Marilyn Johnson, Henry A. Plotkin, Gordon J. Schochet, David C. Schwartz, Sandra K. Schwartz, and Vicki G. Semel. Mark A. Schulman must be individually thanked. In addition to comments on other chapters, he originated and performed the analysis that is the core of Chapter 9. I am grateful for his willingness to allow me to include in this book a study that owes all of its sophistication and insight to him.

Conversations with other colleagues have been less immediately relevant to this volume, but highly valued. These advisers include: Anthony Champagne, Kathleen A. Frankovic, Richard Lehne, Wilson C. McWilliams, Jennifer V. Plotkin, Neal M. Pomper, Alan Rosenthal, Barbara Salmore, Efraim Torgovnik, my graduate students in the spring of 1973, and my undergraduate seminar students in the following fall.

The quantitative data for the book were made available by the Inter-University Consortium for Political Research and were originally collected by the Survey Research Center and the Center for Political Studies of the University of Michigan. Neither the original collectors of the data nor the Consortium bear any responsibility for the analyses or interpretations presented here. In addition, Angus Campbell deserves special gratitude for permitting me access to previously closed variables on attitudes toward racial integration in 1972. As a user, I also gladly acknowledge the genius of the *Statistical Package for the Social Sciences*, developed by Norman Nie, Dale Bent, and C. Hadlai Hull.

My analyses of these materials were made possible through the able instruction and data management of Stephen Salmore. Further contributions were made by Leonard Champney, Genia Graves, Virginia Hans, Laura Greyson, Shelley K. Hartz, and Steve Koffler. Pressed by deadlines, the final typing was done by Vera Lee, Karen Osowski, Edith Saks, Cindy Wilk, and an inestimable secretary, Mary Wilk.

This book was supported financially by grants of the Rutgers University Research Council and Faculty Academic Study Program, which paid for a semester's leave and other expenses; by the Rutgers University Center for Computing and Information Services, which provided grants for data analysis; and by an Eagleton Institute of Politics' subvention for typing. I also acknowledge the courtesy of the *American Political Science Review*, the *American Journal of Political Science*, and *Society*, which have permitted me to include here revised versions of published articles. William Oman of Dodd, Mead has provided both psychological and material support.

In the long causal sequence that precedes any book, one's kinfolk have strong, if indirect, effects. I have tried to recognize these distant influences in the dedication. More immediate contributions have been made by my own family. Marlene not only has read the manuscript, but lovingly has reminded me that a gamma correlation is not the alpha and omega of life. Marc, David, and Miles kindly have provided me the opportunity to share in their continuing growth into reasoning citizens and decent men.

Gerald M. Pomper

CHAPTER 1

THE OBSCURE
AMERICAN VOTER

Who is the American voter?

Although founded on the premise that legitimate government requires "the consent of the governed," the United States has long puzzled over its own electorate. The power of the voters has been proclaimed and restrained, as the wisdom of their choices has been praised and condemned. The self-portrait of the American voter is of both a hero and a villain.

The conflict in American attitudes has been evident throughout the nation's existence. Alexander Hamilton contemptuously concluded, "your people, sir, are a great beast," but still argued for direct popular election of the Congress.[1] George Mason, on the other hand, was one of the most democratic members of the Constitutional Convention of 1787, but found popular election of the president as irrational as "to refer a trial of colors to a blind man."[2] Even as James Madison insisted that "a dependence on the people is the primary safeguard of good government," he supported institutional barriers against "the superior force of an interested and overbearing majority."[3] As Hamilton wryly observed, the persons "most tenacious of republicanism were as loud as any in declaring against the vices of democracy."[4]

Our uncertain stance toward the voters has been evidenced in ambiguous institutions. Popular sovereignty is recognized in electoral choice of a half-million officials from precinct committeemen to president. The wisdom of the voters is assumed in asking them to decide on state constitutional amendments and legislation by referenda and to determine the details of school budgets in local votes. Yet popular decisions are severely limited by restrictions on terms of office, judicial review, fixed tenure of

1

officials, and the reservation of important functions to nonelected commissions and public authorities. The world's first mass democracy also imposes the most elaborate legal restrictions on the right to vote. The world's most powerful person, the president, is still formally elected by an unknown Electoral College of 538 members.

In calm times, the nation seemed able to live with its equivocations and its shadowy electorate. Geographically isolated, growing ever more prosperous, smug in its missionary zeal, the United States only episodically confronted fundamental questions of democratic theory. There were challenges, to be sure, in population expansion, slavery, and industrialization, but political institutions did not change fundamentally. The United States remained at an arrested stage of political development,[5] a classic preserved from the seventeenth and eighteenth centuries. Even the Marxist revolutions that won power in a fourth of the globe failed to impinge on America. A conservative like Justice Holmes typified the self-assurance of the nation when he defended the civil liberties of communists. "If in the long run the beliefs expressed in proletarian dictatorship are destined to be accepted," he argued, "the only meaning of free speech is that they should be given their chance and have their way."[6] Confident of American institutions, Holmes saw no threat to political stability in the doctrines that would influence every other polity.

Today, however, America's self-confidence is irrevocably shattered; complacency about its political institutions no longer exists. The airplane and the telephone ended the nation's isolation, and the nuclear-armed ballistic missile ended its geographical security. Photographs from outer space have revealed the truth that the United States is only a small neighborhood within the global village. The nation's economy, once self-contained, now depends on decisions made in the gold markets of Europe or at the oil wellheads of Saudi Arabia. The dogma of growth has been challenged by the specters of overpopulation, air and water pollution, and the disappearance of open space. The missionary benevolence of America has been rejected abroad and abandoned at home after the nightmare of bringing "democracy," death, and destruction to Vietnam. Racial conflict mocks the national promise of equality.

In the last decade and a half, change has come most dramatically to America. The nation's youngest elected president could confidently promise on his inauguration in 1961, that it would "pay any price, bear any burden, meet any hardship, support any friend, oppose any foe to assure the survival and success of liberty." Such pride soon disappeared. A scarce dozen years later, another president would be satisfied with the withdrawal of American troops and the return of prisoners-of-war from Vietnam, even while he began to worry about the possibility of his impeachment and removal from office.

These years have encompassed a wrenching, if not a revolution, in virtually all American institutions, within and outside of politics. The family has been challenged by its loss of economic and socialization functions, spatial separation of generations, divorce rates as high as 50 percent, and the decline of birthrates below the level of population replacement. New contraceptive methods have contributed to a sexual revolution that likely will lead to the ending of premarital virginity. Universities have opened their doors to ethnic minorities and their offices to women, ended traditional curriculum requirements and parietal rules, and begun to share decision-making power with students. After a quarter of a century, the military draft has ended, as the armed forces entered a competitive labor market to meet reduced quotas. Television networks now dominate communications, as competitive newspapers and general-purpose magazines have disappeared. Economic power has become increasingly centralized with the development of conglomerate corporations. In one of history's greatest mass migrations, a majority of blacks have come to live outside of the South.

The political changes during these years have been equally significant, but more traumatic. A nation that prided itself on the use of ballots in place of bullets now finds the rifle and the handgun to be as relevant to political decision as the television camera and the voting machine. Assassination of John Kennedy made American entrapment in Vietnam inevitable; assassination of Martin Luther King and Robert Kennedy marked the end of their dream of an integrated society. American college students have been killed by other American youths at Kent State University and Jackson State University. Urban ghetto revolts from 1965 to 1968 occurred in almost every urban community in the nation, leading to hundreds of deaths and to destruction of neighborhoods that continue today to resemble bombed cities.

These events have challenged the accepted political institutions of the United States. Revered symbols such as the flag, the Supreme Court, and the presidency have been derogated. Since 1960, the once-inviolate Constitution has been amended four times; a fifth revision impends; and new proposals range from campaigns to permit school prayers and prohibit abortion, to the complete revisions urged by the Center for the Study of Democratic Institutions and the Black Panthers. Protest marches, civil disobedience, and mass demonstrations have become new and accepted methods of political action. Pioneered by southern blacks, these tactics were adopted by antiwar protesters, and have now been accepted by white opponents of integration and school busing. The potential for widespread civil conflict has risen as each group has turned away from traditional behavior.

The ultimate effect of these social and political changes is unknown.

The complacent tradition of American politics would predict that the new forces eventually would be peacefully suffered and absorbed by the political system. Given their survival over a long period of time, the persistence of governmental institutions is likely. The voices of dissent and protest are clamorous, but disaffection is overtly evident only among relatively small and isolated minorities. Even among these persons, violent protest has apparently diminished. In the larger society the airplanes still run on time; officials receive their pay regularly; and drivers stop at red lights. Breakdown or revolution is possible, but muddling through is a safer bet.

Other possibilities remain. To recall past violence and discontent is not a mere exercise in history, for the political changes underlying the violence will continue to affect the nation. Although mass urban violence has declined, deliberate attacks on policemen and nihilistic kidnappings and assassinations have spread. Although college campuses are superficially quiet, the political disaffection of the young continues. Blacks, once passive or optimistically integrationist, have turned increasingly to support of "black power" and even to separatist ideologies. While most Americans still obey the law and pay their taxes, barely a majority voted in the last presidential election; fewer than half believe the government operates for the benefit of all citizens; and only a quarter consistently support the president.

Further political change may be impending. Even if relatively few voters personally protested in recent years, all of the electorate witnessed and agonized over these events and surely were affected to some degree. The tragedies of the 1960s and 1970s were not remote performances, but the acts of Americans committed in full view of their fellow citizens. Personally or vicariously, it was the voters and potential voters who sat at lunch counters in Greensboro or abused those who sat; who saw their children dynamited in Birmingham or set the charges; who rallied to protest or support the war in Vietnam; who rode or destroyed school buses in Michigan; who shot or were shot in Watts and Newark and Detroit; who wrote letters and signed petitions and paid for advertisements; who cried at the shootings of John Kennedy, Martin Luther King, Robert Kennedy, and George Wallace; who fought on both sides of police barriers at the 1968 Democratic Convention in Chicago; who resisted and attended the marches to Washington, Selma, Cicero, and the Pentagon.

These searing experiences have been branded onto the minds of Americans, compelling new thought. The turmoil of the United States has revived basic issues of political dispute, leading to renewed debate over the premises and practices of American democracy. The electoral process, central to national institutions, has been central in the theoretical argument also. The challenge to political institutions necessarily has called into question the role of voting, the character of the electorate, and the quality of its choices. As Americans have tried to understand the torment of their nation, they have also tried to understand themselves. Although the hazy portrait of the American voter could remain untouched in periods of calm, such unconcern was inappropriate, indeed impossible, amid the shocks of recent years.

TWO VOTER PORTRAITS

The recent anguish of the United States has not only been intense, but surprising in its very existence. Academic observers and practicing politicians were convinced before 1960 that the nation had reached "the end of ideology"[7] and that politics had become no more than disputes over which men should apply which means to the achievement of consensual goals. Alexis de Tocqueville might have been forecasting the Eisenhower presidency when he wrote: "In the absence of great parties the United States swarms with lesser controversies, and public opinion is divided into a thousand minute shades of difference upon questions of detail. The pains that are taken to create parties are inconceivable, and at the present day it is no easy task. In the United States there is no religious animosity . . . there is no jealousy of rank, there is no public misery to serve as a means of agitation."[8]

The storms that broke after 1960 revived ideology and also renewed interest in the character of the parties and the electorate. The accepted portrait had depicted the voters as relatively uninterested, unknowledgeable, unconcerned with public policies, and unfree of social and political restraints. But, over the years, a disparity developed between this portrait and the realities of intense and expanding popular participation in the multitudinous forms of political action. The allegedly "silent generation" of the 1950s was succeeded by brash youthful protesters. The passive Negro of the traditional South was replaced by the angry black militant. The loyal partisan gave way to the issue-oriented voter. As the disparity grew, a revised portrait of the electorate became necessary.

The Dependent Voter. Two portraits of the American voter have been drawn. There are some similarities in these two portraits, but their foci are substantially different. The first is that of the dependent voter, based on a series of surveys of presidential elections beginning in 1940. The focus of this portrait is on the long-term factors affecting the electorate and the voters' consequently limited attention to contemporary issues and individuals. Although the findings are sometimes distorted when retold, the central thrust of these studies is denigrating to the electorate. It is described as choosing candidates because of influences established considerably before a given campaign, such as social characteristics, or traditional party loyalty. Dependent voters pay little attention to political events generally, and even less to specific issues of public policy.

The dependent voter does not rely primarily on his own resources and opinions in making political choices. Rather, he relies on the cues of his social groups—his economic class or race or accustomed party. Following these cues often may serve an individual's objective interests, but the association is highly contingent. The dependent voter does not make an autonomous choice on the basis of the issues and candidates. He relies instead on indirect and uncertain relationships.

"It is abundantly clear," as one author summarized this description, "that the voter of today does lack both high political interest and an urge to participate in the political discourse. The voting studies indicate that political discourse is limited, sparse and desultory. Indeed, most voters make up their minds, and act ultimately on that decision, even before the campaigns begin. Family background, cultural milieu, all of the inchoate pressures of 'socioeconomic status' seem subtly to work on the voter in a process which is neither rational nor accompanied by high interest."[9]

Substantial research supports these conclusions. In particular, the voting studies provide data on two related subjects: the political capacity of individual voters and the causal influences on balloting. Dependent voters are deficient on both grounds. Few give serious consideration to public matters. Even the majority who do vote are not greatly concerned over the outcome. Beyond voting, most refrain from further participation in organized political life, such as financial contributions, attending political rallies, or membership in community organizations.[10]

The capacity of dependent voters for informed judgment is limited. On the two most vital issues of the 1948 campaign, for example, only a sixth of the voters could report accurately the position of both Harry Truman and Thomas Dewey.[11] On a longer series of issues in 1956, no more than a third was able to offer an informed opinion on any particular policy relevant to the election choice.[12] A broader perspective on politics is still rarer. In 1956, only 2.5 percent of the population were "ideologues," who "clearly perceived a fundamental liberal-conservative continuum on which various of the political objects might be located." If less elaborate conceptual schemes of politics are included, this group still constituted only an eighth of the population.[13] Similarly, when asked to explain such terms as "liberal" and "conservative," only 15 percent could provide an extended explanation.[14]

In place of individual judgment, group influences determine the dependent voter's choice. "A person thinks, politically, as he is, socially,"[15] for "his vote is formed in the midst of a group decision—if, indeed, it may be called a decision at all."[16] Therefore, "the Catholic vote or the hereditary vote is explainable less as principle than as a traditional social allegiance. The ordinary voter, bewildered by the complexity of modern political problems, unable to determine clearly what the consequences are of alternative lines of action, remote from the arena, and incapable of bringing information to bear on principle, votes the way trusted people around him are voting."[17]

Of the various influencing groups, the most important for this voter is his party. Affinity to the Republicans and Democrats is not unique, but provides a social reference point, much like membership in a union or religious community. Party "is a type of social group, a group that happens to be political. Attachment to this group is therefore psychological in character, and is not essentially a political phenomenon."[18] The theme of electoral studies, thus, has been "primarily the role of enduring partisan commitments in shaping attitudes toward politics."[19] The voter's evaluations of candidates and issues are distorted by his partisanship. His choices are "guided by essentially nonrational political partisanship that is culturally transmitted from generation to generation in the course of normal socialization processes—the same as is 'character,' 'breeding,' or any other of the abstruse terms used to describe a cultural heritage."[20]

While partisanship strongly affects voting choices, this connection is not based on policy preferences. Party loyalty has not been founded on a general liberal or conservative posture, nor on opinions about international issues, and has been related to only five of twenty-four specific policy questions. Both Democrats and Republicans have favored such proposals as federal aid to education, while large proportions in both parties have been unenthusiastic about suggestions such as public ownership of natural resources.[21]

Unable to focus upon issues, dependent voters cannot substantially affect public policy. Only a small proportion of the electorate meets democratic ideals: "Once below the higher deciles of the population, there are major barriers to understanding that disrupt the processing of even that information about public policy to which the person attends." As a result, the citizenry "is almost completely unable to judge the rationality of government actions; knowing little of particular policies and what has led to them, the mass electorate is not able to appraise either its goals or the appropriateness of the means chosen to serve these goals."[22] Policy decisions are necessarily left to unmandated government officials, for "individual voting decisions have no direct consequences for public policy; and conversely, the actions of government from election to election have no discernible resonance in the minds of voters."[23]

The portrait of the dependent voter has been widely accepted as a faithful likeness, but varying ideological judgments have followed. The conservative conclusion has been to employ the findings to develop a new normative theory of democracy, aptly termed the "theory of democratic elitism."[24] The electorate, pictured as unresponsive and unknowing, is potentially dangerous according to this theory.[25] The inability of the undemocratic mass to affect policy is therefore seen as desirable, since decisions will be left to those more informed and more supportive of American institutions. Furthermore, voter apathy, ignorance, and lack of principle are actually beneficial, for such attitudes promote stability and moderation.[26] The prevalent absence of commitment softens the clashes of the few intense partisans and ideologists. Individual vices become public virtues, for "the very low affect of most voters, their lack of ideological commitment, and the low faith in the efficacy of politics makes political concord relatively easy to achieve."[27]

The same portrait, however, has been employed for very different purposes. Radical writers have seen the voting studies as demonstrating the disappearance of democracy in America. In their view the public citizen has been reduced to the mass man: "He cannot detach himself in order to observe, much less to evaluate, what he is experiencing, much less what he is not experiencing. Rather than that internal discussion we call reflection, he is accompanied through his life-experience with a sort of unconscious, echoing monologue. He has no projects of his own: he fulfills the routines that exist."[28] Under these conditions, the choices of voters are easily manipulated. "The prevailing level of opinion has become a level of falsehood," where officials are "elected under conditions of effective and freely accepted indoctrination."[29]

These conclusions, whether conservative or radical, are alike in their basic contempt of the electorate. If voters are essentially nonrational, their choices can be deliberately controlled. Issue appeals can be abandoned, while the uninformed, conceptually limited, and indoctrinated electorate is approached through attention-getting but irrelevant campaigns. A winning smile or religious enmity or an empty slogan will promote political careers better than a concern with relevant problems. An academic portrait of the dependent voter is the unintended intellectual foundation of the merchandized candidate.[30]

The Responsive Voter. National events have spurred revisionary research on electoral behavior. In recent years, political involvement has clearly increased, although the locus of participation has been not only in polling places but still more in marches, gathering of petitions, and demonstrations. Accepted political truths are called into question when the Republicans nominate a pure ideological conservative for president and the Democrats choose a pure ideological liberal, when the South becomes heavily Republican and Congress consistently Democratic, and when benevolent presidential power turns toward autocracy. New issues of race, war, and life-style have reached and divided the citizenry. The substance of politics is no longer Tocqueville's "lesser controversies," but the ultimate questions of who should live and who should die.

In this context, an alternative portrait of the electorate has been drawn, that of the responsive voter. The character of this voter, and the influences upon his choices, are not permanent, but change with the circumstances of the times and with political events. Issues are often important to the responsive voter. In the proper environment, public questions and the candidates' issue positions become critical to the electoral decision. Variety in electoral behavior is most evident, not determinism.

The variation in the stimuli provided by political leadership, parties, and candidates is particularly important in this view of the voter, for the popular response will be strongly conditioned by these stimuli. "The voice of the people is but an echo," wrote V. O. Key. "Even the most discriminating popular judgment can reflect only ambiguity, uncertainty or even foolishness if those are the qualities of the input into the echo chamber. If the people can choose only from among rascals, they are certain to choose a rascal."[31] When issues are raised effectively, however, the popular reaction changes. "In the moment of truth in the polling booth, how the parties and candidates look on the issues seems the most relevant cue for much of the American electorate if conditions permit issues to be used."[32] This argument is the basic undercoating of the responsive-voter portrait.

Responsive voters are affected by their social characteristics such as race and economic position. However, these characteristics are essentially permanent in nature. If they alone affected ballot choices, every election would have the same result, and there would be neither short-term nor long-term shifts in the vote. In fact, other influences also are important, and elections cannot be understood by emphasizing single features. Rather than determinism, analysis reveals that "social characteristics move into and out of the zone of political relevance, that they 'explain' the actions of some people and not those of others, and that insofar as social characteristics determine political preference they encounter considerable friction."[33]

There is a further problem in the deterministic approach, for it does not explain the particular partisan direction of a social group. While businessmen or blacks each have distinct group interests, there is no inherent, nonpolitical reason why these interests always must be expressed as black support of the Democrats or business backing for the Republicans. Historically, in fact, each group has changed its partisanship. Sociological influence "indeed explains a certain uniformity of choice but not the political direction of the choice. An explanation will always have to be sought in outside factors, and it is probable that, in the last resort, these factors will be the activities of the parties and the government in the present and past."[34]

While the responsive voter evidences party loyalty, this attachment does not determine his vote. In the aggregate, in fact, the combination of steadfast independence and temporary defections from party loyalty means that "electoral dynamism of some sort seems almost as normal as electoral stability."[35] On the individual level, partisanship does not necessarily mean loyalty devoid of issue content, but may indeed be a rational course for the voter. To vote along party lines can be an efficient means for the individual to reduce the personal costs of participation, while still expressing his general judgment on the government and opposition.[36] Adhering to a party can also be an effective expression of the voter's particular interests.[37] "There is a rational component to party identifications rooted in group norms,"[38] for the interests of a group may be best expressed by support of a particular party. Blacks' support of the Democrats, or businessmen's support of the Republicans may not be thoughtless conformity to a social group, but an expression of a policy preference. Moreover, over time, there is an increasing parallelism between the electorate's issue positions and its partisan choices.[39]

The fact of group or party loyalty therefore can be viewed in two different ways. In the portrait of the dependent voter these facts are interpreted as demonstrating the inattention and incapacity of the electorate. In the portrait of the responsive voter, the same facts may be interpreted as consistent with the issue and candidate preferences of the voters. The accuracy of the second interpretation will be tested by the consistency between these preferences and actual ballot choices. A businessman voting Republican simply to follow his social group is dependent on that group for political guidance, while a businessman voting Republican to promote his policy objectives is responsive to contemporary issues.

Contrary to the deterministic portrait, the responsive voter evidences considerable awareness of ideology and issues. However, voting choice may be reasonable but inarticulate, for "the reasoning that lies behind the choice is often made in private language which the chooser never learns to translate into words intelligible to others because there is ordinarily no need for him to do so."[40] Direct questions may underestimate voter awareness. When other techniques are employed, popular attitudes become more comprehensible.[41] For example, lengthy interviews, even among persons of limited education and articulateness, evoke an underlying ideological viewpoint.[42] Another method is to rely on multiple questions, rather than a single indicator, as an index of consciousness. Through these broader techniques, over a fifth of the electorate was found to be ideologically aware in 1956, using concepts such as liberalism and conservatism explicitly, or by implication in references to "the individual and the state, the role and power of government, welfare, free enterprise, and posture toward change."[43] These proportions increase substantially in later elections.

The public judgments of the responsive voter can have a substantial impact on his vote, depending on the salience of issues and the campaign strategies of a particular election. Many persons change their partisan choice from one election to the next, and these changes are closely related to their positions on the issues and their assessment of the abilities of the candidates. The resulting portrait "is not one of an electorate straitjacketed by social determinants or moved by subconscious urges triggered by devilishly skillful propagandists. It is rather one of an electorate moved by concern about central and relevant questions of public policy, of governmental performance, and of executive personality."[44]

But the electorate can choose only from the options presented to it, and these alternatives are not always distinct on any single issue, and are never distinct on all dimensions of judgment. Even when the choices are clear, the individual voter is unlikely to agree fully with one candidate on all questions. In a contest between a rabid segregationist and an advocate of compulsory statewide busing, for whom does the gradual integrationist vote? He is likely either to ignore the issue or to select the candidate closer to his own intermediate position, even though dissatisfied partially with both. Fuller explanations of elections must consider not only the voters, but also the alternative candidates and parties, and the voters' closeness or proximity to them on various attitudes. "It is not theoretically sound, nor even particularly logical, to attempt to explain a voter's behavior solely on the basis of his own positions on issues, disregarding his perception of the locations of the candidates and/or parties on those same dimensions."[45] The behavior of the voters varies with the character of the available choices.

Electoral sensitivity to issues has been particularly evident in recent presidential contests. A concern for specific issues is evident in 1964 and is as closely correlated to the vote as party identification itself.[46] Evaluations of policy on Vietnam and civil rights, and of the performance of the Johnson administration were the vital influences in the 1968 contest;[47] while "overall relative proximity to the candidates and parties on the issues is the best predictor of the vote,"[48] surpassing party identification in its effect. Again in 1972, "ideology and issue voting in that election provide a means for better explaining the unique elements of the contest than do social characteristics, the candidates, the events of the campaign, political alienation, cultural orientations or partisan identification."[49]

The portrait of the responsive voter that appears in these recent elections has been drawn by different methodological instruments than were used to draw the dependent voter. The different results may have been obtained, then, from variations in technique. Yet it seems more likely that the differences reflect variation in behavior in different periods. Time itself must be considered as a crucial contextual variable. Rather than being an unchanging behavior, voting varies with circumstances, for "elections differ enormously in their nature, their meaning and their consequences."[50]

Any conclusions drawn from a given election may therefore reflect, not permanent voter characteristics, but rather that contest's particular influences—composition of the parties, specific issues or their absence, and the given candidates. The basic findings of electoral stability in the pioneering voting studies are not necessarily enduring truths, but may be a product of "investigator's misfortune" in analyzing campaigns in which the tides of change were weak.[51] The particular conclusion of low ideological awareness among the voters during the Eisenhower period may have resulted from the generally low level of ideological stimulation during this period.

The different circumstances of the 1960s and 1970s parallel change in the electorate. In explaining the greater impact of policy issues in the latter period, the simple fact that research is conducted in a different environment is more important than changed techniques. Whatever the measure employed, ideology was more evident after 1960 than in earlier years.[52] Even if they deliberately replicated previous research, analysts would find an immense increase in the internal consistency of the views of the American public, which can only be explained by its reactions to the times.[53]

There is no single answer, then, to the question, "who is the American voter?" The question must be further specified by "when" and "where," as we shall attempt to do in this book. Certainly American voters are not persistently interested and active, and surely the Jeffersonian dream of independent yeomen discussing politics learnedly is unachievable. Coherent and well-argued political philosophies are no more to be expected at shopping centers than in college classrooms. Yet, if voters are unlikely to be philosopher-kings, neither must they be regarded as insignificant helots. Americans are concerned about their futures and their country's future. Recent research argues that they can understand issues and can express their concerns. Although those concerns may be expressed in the streets, they can also be expressed at the polling place. Not fixed in their allegiances by party tradition or group memberships, the electorate can respond differently when the times and the alternatives favor change. For the future, the behavior of the voters will depend on what the future brings into their view.

THE FUTURE AMERICAN VOTER

Two alternative portraits of the electorate have been sketched above. One emphasizes stability in voting behavior, with the largest proportion of the vote dependent on enduring factors such as group membership and partisanship; neither coherent ideologies nor the particular issues of the times are seen as having major impact. The other portrait places more emphasis on change, on the responsiveness of the electorate to new stimuli in the environment, and on the electorate's ability to grasp coherent, internally consistent, belief systems and to effectuate policy preferences in its vote.

Both of these portraits are based on competent research and can be partially reconciled by including time as an important variable. The dependent voter is more common in an inertial era such as that of the Eisenhower administration, while the responsive voter is more evident in periods of turmoil such as the Kennedy, Johnson, and Nixon years. This evenhanded generalization, however, immediately raises new questions: Which voter predominates in "normal" times, and which in exceptional ones? What is to be expected most of the time, relative passivity on the part of the electorate or relative concern?

Ladd and Hadley argue that the model of voter responsiveness is the one that usually applies: "Always manifesting ample internal disagreements, Republicans and Democrats have nonetheless been in clear policy conflict throughout the 1930s, in the course of Truman's presidency and into the early Eisenhower years, and now again in the 1960s and 1970s." In an unusual period such as the late 1950s, but only rarely, the voters will "not be distinguished by notable differences in issue positions, will not consider policy judgments very important to their electoral choice, and will not perceive the parties as programmatically distinct."[54]

Probably the more common view is that it is the recent period, particularly the turmoil of the 1960s, that is unusual. Voter inactivity is seen as the likely condition of American history.[55] The rise in citizen awareness and activity is seen as a unique response to unique circumstances, and it is therefore concluded that popular opinion was abnormally stimulated and crystallized in the recent conflictful period.[56] Popular analyses tend in similar directions. Commentators refer to quiet on college campuses, the ending of American involvement in Vietnam, abolition of the draft, and the absence of large-scale urban violence. Given the absence of unusual conditions, the unusual degree of voter consciousness will recede.

The 1972 election provided an early and partial test of these arguments. In its platform, the Republican party emphasized its performance in achieving a degree of stability domestically and a reduction of American military commitment abroad. By objective standards as well, there was less overt turmoil in the nation. If voter responsiveness were the result only of severe disturbances, we would expect a regression toward the characteristics of earlier times. In the data to be analyzed below, however, there is little evidence of such regression. The awareness of issues, and their effect on the vote, do not decline. A preliminary conclusion is that the model of voter responsiveness applies even to a more "normal" time.

More generally, there are theoretical reasons for believing that the new portrait of the voter is drawn in permanent oils, not erasable crayons. The total system has changed, not only individual voters. Recent turmoils can be seen, not as passing events, but as evidence of a major change, the political modernization of the United States.

At first reading, it would appear strange to apply the concept of modernization to the United States, which has often been characterized as the model for developing nations.[57] However, America's development has shown more of an economic than political character. Its technology, systems of mass production, and consumer goods indeed are prototypes for the world. Its political institutions, on the other hand, have not progressed, Huntington argues, beyond the state of the "Tudor polity" of Elizabethan England. Where the genuinely modern state has rationalized centralized authority, power in the United States is deliberately fractured, checked, and limited. Where we find in the modern state specialized structures of authority, we find in America separated institutions and shared powers. Where modern parties attempt to mobilize the entire population, Democratic and Republican parties have only limited effect on most citizens' lives. "The United States thus combines the world's most modern society with one of the world's most antique polities."[58]

In contrast to the past, the nation today is undergoing rapid political modernization, and this development is the root cause of the change in electoral behavior. The modernizing process is evident in four trends: increased political participation, the loss of traditional authority, national integration, and the growth of ideology.

Increased participation is one of the signs of modernization. It is evident even in the relatively privileged middle class, which is turning to politics as a new form of leisure activity and social service. But new involvement is more marked among those who previously have been excluded from sustained political action. Although they have not been fully socialized into the parties, large numbers of blacks, the poor, women, and the young have been brought into politics. Their political action is not always through the electoral process; but demonstrations, takeover of buildings, deliberate violence, and construction workers' marches can be even more potent political acts. The United States today bears the marks of a society in which large numbers of people are rapidly entering the political system and making demands on it, though not through the established party organizations.

Modernization also involves the loss of traditional authority and prestige, and this feature is also notably visible in contemporary America. The destruction of the southern racial code by blacks insistent on equality, the forced resignation of the vice-president and the virtual impeachment of the president, the castigation of male chauvinists by women's liberation advocates, the disregard for legal restraints in the smoking of marijuana, and the beating of college students by policemen—these diverse phenomena are alike in being attacks on past authority or previously privileged groups. Those previously subordinate in status no longer accept the legitimacy of the traditional hierarchy.

A third major feature of the current political modernization is the movement toward the nationalization of American society. This development is not new, but it represents a clear source of the current tensions. The United States is now economically centralized by its mature capitalistic industries. The issues we face are now national issues: race, war, pollution, urban life. Through television, universal education, and residential mobility, we have developed a common political discourse in an increasingly homogeneous society. Even our formal governmental institutions evidence the beginning of centralization, notably in the growth of the unchecked presidential power and the national bureaucracy.

Lastly, in a period of modernization the type of political demand changes. Particularistic claims—such as an individual's demand for a patronage position—become less dominant. The stress comes to be more on group demands. As group consciousness heightens, ideologies develop, functioning to present a unified explanation of the political world to group members, to increase the solidarity of the group, and to make wide-ranging demands on the polity. The movement to black unity is probably the clearest contemporary American example of the development of ideology through an increase in group consciousness. This form of political modernization is also found among other groups. A new awareness of identity is evident among other minorities, students, women, and white ethnic groups.

Group consciousness often means the escalation of political conflict, because demands are phrased in collective, ideological, moralistic—and therefore nonnegotiable—terms. The redefinition of political disputes is now evident in the United States, where conflicts seem to involve very basic values rather than merely opposing interests. The polarization of hawks and doves was not only a question of specific policy in Vietnam; it was a difference over the values of patriotism, anticommunism, and military involvement. The dispute between young and old is not on policy issues, where there is actually relatively little difference of opinion; the conflict, where it exists, is over life-styles. The conflict over race is not only—and perhaps not primarily—over integrating a suburban school or ending discrimination in construction. It involves issues of the meaning of equality, of the differences between achievement and ascriptive criteria, and of the personal psychological defenses involved in racism.

These modernizing trends will be continually reflected in the behavior of the electorate. The outlook is for participation rather than disinterest, for change rather than tradition, for national rather than local power, for ideological rather than individual demands. This political development in the United States brings the portrait of the responsive voter into higher relief. The shift from the dependent voter is not total, nor necessarily constant, but it is likely to be permanent.

The behavior of the electorate will continue to be greatly affected by the external environment. When events raise certain issues to prominence, voters will be able to respond. Particularly critical is the role of political leadership. It remains unlikely that voters will be able to seek out for themselves the information necessary to create an organized view of the political world. The electorate is capable of responsiveness, but the parties and candidates must find appropriate stimuli for creating a response. The underlying trends toward modernization are creating the conditions for a participatory and aware citizenry, as well as increasing the stridency of conflict.[59]

Surely the issues affecting the lives of American men and women will not disappear. Political leaders can make the ballot relevant to the resolution of those issues, or they can ignore them and thereby foster alienation and fury. After the leaders choose their course of action, the voters too will choose.

The following chapters are a detailed examination of the factors affecting electoral behavior, particularly the vote for president, from 1960 to 1972. The continuing emphasis in these chapters will be on two questions: the relative importance of issue concerns as against the long-term social and political memberships of the voters, and the variation in voter response over the course of the four presidential contests emphasized in the analysis.

Since party loyalty has been established as the most important influence on the vote, we begin with an examination of the changing distribution and effect of partisanship, the differences between the partisans and Independents, and the sources of Democratic and Republican affinity. Next, we analyze four demographic characteristics of the population —social class, sex, age, and race—and their relationships to such behavior as voting participation, opinions, and vote. For each of these fixed characteristics, an assessment is made of its relative impact on the vote, when compared to the impact of issues.

We then turn to a more direct examination of issues. In Chapter 7, the unrestricted answers of respondents are employed to discover the problems of greatest concern to the voters over this period, their evaluations of parties and candidates, and the relative importance of evaluative dimensions in past presidential contests. In the following chapter, we trace the changes in voters' loyalties, issue preferences, and perceptions of the parties. The various strands of data are then put back together in a causal analysis of three presidential elections. This procedure summarizes the comparative and variable impact of partisanship, social characteristics, and political attitudes. In conclusion, implications are drawn from the findings for the future of American politics.

This analysis, hopefully, is more than an academic exercise. The argument essentially represents a statement of faith in democratic elections, a belief that they are concerned with important questions and that voters can deal meaningfully with these questions. Despite America's long experience with free voting, the utility and significance of popular elections is still debated today. At one time, the debate was conducted between aristocratic Federalists and democratic Republicans. Today, that debate continues among political scientists.

Tocqueville might have been writing of these academic factions in observing that "the greater part of them are more or less connected with one or the other of those two great divisions which have always existed in free communities. The deeper we penetrate into the inmost thought of these parties, the more we perceive that the object of the one is to limit and that of the other to extend the authority of the people. . . . I affirm that aristocratic or democratic passions may easily be detected at the bottom of all parties, and that, although they escape a superficial observation, they are the main point and soul of every faction in the United States."[60] This book constitutes one vote for the democratic faction.

CHAPTER 2

PARTY LOYALTY
AND PARTY CHOICE

To study America is to study American parties. As the Constitution itself was spawned by a "reform caucus,"[1] national life has been continually nourished by organized factions and their leaders. Territorial expansion, emancipation of the slaves, and social reform have been the work of politicians such as Jefferson, Lincoln, and Roosevelt. Selecting the candidates and organizing the ballot, those who hold power today are identified with the Republican elephant and the Democratic donkey. The voters choose not only individuals, but parties as well.

The pervasiveness of party is reflected in the portrait of the dependent voter. Loyalty to party is the focal point of the portrait. This voter's affinity to Republicans and Democrats is established early in life, largely on the basis of habit and group tradition. This loyalty affects all political perceptions and behavior, particularly the crucial act of voting. "Partisanship is the most important single influence on political opinions and voting behavior," emphasizes a leading analyst. "Many other influences are at work on voters in our society, but none compare in significance with partisanship ... the feeling of sympathy for, and loyalty to, a political party which an individual acquires (probably) during childhood and which endures (usually) with increasing intensity through his life."[2]

In less sophisticated language, Theodore Roosevelt learned of the tenacity of partisanship while campaigning in the erstwhile Democratic South. As this Republican president was speaking, he became disturbed by a member of the audience who turned aside all of Roosevelt's arguments with the incantation, "My granddaddy was a Democrat, my daddy was a Democrat, and I'm a Democrat." Ultimately enraged by this display of blind loyalty, Roosevelt confronted the voter: "Well, if your grandfather were a Republican, and your father were a Republican, what would you be?" The answer was quick, "Why I'd be a damn fool, of course."

Whatever the terms of discourse, the influence of partisanship on electoral behavior is widely accepted. Analysis of any given election typically begins with the premise of sheer persistence: Democrats will vote for the Democratic candidate and the Republicans for the Republican nominee. While the particular circumstances of a campaign may change expectations, the presumption is "that the normal vote associated with any population depends entirely on the underlying distribution of party loyalties, and that the actual vote in any election, although influenced by short-term forces, still is largely determined by that distribution."[3]

In normal times the premise is reasonable—but modern times are unlikely ever again to evidence the tranquillity of the 1950s. As instability has developed in the total society, political constants too have declined. Partisanship has become less widespread and less determinative of the vote. Despite the fact that Democrats are far more numerous than Republicans, the party has won only one convincing national victory in the last two decades and has occupied the White House for only two of the last six administrations. Despite the fact that Republicans have elected presidents frequently, they have controlled the Congress for only two years in the past quarter of a century. Party loyalties no longer explain election outcomes. Candidates cannot march to victory at the head of a partisan army. It is now necessary to mobilize irregulars and occasional volunteers. A reliance on sunshine loyalists has brought us to a time that tries politicians' souls.

CHANGING PARTY LOYALTIES

Our consideration of partisanship, and of the other topics in this book, depends on data collected in national surveys by scholars at the Survey Research Center of the University of Michigan. In each presidential election since 1948, a sample of up to 2,000 persons has been carefully selected, representing in miniature the civilian voting-age population of the United States. These persons have then been interviewed twice, once before and once immediately after Election Day, with each interview typically lasting over an hour. Because the sample size is large, and because the necessary procedures have been followed meticulously, we can have great confidence in the validity of the results. Within known statistical limits, the answers of those interviewed correspond to the opinions of the nation.

The relevant data on partisanship consist of the "party identifications" of the voters. A basic question in each survey concerns the individual's psychological self-identification with the parties. Respondents have been asked to classify themselves as Republicans, Democrats, or Independents, and have then been invited further to indicate if they are "strong" or "weak" Democrats, "strong" or "weak" Republicans, Independents who "lean closer" to one party or another, or completely autonomous. In most of the analyses that follow, we will consider the voters in five groups: all Independents as a single group, strong Democrats, weak Democrats, strong Republicans, and weak Republicans.

For the dependent voter, partisanship is the enduring core of his political beliefs, the principal cue to his behavior. Emphasizing this factor even when the public shifts its actual votes, observers have found "a serene stability in the distribution of party loyalties expressed by the same public," as well as "a remarkable individual stability in party identification even in this period of extravagant vote change."[4] In the contemporary period, however, this stability is eroding. Paralleling the general disruptions of American society since 1960 have come disruptions in partisanship. Less hidden by the cloak of traditional loyalties, the responsive voter has become more visible.

Changing party loyalties can be demonstrated in various ways. First, we may examine the overall distributions of self-identification over time. The belief in stable partisanship has been based partially on the similar percentages in each party's camp from one election year to the next. Thus, since a total of about 45 percent in past years classified themselves as Democrats (whether strong or weak adherents), there appears to be a massive bedrock of support for the party of Franklin Roosevelt and John Kennedy. It is at least theoretically possible, however, that a constant overall distribution masks internal but opposing shifts of loyalties. For every defection from the Democrats, there could conceivably be a compensating conversion from the Republicans.

On the other hand, a change in the total pattern necessarily does involve individual change. If there are more or fewer Democrats over time, there has been a real alteration in party identification. The data presented in Figure 2.1 show considerable change in the past four presidential election years. The clearest trend is the loosening of party ties in the United States, particularly demonstrated by the growth in self-identified Independents. Previously less than a quarter of the electorate, and less numerous than the supporters of either major party, Independents now constitute over a third of the total citizenry, considerably outnumber the Republican identifiers, and threaten to overtake the Democrats as well. In the distribution of party loyalty, the most important novelty is the widespread and growing absence of party loyalty.[5]

The weakening of the bond of party is evident even among those who still consider themselves Democrats or Republicans. Loyalty is increasingly flabby, as weak partisans now outnumber those who strongly assert their party identification. Until 1964, strong and weak partisans were

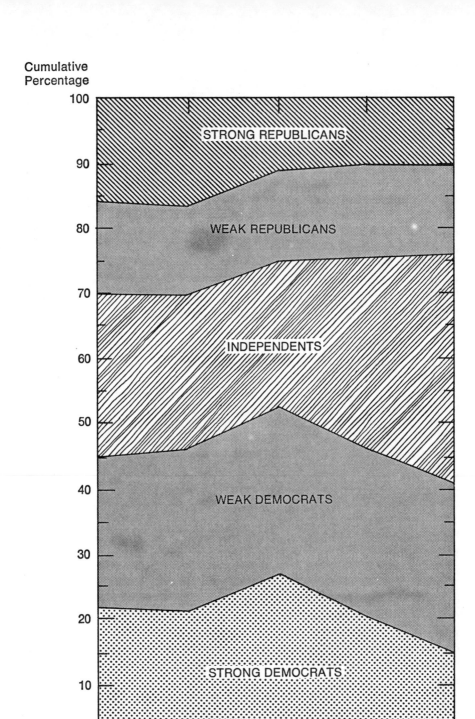

FIGURE 2.1 / PARTISAN LOYALTY FROM 1956 TO 1972

approximately equal in number; in 1972 the fainthearted predominated within the party ranks by better than a 3-2 margin.

These trends apparently show the decay of partisan vigor. It is possible, however, that they can be simply explained, and without discomfort to the parties, by reference to the changing age distribution of the electorate. In recent elections, the children of the postwar "baby boom" have begun to vote, and their ranks have been further swollen by the enfranchisement of 18-year-olds. The reduced partisanship of the total electorate may be simply a demographic artifact of its more youthful character. Possibly, as these youths mature, they will return to more normal patterns of partisanship. Such an effect of age would be expected of the dependent voter, while a responsive voter would be expected to show an independence based on his reactions to the politics of the times.

To test this explanation, the respondents in each election survey are classified into five political generations on the basis of the time at which they were eligible to cast their first votes for president.

The generations are defined by political milestones. Much of recent American politics has been shaped by the events of Franklin Roosevelt's presidency, which saw the worst economic crisis in the nation's history, the approach of social revolution, the creation of a national welfare state, the reversal of party fortunes and the creation of a Democratic party majority, and the waging of the world's most extensive and most destructive war. The three oldest generations are defined in reference to these events: constituting the pre-New Deal group, those who came of voting age for the presidential elections from 1932 to 1944, and those who entered the electorate after Roosevelt's death in the postwar elections of 1948 through 1956. The two youngest generations are those that have gained political maturity during the upheavals of recent times: including those who first voted from 1960 to 1968, and the large group of the newly enfranchised in 1972.

A generational analysis of partisanship, as in Table 2.1, does show an effect of age. In any of the last four elections, the proportion of Independents increases from older to younger cohorts. In 1972, the disparities are particularly great. While less than a fifth of the pre-New Deal group is free of partisan loyalties, this stance was assumed by more than half of the new voters given a choice between a Republican Nixon and a Democratic McGovern.

However, the general loosening of party ties cannot be attributed exclusively to the entrance of the new voters. If we examine the same political cohorts over the four elections, we find noticeable change in all of the groups. The willingness to abandon partisanship is relatively slight among the two oldest groups, shaped in the heated political crucible of the New Deal. But even they evidence attitudes considerably different from earlier behavior. Given the historical record of actual voting, we might

TABLE 2.1 / PARTISAN IDENTIFICATION BY POLITICAL GENERATIONS*

	Strong Democrat	Weak Democrat	Independent	Weak Republican	Strong Republican	(N)
Pre-New Deal						
1960	22.9	23.1	16.6	16.8	20.6	(637)
1964	30.7	20.7	14.6	15.4	18.5	(410)
1968	26.5	25.9	16.9	13.1	17.5	(343)
1972	20.5	24.8	19.6	15.8	19.3	(419)
New Deal						
1960	20.3	25.3	26.8	13.9	13.6	(679)
1964	27.8	26.8	22.5	13.1	9.9	(497)
1968	20.2	26.2	26.4	18.0	9.3	(451)
1972	20.5	26.9	25.3	15.3	11.9	(620)
Postwar						
1960	20.9	27.3	26.9	11.2	13.7	(498)
1964	25.1	27.5	25.9	13.6	8.0	(375)
1968	23.3	25.7	31.5	13.0	6.6	(378)
1972	15.7	25.9	35.3	13.1	10.1	(567)
The 1960s						
1960	3.7	40.7	29.6	11.1	14.8	(54)
1964	22.9	25.7	32.9	12.0	6.4	(249)
1968	11.6	24.9	43.2	14.4	5.9	(354)
1972	8.9	24.8	46.0	13.4	6.9	(642)
New Voters						
1972	8.7	27.1	50.9	7.0	5.4	(391)

*Cell entries are percentages adding horizontally by rows to 100 percent, except for rounding errors.

expect the pre-New Deal group to identify with the Republicans and the New Dealers to be overwhelmingly Democratic. While contemporary party identifications incline in these directions, the distributions show more similarity between these groups than might be expected. In the postwar group, considerable movement away from strong partisanship and toward independence is apparent. Although aged 37 to 48 by 1972, this middle-aged group has not yet ossified into party loyalty.

The most evident changes in partisanship occurred in those persons who came of political age in the turbulent 1960s. With each succeeding election, this group became increasingly disaffected from both major parties, and less willing to make a strong commitment to either Democrats or Republicans. These changes cannot be explained by the successive additions of newly enfranchised, presumably unaffiliated, voters. If these increments were the vital factor, disaffection should be evident in 1964 and 1968, as new voters were added, but not in 1972, when all members of this cohort had previously reached voting age. In contrast, strong partisan fidelity grows in 1964, but diminishes sharply in 1972.

The more tenable explanation for this generation's evolving loyalties are the events it has endured. Rather than "growing up" and accepting the established parties, it has spurned the leaders who were unable to resolve an escalating war, to promote jobs and economic security, to quiet the discontent in the streets, or even to protect themselves from assassination. Limited party loyalties are even more evident among the new voters of 1972, whose political memories are completely unclouded by earlier innocence. Rather than inevitably adhering to the major parties, the two youngest cohorts have broken with past patterns, while responding to the events of their public lives.

A second way to examine change in party loyalties is by following the same individual voters through the years and repeatedly asking their party identification. To actually conduct such an inquiry over many elections, however, is virtually impossible.[6] A substitute technique is to ask voters to recall any past changes in their partisanship. Such questions are subject to considerable error and rationalization, since most people do not have vivid memories of their electoral past. However, these biases are likely to be the same in every survey. While we cannot put too much credence in the specific percentages, comparisons can still be made among different periods.

The reports of past identifications further indicate an erosion of party loyalty. Twenty years ago, some two-thirds of the respondents averred that they had been constantly devoted to the Democrats or Republicans, and this degree of attachment was reduced only slightly in 1960 and 1964. In the last two presidential contests, however, reported constancy has declined substantially, to 58 percent in 1968, and to little more than half of the total electorate in 1972.[7] Lifelong fealty to the parties is no longer prevalent, nor is current devotion particularly strong. The parties are not built on bedrock, but on shifting sands.[8]

A third test of partisan stability is to examine the transmission of party loyalties from parents to children. In the dependent portrait of the voter, considerable emphasis is placed on the inheritance of Democratic and Republican affinities. In accepting the political faith of their fathers and mothers, as Theodore Roosevelt discovered, voters obviously are not responding to current issues, but are only adopting the norms of their social groups. Family milieu, rather than political environment, affects this electorate.[9]

While a high degree of political inheritance existed in the past, the relationship is considerably weaker today. Illustratively, inherited partisanship previously was evident among 80 percent of the children of parents interested in politics and with a Democratic loyalty, and in 72 percent of the offspring of interested Republicans.[10] By 1972, such inheritance is manifested by only 63 percent of the descendants of active Democrats and 59 percent of the interested Republicans. A similar decrease occurs among voters from politically quiescent homes, where the transference of partisanship takes place today in little more than a majority of cases.[11]

The decreased transmission of partisanship can be specified further, by analyzing the five political generations. In the table below, we divide the population by two variables: the respondent's own party identification in 1972 and the loyalty he attributes to that parent, whether mother or father, who was more interested in politics.[12] This analysis shows considerable decline in the direct inheritance of Democratic or Republican partisanship from parents to children. Those entering the electorate before the New Deal remain generally faithful to the remembered party of their parent (65 percent of the group). There is a regular regression in loyalty to the two major parties from this steadfast generation to the youngest cohort, where fidelity is far less common (only 44 percent of all the new voters).

To assess the relationship between the two factors, the statistical method of ordinal correlation can be employed. The method, used extensively in this book, gauges the degree of association between two variables, each arranged in a definite order. In Table 2.2, a high correlation shows that parental partisanship or independence is closely related to the

TABLE 2.2 / TRANSMISSION OF PARTISANSHIP BY POLITICAL GENERATIONS*

a) Pre-New Deal

Respondent's Partisanship	Parent's Partisanship		
	Dem	Ind	Rep
Dem	36	1	8
Ind	10	1	6
Rep	8	1	29
	N=335	G=.69	

b) New Deal

Respondent's Partisanship	Parent's Partisanship		
	Dem	Ind	Rep
Dem	41	2	5
Ind	13	3	8
Rep	7	1	20
	N=523	G=.71	

c) Postwar

Respondent's Partisanship	Parent's Partisanship		
	Dem	Ind	Rep
Dem	37	1	4
Ind	18	4	12
Rep	10	1	13
	N=486	G=.58	

d) The 1960s

Respondent's Partisanship	Parent's Partisanship		
	Dem	Ind	Rep
Dem	32	1	2
Ind	21	9	15
Rep	4	2	14
	N=546	G=.76	

e) New Voters, 1972

Respondent's Partisanship	Parent's Partisanship		
	Dem	Ind	Rep
Dem	34	2	3
Ind	25	9	14
Rep	3	1	10
	N=339	G=.70	

*The entry in each cell is the percentage of the total cohort, among 1972 voters, with both the designated party self-identification and the party identification attributed to the parent with greater interest in politics.

respondent's loyalties. The precise relationship is measured here by a statistical coefficient designated as gamma, or G, which varies from zero, when there is no relationship, to 1.0, when the two factors are completely associated.

These data, and the statistical measures, substantiate the changing trends of American politics. The great impact of the Depression years led large numbers of persons entering the electorate around that time to switch completely from the party of their parents. As the parties responded to the problems of the time, the voters' choices were realigned. Class divisions previously disguised became manifest when the vital issues centered on the distribution of wealth and likelihood of bodily survival. Habitual acceptance of parental faith was less likely when the objects of faith provided little solace. In the crises of the time, new thought was stimulated. In all, 14 percent of the three older generations crossed the great divide in both directions between the Republicans and Democrats. The change is most marked in the lower ordinal correlation within the postwar generation, most of whose parents began to vote before the New Deal.

In more recent times, defection from the parent's faith has resulted in partisan independence, rather than adherence to the opposition. Dissatisfied with their political inheritance, the newer generations have not been attracted either by the obvious alternative. Since the change in loyalties has been less complete than in previous generations, the ordinal correlations are relatively high. However, these newer groups have many voting years before them, and may still show complete transformation from the political faith of their parents.

Both of the major parties as presently constituted are unappealing. This reduced transmission of party loyalty partially accounts for the lessened degree of partisanship previously noted in the total electorate. As new independent voters have entered the system, they have replaced more loyal partisans. Joined by older persons who have loosened or removed party bonds, these voters have made voting less static and more potentially responsive. Partisanship is less extensive, less persistent, and less continuous across generations. It is therefore less explanatory as well.

SOURCES OF PARTISANSHIP

Party loyalty, however extensive, reflects the individual's social and political environment. In the dependent portrait, Democratic and Republican identification is associated with the voters' demographic characteristics. Findings of a relationship between social and political characteristics are then oversimplified "to a conception of voting not as a civic decision but as an almost purely deterministic act. Given knowledge of certain characteristics of a voter—his occupation, his residence, his religion, his national origin, and perhaps certain of his attitudes—one can predict with a high probability the direction of his vote."[13]

The original emphasis in explanations of voting was on factors related to social class, such as income and occupation. The election of 1960 brought increased awareness of the importance of religion. With the development of black consciousness, and of white reactions to it, the effect of race and ethnic group has been stressed. The advent of the youth culture and of women's liberation has stimulated discussion of the effects of age and sex on political behavior.[14]

These interpretations are alike in seeing political attitudes such as partisanship as determined by nonpolitical forces. A person's Democratic or Republican loyalty is not explained by his views on policy questions and his evaluation of party nominees. Instead, the emphasis is on his categorical memberships, whether class, religion, race, sex, or age. Loyalty, like love, is blind, for the voter's vision is so fully shaped by his social groups that he sees only what supports his preconceptions.

When political factors are introduced in these explanations, they are secondary and remote in time. The presumed southern support of the Democrats is attributed to the Civil War, when the opposition Republicans led the subjugation of the region;[15] Catholic loyalty to the same party is related to the distant candidacy of Al Smith for president in 1928 or to the aid provided Catholic immigrants by the classic urban machines;[16] working class and black support is held to be a reflex developed forty years ago. Once established, loyalties become habits, not judgments subject to reconsideration. These remote influences continue to have a present effect because of the intergenerational transmission of partisanship and the social reinforcement of political tradition. Dependent voters are common, according to these explanations, typified by Theodore Roosevelt's heckler, declaring their loyalty to the party of their granddaddy and daddy, without regard to contemporary events.

In fact, voters fixed in their party loyalties by group cohesion are not readily apparent in the American electorate. We have already discovered the shrinkage of partisanship and its diminished direct transfer between generations. Party loyalty remains widespread even with these changes, but it is not a simple reflection of social characteristics. The influence of social groups would be evident in marked differences in the party identifications of opposed regions, classes, races, and religious communities. Few such marked contrasts exist, and the tendency is for these categorical aggregates to become more alike over time, as seen in Table 2.3. Rather than the parties being divided along social lines, they are coming to resemble one another demographically.

The effect of class is illustrative. If social position dictated political preference, most workers should be Democratic and most of the middle class Republican, but such polarization has never been evident. A deterministic premise would also predict growing Republican strength. As the growth of the American economy has brought ever-larger proportions of the electorate to the white collar estate, many would be expected to

TABLE 2.3 / DEMOGRAPHIC CHARACTER OF THE PARTIES*

	1960					1964				
	SD	WD	I	WR	SR	SD	WD	I	WR	SR
Education										
Less than High School	24.3	26.7	22.6	12.2	14.3	35.1	28.7	18.7	10.3	7.2
High School	21.6	27.7	24.5	15.3	10.8	24.8	26.1	24.0	15.4	9.7
Some College	17.0	22.2	22.7	15.8	22.2	20.2	19.6	29.5	15.1	15.6
College Graduate	13.2	20.5	26.8	16.3	23.2	18.6	20.9	23.2	17.4	19.8
Region										
South	25.0	35.6	18.0	8.8	12.7	36.5	32.1	16.7	7.2	7.4
Non-South	18.8	20.6	26.1	16.7	17.7	23.2	22.5	25.5	16.2	12.6
Race										
White	20.3	25.7	22.5	14.6	16.9	24.3	25.3	23.6	14.6	12.2
Black	28.6	21.8	31.3	10.2	8.2	54.4	22.8	15.4	5.4	2.0
Occupation										
White Collar	14.4	27.3	24.6	15.6	18.1	21.3	23.6	26.2	14.7	14.2
Blue Collar	22.2	26.8	26.9	13.4	10.8	31.5	27.1	24.9	11.1	5.4
Class Identification										
Middle Class	16.3	20.8	21.1	18.2	23.6	21.3	21.7	23.7	16.9	16.4
Working Class	23.5	27.7	23.5	12.5	12.7	32.5	28.7	22.3	10.4	6.1
Religion										
Protestant	18.9	23.4	22.3	15.3	20.1	26.5	24.7	20.2	15.8	12.8
Catholic	28.6	32.8	23.0	10.0	5.6	31.1	27.3	24.7	8.4	8.4

*Within each year, percentages in each cell add horizontally by rows to 100 percent, except for rounding errors. SD = Strong Democrat, WD = Weak Democrat, I = Independent, WR = Weak Republican, SR = Strong Republican.

assume the appropriate Republican loyalty.[17] In reality, no such growth has occurred in the GOP. Economically mobile voters have carried their Democratic loyalty with them into the middle class, eliminating the Republican advantage in this group.[18] At the same time, there has been some diminution in Democratic strength in the party's former stronghold, the working class, and a general increase in independence from partisanship. The total result is to diminish sharply the economic polarization of the parties. On the basis of class, as on other demographic characteristics, citizens emphatically do not think politically as they are socially.

The total effect of demographic factors on party loyalty can be evaluated through the statistical method of multiple regression. In this method we employ a series of independent variables—such as party identification, occupation, religion. The relative effect of each demographic variable is shown by a statistic known as the beta weight. The greater the beta weight, the greater is the effect of the particular variable it represents when the effect of all of the other factors is controlled. Another statistic, R^2, measures the total effect of all the independent variables together. In our example, R^2 measures the percentage of the variance in party identifications that is explained by a combination of eight demographic variables—occupation, class identification, education, race, religion, region, sex, and age. In the four elections from 1960 to 1972, all of the eight demographic variables together have had relatively little effect

TABLE 2.3 / DEMOGRAPHIC CHARACTER OF THE PARTIES* [Continued]

	1968					1972				
	SD	WD	I	WR	SR	SD	WD	I	WR	SR
Education										
Less than High School	30.1	30.4	21.1	10.9	7.5	20.8	28.1	28.9	12.1	10.1
High School	17.9	27.9	28.7	16.0	9.5	13.1	27.6	37.5	12.4	8.7
Some College	12.4	22.7	37.9	16.7	10.4	12.2	25.2	38.8	12.3	11.4
College Graduate	13.3	14.8	37.4	19.2	15.3	8.8	19.2	39.0	20.1	13.0
Region										
South	27.0	29.1	30.9	8.5	4.5	17.8	32.1	30.5	10.6	8.9
Non-South	17.3	24.2	28.8	17.5	12.1	13.7	23.0	37.5	14.6	11.2
Race										
White	16.3	25.1	31.5	16.5	10.7	12.7	25.0	36.6	14.5	11.3
Black	57.6	29.9	10.4	0.7	1.4	37.2	31.8	23.4	3.8	3.8
Occupation										
White Collar	14.4	21.4	34.7	18.5	11.0	11.6	22.1	37.1	16.7	12.5
Blue Collar	22.6	29.0	29.3	11.5	7.6	17.0	29.2	35.8	9.7	8.3
Class Identification										
Middle Class	14.6	23.4	32.6	17.4	12.0	17.2	28.9	33.5	11.5	8.9
Working Class	25.0	27.9	26.7	12.6	7.8	12.6	22.5	37.1	15.6	12.2
Religion										
Protestant	19.5	24.4	27.4	16.9	11.8	13.3	24.6	33.6	15.8	12.7
Catholic	23.4	29.7	31.5	9.6	5.7	19.3	31.7	34.9	8.1	6.0

*Within each year, percentages in each cell add horizontally by rows to 100 percent, except for rounding errors. SD = Strong Democrat, WD = Weak Democrat, I = Independent, WR = Weak Republican, SR = Strong Republican.

on the voters' partisanship. About 16 percent of the variance in partisan identifications could be explained by these variables from 1960 to 1968, and but 9 percent in 1972 as measured by R^2. The relationship between the social groups of the voter and his party loyalty was only moderate in the past, and fell further in the last presidential election.[19]

One additional factor can be employed to explain party loyalty, the tradition of partisanship itself. While the transmission of political fidelity has decreased in recent times, the process remains of major significance. Children do not always remain in their parents' party, but they are far less likely than others to join the opposition. To assess the importance of such transmission, this factor is added to the original eight demographic variables in a second multiple regression. This enlarged analysis shows that as demographic factors have become less determinative, family inheritance has become the main support of party loyalty. Table 2.4 presents the detailed results of the second multiple regression.

Party loyalty can be described as a ship held stably to its moorings by a series of ropes representing the various demographic variables. These ropes have largely parted, leaving intergenerational transmission as the remaining, but weakening, anchor. With parental partisanship included in the multiple regression, a total of about 30 percent of party loyalty can be explained, with the proportion slowly decreasing. By 1972, of the total nine variables, taken independently, only the relationship between paren-

TABLE 2.4 / THE SOURCES OF PARTISANSHIP
(Beta Weights, Multiple Regression of Democratic Identification)*

	1958-60**	1964	1968	1972
Parental Partisanship	.40	.40	.35	.47
Occupation	−.08	−.05	−.00	−.07
Class Identification	−.08	−.09	−.03	−.05
Education	−.07	−.13	−.14	−.06
Race	.09	.15	.23	.06
Religion	.12	.06	.11	.10
Region	.22	.10	.11	.03
Sex	.02	.01	.01	−.01
Age	−.03	.03	−.03	−.01
Total R^2	.325	.309	.286	.288
Unique R^2, parental partisanship	.139	.144	.109	.197
R^2, parental partisanship as First Variable	.231	.215	.193	.257

*The magnitude of the coefficient indicates the independent effect of the given variable on party identification. Positive relationships show that Democratic loyalty is related to Democratic parental partisanship, white collar occupations, middle class identification, higher education, Catholic religion, black race, southern region, male sex, and older age. Negative relationships show that Democratic loyalty is related to the opposite social characteristics.

**The 1960 sample is largely composed of persons previously interviewed in 1958. Since questions on parental partisanship were not repeated in 1960, the results of the 1958 survey are used.

tal partisanship and current party identification results in an impressive beta weight. Once this factor is taken into account, none of the demographic variables has a direct, unique effect on current party loyalty.[20]

The importance of family inheritance can also be demonstrated by attention to the bottom rows of Table 2.4, detailing the amount of explanation provided by the listed variables. The first of these rows is the total R^2 the variance explained by all of the nine independent variables together. To locate the specific explanation provided by any single factor, such as parental partisanship, we must consider the order in which variables are included in the multiple regression. The explanation attributed to the first variable is inevitably exaggerated, because it gets "credit" for all of the joint effects shared with other variables. The unique explanation provided by any single variable can be found by holding it back to the end of the procedure. The beta weights remain the same in all of these operations.

In Table 2.4, the larger R^2 associated with partisanship results when it is entered first in the regression; the smaller when it is held back to the end. The second row represents the proportion of the variance which may be uniquely attributed to parental partisanship, aside from any overlap with the demographic variables. By 1972, this unique contribution of tradition constitutes the bulk of the total explanation. The last row shows the explanation provided by parental partisanship as the first variable.

The steadfastness of the party faithful is highly problematical. Loyalty is hardly supported any longer by associations with the basic group memberships of the voters, but becomes ever more reliant on traditions that are themselves increasingly rejected by the new political generations. The ship of party loyalty is now held largely by an aging rope. If this rope fails to hold, the parties will be cast adrift.

THE NEW INDEPENDENT VOTER

A marked change has occurred in American electoral politics. Party loyalty is less prevalent throughout the electorate, less constant within and between generations, and less rooted in the underlying group life of the nation. The voter is increasingly independent—of party ties, of fidelity to his parent's politics, of his groups' norms. The future decisions of the electorate are likely to be the decisions made by self-identified Independents. It is therefore necessary that we examine this group in detail. The new Independents may provide subjects for a new portrait of the dependent voter, one controlled by campaign manipulation rather than by habitual partisanship. Or they may evidence the capacity for political activity and awareness of issues expected of the responsive voter.

Until the advent of survey research, the Independent voter was usually praised for his individualism and emancipation from "blind party loyalty." Reform movements commonly have been supported by persons without partisan affiliations and have been directed against the institutions of party government.[21] Empirical research, on the other hand, led to the very different conclusion that Independents were the "least admirable voters,"[22] not paragons of civic virtue. "They have somewhat poorer knowledge of the issues, their image of the candidates is fainter, their interest in the campaign is less, their concern over the outcome is relatively slight, and their choice between competing candidates, although it is indeed made later in the campaign, seems much less to spring from discoverable evaluations of the elements of national politics."[23]

This lowly estimate of the Independent voter has become accepted truth in American political science, but political trends require a new description. The recent growth in the proportion of Independents has come from persons of advanced education, the young, and those of higher social status—individuals who presumably are able to analyze political issues and to make sense of campaigns. As a total group, the Independents still include many who are disinterested and unaware, but their new recruits "have largely been concentrated among precisely those strata in the population most likely to act through and in the political system out of proportion to their numbers. This may point toward the progressive dissolution of the parties as action intermediaries in electoral choice and other politically relevant acts. It may also be indicative of the production of a mass base for independent political movements of ideological tone and considerable long-term staying power."[24]

A more complimentary view of Independents also results if the group is defined differently, by behavior rather than by self-identification. Those who switch votes from one election to another—behavioral Independents, regardless of declared partisanship—are about as educated, concerned, and aware of policy questions, as those who stay with the same party. "Those who switch do so to support governmental policies or outlooks with which they agree, not because of subtle psychological or sociological peculiarities."[25] The reasonable behavior of switching voters is consistent with the data on the new Independents. To avoid the problems of fallible memories, however, the analysis that follows will depend primarily on the voters' current self-identifications.

Independents are worthy of both praise and disapproval. By making a simple distinction between politics and elections, we can comprehend their two concurrent characteristics, disinterest in elections and awareness of politics. Most of the measures used to evaluate the political consciousness of voters relate to election campaigns and parties. Yet the Independents, by definition, do not feel an identification with the parties and therefore cannot be expected to feel very involved with the results of party contests. It is still possible for an Independent to be concerned about the political world, and knowledgeable about its issues and contexts, yet rationally to decide that he is indifferent specifically to the Democrats and Republicans. To judge by recent evidence the unaffiliated voter is as qualified a citizen as the party loyalist. The Independent is not indifferent. Rather he is simply—and tautologically—unconstrained by partisanship.

Three kinds of evidence of political awareness in 1972 are presented in Table 2.5. In regard to purely factual knowledge, Independents are as well-informed as the weak partisans and close to the level of accuracy of the strong partisans. Even though these factual questions relate to electoral politics, the unaffiliated know basic facts in about the same degree as other citizens. In regard to electoral politics, Independents do show less activity and do conform to the accepted description of limited involvement. They vote less, change votes more frequently, express less interest in the campaign, and give political contributions less often. In other words, Independents act independently.

More significant is the fact that Independents' indifference to elections is not paralleled by apathy toward all politics. On five of six measures of more general involvement, the unaffiliated are more active, aware, or confident than the weak partisans, although they do evidence less subjective efficacy, the belief that "people like me have political power." However, even compared to the strong partisans, Independents are somewhat more likely to write letters to public officials and to vote on all public referenda—forms of political activity distinct from party competition.[26] These Independents "may have declined to identify with either major

TABLE 2.5 / STRENGTH OF PARTISANSHIP AND POLITICAL AWARENESS, 1972*

	Strong Party Identifiers	Weak Party Identifiers	Independents
Accurate Factual Knowledge			
Limit on Presidential Term	93.1	89.1	89.2
Length of Senator's Term	43.0	45.0	44.7
Length of Congressman's Term	59.7	57.7	56.8
House Majority Party Before Election	92.5	87.8	87.1
House Majority Party After Election	86.2	84.4	81.5
Electoral Political Activity			
Have Voted	82.9	73.6	66.3
High Interest in Political Campaigns	48.6	25.2	27.2
Low Interest in Political Campaigns	18.0	29.4	29.6
Change Vote between Elections	27.1	58.9	74.2
Give Money to Parties	15.3	9.1	8.4
General Political Activity			
Subjective Efficacy	62.6	60.2	57.6
Understand Politics	30.0	22.9	27.2
Talk to Others About Politics	37.1	28.6	31.8
Write to Public Officials	28.5	24.6	29.9
Vote on All Ballot Referenda	70.8	69.1	74.4
High General Interest in Politics	44.9	32.1	36.0

*Cell entries are percentages of the given group evidencing the designated behavior.

party not because they are relatively politically unconscious, but because the structure of electoral politics at the present time turns upon parties, issues, and symbolisms which do not have much meaning in terms of their political values or cognitions."[27]

If today's Independents are truly as aware as partisans, their consciousness should be evident in their concern for issues and their knowledge of the candidates' positions on these issues. In the past, the unaffiliated voter was also uninformed. But as more recent times have made issues more dramatically salient, the contemporary Independent has responded, largely eliminating the cognitive gap between partisans and nonpartisans. On ten major issues of 1972, there are almost none that show major differences by strength of partisanship, either in the position held on the issue or in the perceived positions of both major candidates. We are not concerned here with the direction of the voter's opinion nor with the objective accuracy of his perceptions of the candidates' views. A necessary condition for rational political decision is that the voter have an opinion which he can relate to those of the candidates.[28] Independents in 1972 fulfill this condition at least as well as strong partisans and tend to be even better equipped than the weak partisans.

Political awareness is as likely among Independents as among partisans. While the swelling of the ranks of the unaffiliated surely betokens a change in American politics, it does not necessarily forecast its domination by uncaring and unknowing barbarians. The implication rather is that the nation's mass behavior will be less centered around loyalty to the existing organizations. Political direction will come from other sources—revised parties, new parties, or novel mass movements.

These developments have been facilitated by the growth of new sources of information for the voters. Parties have been important to the electorate not only as emotional symbols, but as means of acquiring costless advice. Those who were strongly committed to the Democrats and Republicans used their loyalty as convenient cues for issue positions and candidate appraisal.[29] When the Democrats favored Medicare or nominated John Kennedy, the party's devotees were prompted to support the program and to vote for the candidate. These cues continue, but they are now less important as sources of information. Independents, devoid of party clues, previously were disadvantaged in acquiring political knowledge. Currently, two general changes enable Independents to be relatively as knowledgeable as partisans.

The first change is in the nature of the salient issues. Party cues are most relevant on issues that have shaped the present alignment of Democrats and Republicans, particularly questions of social and economic policy. Having the benefit of this prompting, partisans are more knowledgeable than Independents on such issues as government guarantee of jobs or health insurance. Thinking in an appropriate factional mode, the committed voters can more easily take a position and place the candidates on such questions. On other issues, however, party clues are less relevant. Since questions of Vietnam, law and order, campus unrest, or the legalization of marijuana have not been part of the established battle lines, a partisan vision does not facilitate a sighting on these issues or on perception of the candidates in regard to them.[30] On such matters, Independents are more likely to have an opinion and to know the candidates' stands.

Party cues are particularly important in the absence of other sources of information. Thus, a second important change has been the development of alternative means of acquiring political intelligence. The mass media are major sources, providing essentially costless and reliable information independently of the parties, and leading to a reduced impact of partisanship on voting.[31] Another source is formal education. With more schooling, persons are better able to assimilate political data and to use the information they acquire outside of factional channels. The growth of Independents has come particularly in those persons with sufficient education to permit freedom from party cues.

The effects of party cues and education are illustrated by the issue of government support of health insurance. As this policy question is closely related to the traditional alignment, party loyalty facilitates the holding of an opinion and the awareness of candidate positions. These hints are particularly important for persons of lower educational achievement. Among persons without high school training, strong partisans are half again as likely as Independents to know both nominees' views and significantly more likely to have an opinion of their own. In this educational stratum, the unaffiliated indeed seem less capable than the partisans. By contrast, among college graduates, Independents show more awareness of candidate views, by a 10 percent margin, and also themselves hold opinions more frequently. For these voters, party cues are less necessary as information sources.

These broad trends are likely to persist. The issues of America as this century wanes will be ever more different from those of the New Deal. Higher education and other sources of information uncontrolled by the parties will proliferate further. Independent voters will become more numerous and more influential. Their presence, however, need not be alarming, for they no longer differ from committed partisans in their knowledge and general interest in politics. They have the capacity to respond, if the parties and their leaders make themselves and their causes relevant to the concerns of voters.

THE EFFECTS OF PARTISANSHIP

Party loyalty is important for its effects on actual behavior—its influence on the balloting that is central to the democratic process. According to the dependent portrait of the voter, his major attitudes and his electoral decisions are critically determined by his partisanship. Drawn sightless, the blind partisan not only unthinkingly casts a ballot as his unshakable faith requires, but interprets the world in order to justify that vote. The contrasting responsive voter may also be a strong partisan, but this loyalty is an amendable "standing decision" to support his customary party. Such party votes, however, require consistency with his partially autonomous preferences on contemporary issues and candidates.

Both perceptual distortion and autonomous evaluation of political objects can be observed in voters. The former is illustrated in the 1948 election, when partisan Democrats who favored the Taft-Hartley labor law still voted for President Harry Truman, who campaigned for the law's repeal. These voters "removed" the discrepancy by misperceiving Truman's position to be support of the very statute he attacked as a "slave labor law."[32] Conversely, accurate perceptions were evident in 1972, when almost all voters, regardless of party or their own position on Vietnam, regarded McGovern both as favoring withdrawal from the war and as relatively more of a "dove" than Nixon.[33]

While partisanship surely does affect perception, its effects vary considerably. Voters' evaluation of the candidates' personal characteristics is illustrative. Not surprisingly, Democrats tend to have favorable reactions to their party's standard bearers, while Republicans view GOP nominees positively. The only surprise is that partisan bias is not complete on a dimension so closely related to actual electoral choice. Nevertheless, in 1964, even Republicans were more favorable to Lyndon Johnson than to Barry Goldwater, while in 1972, Democrats evaluated Richard Nixon more positively than George McGovern. Other elements of politics, more removed from the immediate ballot choice, show still less partisan bias. Voters of all persuasions tend to favor Republican administrations on issues of foreign policy, while seeing the Democrats as more receptive to the interests of distinct economic groups, such as farmers and workers.[34]

A more general illustration is found in descriptions of the parties as liberal and conservative. Regardless of their own preferences, there is a general consensus in the electorate on the ideological positions of the parties. Even in 1960, voters were inclined to characterize the Democrats as relatively liberal and the Republicans as relatively conservative, and the consensual proportion grew to three-fourths of the total by 1972. Some distorted perceptions remain, with liberals or conservatives seeing their own party as reflecting their personal preferences. More striking than such possible rationalization, however, is the consensus across parties and ideological groupings. Even at the extremes, only small proportions of liberal Republicans or conservative Democrats believe the Democrats are more conservative.

The most critical effect of partisanship is on voting itself, the act by which the attitudes and perceptions of the citizenry are translated into public action. To authenticate the portrait of the dependent voter, there must be a high correlation between party loyalty and electoral choice. But even if such a correlation exists, the portrait of the responsive voter may still be accurate if voter attitudes and partisanship are consistent with each other.

In the four elections considered here, the relationship of partisanship to the vote is quite high. In each contest, there is a monotonic relationship between the vote and the scale of party identification. Even in electoral disaster, a candidate will receive his greatest support from partisans of his own party, as Goldwater obtained 62 percent of his vote from Republicans and McGovern two-thirds of his from Democrats. The relationship of party loyalty and the vote is never perfect, but it is strong and consistent.

Although partisanship remains a major influence, its relationship to the vote appears to be weakening. From 1960 to 1972, there is a continual decline in the correlation of party identification and the vote, as seen in Table 2.6. In neither party are the voters constantly faithful. While John Kennedy won the vote of nine of every ten strong Democrats, George McGovern commanded the loyalty of only three of every four of these devoted Democrats. Barry Goldwater suffered considerable defection from his own ranks, and even Richard Nixon experienced some slight erosion over the years in his support among Republicans.[35]

TABLE 2.6 / PARTY IDENTIFICATION AND THE VOTE*

	1960		1964		1968			1972	
	Kennedy	Nixon	Johnson	Goldwater	Humphrey	Nixon	Wallace	McGovern	Nixon
Strong Democrat	91.0	9.0	95.3	4.7	84.7	7.7	7.7	73.4	26.5
Weak Democrat	71.7	28.3	82.1	17.9	57.9	27.1	15.0	48.5	51.5
Independent	45.6	54.4	66.2	33.8	26.3	56.6	17.1	33.8	66.2
Weak Republican	13.1	86.9	43.2	56.8	9.8	82.3	7.9	8.9	91.1
Strong Republican	1.6	98.4	9.7	90.3	2.5	95.8	1.7	3.3	96.7
(N)	(684)	(713)	(748)	(358)	(420)	(490)	(116)	(566)	(1014)
Gamma	.85		.79		.73			.68	

*Cell entries within each year add horizontally to 100 percent by party identification rows.

The decline in the effect of party loyalty, as measured by the correlation coefficients, is very evenly paced. Partisanship's diminished effect therefore cannot be attributed to the unusual circumstances of any particular campaign, whether the unique features be a Goldwater or McGovern candidacy, the three-way division of the vote in 1968, or specific issues. Every campaign is unique, for it takes place at an instant in history and resolves singular issues argued by particular contestants. The important point is that voters can and do respond to these unique stimuli, alter their ballot choices, and in these actions reaffirm or subordinate their underlying partisanship. Such is the behavior of a responsive, not dependent, electorate.

The decreasing impact of partisanship also cannot be attributed to the unstable behavior of young voters, for the trend is continuous within each of the five political generations. At each election, the 1960s cohort does tend to show the least partisan fidelity in its vote, but a downward trend is evident in every group, regardless of the time of its initial entrance to politics. Aging does not mean electoral immobility.

Particularly interesting is the New Deal generation, which first became eligible to vote when Franklin Roosevelt was a presidential candidate. Intense experiences in youth commonly affect an individual throughout his lifetime. For this generation, politics was intense in its youth, involving very immediate questions of possible starvation, the loss of farms and homes, and the prospect of death in war. We would expect that the high intensity of politics of the time engendered very strong party loyalties, which would persistently affect later voting behavior. Contrary to this expectation, the correlation of partisanship and the vote among New Dealers has declined virtually as rapidly as in other cohorts, falling slightly below (G=.67) the national figure in 1972.

The partisan solidarity of this group has declined as well. When first coming of age, the New Deal generation evidenced its support of Roosevelt by returning Democratic majorities of 69 percent to 89 percent.[36] By 1972, now aged 49 to 64, the cohort had become strongly anti-McGovern, giving the senator only 29 percent of its vote. This reversal was evident even among the cohort's Democratic identifiers. While four out of five partisans of this generation voted for Kennedy, and nine of ten for Johnson, only two-thirds supported Humphrey and less than a majority followed their own proclaimed loyalties to cast a Democratic ballot in 1972.

The diminished impact of partisanship occurs not only in presidential elections, but also appears in the decreasing proportion of persons who vote a straight ticket for other offices.[37] It is also demonstrated by the increased switching of presidential choices from one election to the next. Such inconstancy is evident in the total electorate, a partial reflection of the growing proportion of Independents. Infidelity also has risen among those who still claim an allegiance to the parties, particularly the weaker loyalists. In this group, half had always voted for the same party in 1960, but only 41 percent were still faithful in 1972 (and still fewer among older respondents). The unusual choices of the period, such as the candidacies of Goldwater, Wallace, and McGovern, provoked responses that overcame the habits of partisan tradition. Party loyalty no longer determines party choice.

THE FUTURE OF THE PARTIES

Over the past two decades, the dependent voter has become less prevalent in America, and the common emphasis on party loyalty in electoral analysis needs to be modified. Fewer voters hold such loyalties, and the electorate is more prone to change. Those who remain committed are weaker in their devotion, both in psychological affect and in the persistence of their vote. The loosening of party ties is particularly evident among younger groups, but the trend exists as well in all generational cohorts. Furthermore, partisanship is now less related to social divisions, but depends increasingly on the slim support of family inheritance.

There also are fewer behavioral consequences of partisanship. The proliferating Independent voter today is generally as confident of his political ability, as knowledgeable of issues, and as interested in nonelectoral politics as his committed neighbor. As new issues develop, and as education and other means of exposure to politics become more widespread, partisanship is likely to decline further as a source of informational cues in elections. While party loyalty remains important, it does not control perceptions—particularly evaluations of Democratic and Republican policies. The ballot itself shows a cumulative independence of partisanship. Changing issues and changing candidates draw different responses from a flexible electorate.

Party alignments will also bend. The lines between Democrats and Republicans, established in the conflicts of the New Deal period, have been breached many times, at many points. Different battle cries are being voiced and different battalions formed. The dominant symbols are not Depression bread lines but protest marches, not factory sit-downs but public sit-ins, not a war against fascism but a war against guerrillas, not a vibrant and revered president but murdered and reviled leaders. The future character of the parties is still unknown, but it will be distinctive.

One hypothetical future is that of "the emerging Republican majority." This new dominant coalition would be based ideologically on advocacy of limited government; geographically on the areas of population growth in the South and West; and socially on the "silent majority" of "middle Americans," particularly whites, Catholics, and suburbanites. All would seemingly join in "a populist revolt of the American masses who have been elevated by prosperity to middle-class status and conservatism."[38] The data developed in this chapter do not support these predictions.

The fact of some Republican electoral victories exists, most spectacularly in the 1972 presidential contest, but the voters have not changed their underlying loyalties in favor of the party. Even before the revelations of Watergate undermined confidence in the Nixon administration, the Republican party lacked the popular base to become dominant in the nation. Throughout the recent period, as seen in Figure 2.1 above, Independents gained more than any group. When the citizenry was willing to choose either party, it predominantly selected the existing Democratic majority. Moreover, among these partisans, the Democrats' advantage has actually grown slightly. They held a 3-2 margin over their competitors even during the Eisenhower presidency. This margin has fluctuated, but the considerable disparity has never been reduced, notwithstanding the party's electoral disaster in 1972.

Nor does a nascent majority loom from the pattern of intergenerational partisanship seen in Table 2.2. Republican elders have been less and less successful in passing on their partisan affinities (even when the diminishing parental proportion is considered). The Republican children of Republican progenitors constitute a rapidly decreasing proportion of the total citizenry. Democrats have had their generational differences as well, but have been relatively more successful in transmitting their political heritage.

Demographic analysis also invalidates the expectation of a Republican conversion. Over the 1960-72 time span, detailed in Table 2.3, the party stands no higher in any demographic group at the end of the period than at its beginning. Economic prosperity has not meant an increase among Republicans, nor is there any discernible change in the proportion of GOP identifiers among Catholics and southerners over the course of the four elections, although these groups are seen as anchors of the new coalition. Among the "middle Americans," those of moderate education and blue collar occupations, there again is no Republican trend, but rather a slight decline in attachment to the party over this time period.[39] The emerging Republican majority is a vision as substantial as the Cheshire cat.

The dominant trend of this period is not toward either major party, but toward independence of both. Loyalty has been generally undermined, although the Democrats have suffered more from this trend because, as the larger faction, they had more to lose. The trend to nonpartisanship has been particularly notable in those demographic groups that constitute the core of the previous Democratic majority, such as southerners, youth, persons of lesser education, Catholics, and those identified with the working class. These losses have been offset only slightly by increased Democratic support among college graduates and blacks.[40]

Unsatisfied with the existing parties, American voters are renouncing their partisan loyalties. Neither Republican nor Democratic leadership has yet demonstrated its ability to deal with the nation's large social changes and developing issues. For a time, political opportunity remains. The electorate is less bound than in the past by the deterministic ties of partisanship, family tradition, and social groups. Allegiance and votes are potentially available from responsive voters, ready to react to new stimuli. The nature and effect of these influences will depend on the initiatives of political leaders. In the following chapters, we will examine a series of factors that may shape the developing character of the American voter.

PARTY LOYALTY AND PARTY CHOICE: FINDINGS

The principal empirical findings of this chapter are listed below in summary form. These statements are not presented as formal hypotheses nor elaborated. For fuller explanation, and for discussion of other points, the reader should review the text and tables. Similar listings will be found at the ends of Chapters 3-9.

1. Party loyalty has weakened considerably, as the proportion of Independents has grown.
   1a. Weak partisan identifiers now predominate over the strongly identified.
   1b. This change is evident even within political generations.
2. Constancy of partisan loyalty has weakened considerably.
3. Transference of partisan loyalty across generations has diminished.
   3a. The direct transference of Democratic or Republican loyalty is lowest among young voters.
4. Demographic differences do not strongly distinguish Republican and Democratic identifiers.
   4a. There is now little class difference in partisanship.
5. While weakening, family inheritance is the principal factor distinguishing Republicans and Democrats.
6. Self-identified Independents are as well informed as those identifying with the political parties, contrary to past beliefs.

7. Self-identified Independents are as active in politics generally as the party loyalists.

   7a. Independents are less involved in electoral politics.

   7b. But Independents are equally informed of issues and candidate positions, and are more informed on newer issues.

8. Perceptions of the parties and candidates are distorted by partisanship.

   8a. But the distortions vary over time and by issues.

   8b. Ideological descriptions of the parties are largely unaffected.

9. The impact of partisanship on the presidential vote has diminished.

   9a. Over the past four elections, the impact of partisanship has continually decreased.

   9b. This decreased effect is evident even within political generations.

   9c. Even among partisan identifiers, fewer than half have always voted for the same party.

10. No "emerging Republican majority" is evident in recent electoral behavior.

   10a. Identification with the Republican party has declined over time and across generations.

   10b. Republican loyalty has not increased in any large demographic group.

CHAPTER 3

THE IMPACT
OF SOCIAL CLASS

Among the many factors that may affect voting, perhaps the most obvious is social class, or the economic status of the population. For half of their waking hours, humans toil, seek work, or travel to and from factories and offices. Their leisure activities, their friends and life-style, even their personalities,[1] are heavily influenced by their jobs and their income. The ballot box can hardly be isolated from the pervasive effects of the cash box.

In the United States, the influence of class has been seen as basic to political conflict, according to one view, since "the most common and durable source of factions has been the various and unequal distribution of property. Those who hold and those who are without property have ever formed distinct interests in society."[2] Controlling these clashing groups was the purpose of the constitutional separation of branches of government and of the various checks and balances, for "the regulation of these various and interfering interests forms the principal task of modern legislation and involves the spirit of party and faction in the necessary and ordinary operations of the government."[3] Contemporary voters accept these characterizations, and the most common descriptions of American parties concern their attitudes toward the interests of various economic groups.[4]

According to another argument, however, the United States is essentially exempt from economic conflict. Because America never endured a period of feudalism, because farmland and opportunity were relatively available, because of external uniformities of conduct, the nation has been seen as a consensual liberal polity, in which the conflict of social classes has been limited and restrained.[5] Alternatively, from a more critical perspective, some argue that class differences indeed do exist, but are hidden by the combined effects of violent repression, ethnic division, and the distractions of mass consumption of goods and media entertainment.[6] The behavioral result would be a similar absence of overt conflict.

In analyzing the effect of social class, we therefore begin with two different expectations. The prevalence of economic influences leads us to assume that these factors will be evident in the vote. The historic appeals of Jackson and Lincoln to frontier farmers, as of McKinley and Truman to industrial workers, underlines the relevance of social class to the vote. On the other hand, the presumed uniqueness of the United States in regard to class conflict makes us skeptical. Not organized on status lines, the major political parties have commonly rejected campaign appeals specifically directed toward exclusive economic interests. "Rather, the situation in the United States [has been] much more one of competing elite parties, each challenging the other's interest and claims to preference; neither of them, however, avowing the 'abolition' of the other."[7]

In investigating the effect of class, we will be reexamining the two portraits of the voter. For the dependent voter, social class is a direct influence, permanent in its effects, with little variation from one political context to another. The dependent voter relies on a nonpolitical characteristic, his economic position, to make electoral choices. At times, these cues may serve his interests well, but there is no assurance of such benefits. If social class is of high and unchanging importance, the finding would authenticate the dependent portrait.

This factor operates differently for the responsive voter. While his class affects his life, its political relevance is indirect, and it becomes salient only when he considers issues and parties which deal with economic matters. The relationship between status and the ballot therefore changes with political influences, such as the character of the election and the policy views of the citizenry. If the relationship between economic status and ballot choice is indirect and variable, the finding would authenticate the responsive voter portrait.

Four sets of variables are used in this analysis. The first includes relatively fixed characteristics of the voter. The most important of these characteristics is social class, but some other stable features—such as time of birth, education, and region—are also reviewed. The second set of variables comprises the voter's class consciousness, his awareness of the existence of relevant economic divisions. The third set includes the citizen's political perceptions, attitudes, and reactions to the changing stimuli of elections. The fourth set comprises the dependent variables, particularly class voting, or electoral polarization between social strata.

Figure 3.1 employs the metaphor of a baseball diamond to picture these variables. In this "game," the rules are uncertain.[8] The object remains to reach home—to explain class voting—but we are not sure how to run the bases. The two divergent views of the electorate—dependent or responsive—suggest different ways to play. A purely deterministic rule-book would demand that all action go from second base to home, since class characteristics (at second base) completely control behavior according to this theory. The given economic differences between classes would therefore result in sharp differences in their votes.

Marxian theory is also deterministic, but takes a longer path, from second to third, and then home. The most important influences on voters remain their class characteristics, but they must be made *aware* of their economic positions. To Marx, conflict between owners and workers, the bourgeoisie and proletariat, is the basic dynamic of all modern societies. The outbreak of revolutionary class struggle, however, awaits the development of consciousness. The great irony of modern history is that capitalism inescapably stimulates consciousness. Eventually, "the advance of industry, whose involuntary promoter is the bourgeoisie, replaces the isolation of the laborers, due to competition, by their revolutionary combination, due to association. . . . What the bourgeoisie therefore produces, above all, are its own grave-diggers. Its fall and the victory of

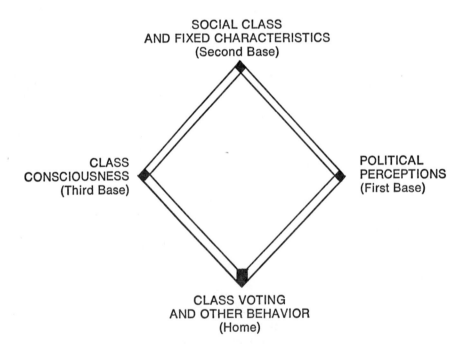

FIGURE 3.1 / THE VARIABLES IN CLASS POLITICS

the proletariat are equally inevitable."[9] Later, Lenin put still greater emphasis on the importance of consciousness and on the necessity of developing a highly disciplined political party to raise the worker's awareness.[10]

In the portrait of the responsive voter, the emphasis is on the variables related to political perceptions, located at first base in the figure. Fixed characteristics and class consciousness will have differential impact on his voting, depending on how the responsive voter perceives them. In other words, this voter's views are not necessarily determined by class, even as modified by subjective consciousness, but can be autonomous. Moreover, the impact of different factors will vary with circumstances, rather than having the permanent effect anticipated for the dependent voter. When playing this unorthodox baseball game, one scores by running from first base to home plate.

CLASS VOTING

The most common and objective measure used to designate class is occupation. The kind of work one does can be readily discovered, changes relatively little over time, and has direct effects on income and life-style. Particularly important is the distinction between manual or blue collar occupations, and nonmanual or white collar ones. The political importance of this distinction is evident in such basic matters as party loyalty. For example, among manual workers in 1972, self-identified Democrats outnumbered Republicans by better than 5-2. Among the white collar workers, the Democratic edge was less than 6 to 5.[11]

As a measure of social class, however, occupation disregards certain important features. Discrepancies often exist between the objective position of a person and her family background, as exemplified by the societal matron employed as a low-wage secretary. Another anomaly comes from income differences, such as exist between the highly paid truck driver and the indigent graduate student. The subjective feelings of individuals therefore must be taken into account in identifying social class.

There surely are many persons whose personal loyalties do not fit their presumed occupational identities, for example, a Horatio Alger hero or a radical intellectual. Taking account of these differences, a second, more subjective measure of social class is commonly employed, class identification. Respondents select their own grouping, almost always calling themselves either "middle class" or "working class."[12] Party identification varies considerably by self-selected status. Voters who identify as working class preferred the Democrats in 1972 by better than 2-1, while those who identify as middle class showed a smaller Democratic edge of 5-4.

There is a third measure of social class. When asked to select their social position, about a third of national respondents do not spontaneously assign themselves to a rank, but must be prompted. We therefore can categorize persons by their "class consciousness," segmenting the sample into those who are "aware" and offer their own classification, and those who are "unaware" and only accept a forced choice. Those aware of class would be expected also to be more affected by economic influences. Politically, the Democratic party receives more and firmer allegiance among persons who are conscious of their class position.

Having clarified the measures of social class, we can investigate the direct relationship between class and the presidential vote—tracing a straight path between second base and home plate on the baseball diagram. A high degree of social division would be evident if a large proportion of manual workers or self-identified working class people supported the Democrats, while the white collar workers or self-identified middle classes voted for their opponents.

Deterministic assumptions would lead to expectations of a strong relationship between class and the vote. To the contrary, there is only limited relationship between either occupation or class identification and ballot choice. In 1968, for example, while manual workers show greater support for Humphrey than nonmanual workers do, the margin is only 47 percent to 36 percent. The correlation between occupation and presidential choice is a very modest .11. The difference between the self-identified working and middle classes is even less, 45 percent to 37 percent, and the correlation still lower, .08.[13] The level of class voting further weakens in 1972, when McGovern receives very similar votes from manual and white collar groups, and the correlation of class and presidential preference is barely significant.

Taken by themselves, these results would substantiate a widespread belief in the decline of class as a significant element in American politics. Writing at the end of the 1950s, the authors of *The American Voter* perceived such a sag. From a relatively high point in the Truman-Dewey contest of 1948, they found a steady decrease, the low point being a correlation of .12 in 1956.[14] The presidential contests of 1968 and 1972 apparently mark a continuation of this trend.

Using a different technique, Alford challenged these conclusions. He found that the level of class difference in the vote had been essentially stable since the period of the New Deal, although the election of 1948 was unusual in the degree of group polarization. Typically, manual workers voted 15 to 20 percent more in favor of the Democrats than nonmanual workers did.[15] Even when Alford's technique is used, however, class polarization appears to have dropped. In 1968, the difference in Democratic vote between the economic groupings is only 11 percent, and in 1972 only 5 percent. These margins hardly constitute a vigorous class struggle.

What is missing in the preceding discussion is a comparison with the data from 1960 and 1964. Vital economic issues—medicare, labor law, aid to education—were raised in these elections. Collaterally, a higher degree of polarization exists than in either the preceding or the following contests. The correlations between class and electoral choice rose in 1960 from the low levels of the 1950s, and then increased further four years later. Responding to their choice between Johnson and Goldwater, manual workers voted Democratic in numbers surpassing the white collar group by 17 percentage points, and the correlation was a more substantial .19. The particular circumstances of the election, in which questions of social class were salient, facilitated class voting.

There is neither an inevitable expression of economic position in the vote, nor an inevitable disappearance of such expression. In any year, we must conclude that voting is not simply determined by class. The path between our second base and home is little used. When the ground is properly prepared, however, an indirect route can be found. We may now consider one of the more complex paths by including third base, or class consciousness, as an additional element. In this variant of the dependent model, we would expect class voting to be more evident among those who are aware of their stations, while less class voting could be explained by the absence of class identity.

Despite the predictions of Marxian theory,[16] we find the opposite result, as specified in Table 3.1. Voters aware of their class do not necessarily join in a heightened political struggle. In 1960 and 1964, the relationship between class identity and the vote among those aware of class is less than, or equal to, the same class identity/vote relationship among those unaware of class, while in 1968 the relationship among the aware voters weakens even when occupation is used as the measure of class position.[17] Only in 1972 does class polarization increase consistently with awareness, but even then the relationships remain barely noticeable.

Awareness of class can lead to political alliances rather than conflicts. Its general effect is not polarization in the vote, but an increased Democratic vote among both lower and higher strata, thus often reducing the statistical measure of polarization. The class character of the parties is not a symmetrical one, in which blue collar workers identify their group interests with the Democrats, and white collar workers view the Republicans more favorably. Rather, when voters conceive of politics in class terms, both occupational categories tend to favor the Democrats. Over the past twenty years, the Democrats have been seen persistently as more favorable to group interests.[18] Middle class voters share this perception of the parties and, when more conscious of class, express these feelings in their votes, as well as in their party loyalties.

The effect of class awareness is slightly different in 1968 from the effect in 1960, 1964, and 1972. As expected, the Republican vote declined among those aware of class and the Democratic vote generally increased.

TABLE 3.1 / CLASS VOTING FOR DEMOCRATIC PRESIDENTIAL CANDIDATES, 1960-72*

	1960	1964	1968	1972
Aware of Class	**By Class Identification**			
Working Class	56.9	78.3	46.6	39.3
	(647)	(392)	(296)	(488)
Middle Class	38.5	55.2	39.7	34.7
	(384)	(286)	(353)	(550)
Tau-b	.18	.24	.07	.05
Unaware of Class				
Working Class	53.0	79.1	42.7	31.3
	(198)	(187)	(178)	(252)
Middle Class	29.5	57.1	33.1	30.8
	(132)	(203)	(127)	(208)
Tau-b	.23	.24	.10	.01
Aware of Class	**By Occupation**			
Manual	60.5	79.1	47.5	40.9
	(403)	(249)	(259)	(423)
Nonmanual	46.0	60.8	38.5	35.3
	(359)	(250)	(286)	(490)
Tau-b	.15	.20	.09	.06
Unaware of Class				
Manual	50.4	74.8	48.4	29.5
	(115)	(155)	(121)	(176)
Nonmanual	42.2	59.3	31.2	29.6
	(128)	(162)	(129)	(216)
Tau-b	.08	.16	.18	.00

*Entries are Democratic percentage of the vote from persons of the designated class and degree of awareness. The numbers in parentheses are the total numbers on which percentages are based. Tau-b is the correlation of class and the presidential vote, with the Wallace third-party vote in 1968 combined with that of the Republicans.

At the same time, George Wallace did best among the working class and increased his vote further among those conscious of class. Beyond his substantially racist appeals, the Alabama insurgent deliberately sought support from those discontented with the distribution of income, status, and privilege. Some voters responded to the racist element in Wallace's campaign, "while millions of others who were not obsessed with race nevertheless felt he cared about the issues that troubled them." Wallace heightened the impact of class awareness by opposing the working class policeman to the privileged student, the middle class shopkeeper to the upper class corporate executive, the burdened factory worker to the elitist bureaucrat.[19]

Another indicator of the effect of consciousness is found in examining those with incongruent class status. Lack of congruence derives from the disparity between the objective occupational position of an individual and his subjective class allegiance. A "false consciousness" is evident in upwards of a fourth of Americans, as in the case of the factory worker who sees himself as part of the "great American middle class" or the liberal professional who identifies as a "worker." Class voting is unlikely behavior for these persons, for they are beset with conflicting pressures from their objective occupational situation and their subjective status allegiance. Even if economic factors are emphasized by a candidate, they will find it difficult to receive consistent cues.

Among those of incongruent status, class voting is sharply reduced in all years. Even in 1964, when class factors were emphasized in the campaign, persons of uncertain class position showed only a low correlation of status and vote. In 1972, with less emphasis on such factors, a relationship was completely absent. On the other hand, among those whose self-identification is consistent with their occupational position, class voting remains evident throughout the entire period.

While status ambiguity consistently depresses class voting, the particular pattern in which this happens varies from one election to another. Typically, persons misidentified as workers give the Democrats a disproportionate share of their vote, while those who "wrongly" consider themselves middle class tend to greater support of the Republicans. In keeping with these expectations of the behavior of the psychologically mobile,[20] in 1964 Johnson received a bonus of 20 percent of the vote from the would-be workers, and Goldwater nearly as many extra votes from the aspirants to the middle class.

In 1968, as seen in Table 3.2, the presence of George Wallace complicated the situation. Those misidentified with the middle class still gave the Republican candidate, Nixon, more votes than their unambiguous peers. On the other hand, those misidentified with the working class showed

TABLE 3.2 / CLASS CONGRUENCE AND THE VOTE*

	1964			1968			
	Johnson	Goldwater	(N)	Humphrey	Nixon	Wallace	(N)
Congruent Class							
Manual Occupations	83.0	17.0	(288)	49.0	38.4	12.7	(292)
Nonmanual Occupations	53.9	46.1	(280)	36.1	57.2	6.7	(299)
(Tau-b)		(.31)			(.13)		
Incongruent Class							
Manual Occupations	66.4	33.6	(110)	42.0	44.0	14.0	(100)
Nonmanual Occupations	74.4	25.6	(125)	36.4	48.5	15.2	(132)
(Tau-b)		(.09)			(.06)		

*Percentages add horizontally by rows to 100 percent, except for rounding errors.

particular support of Wallace. This vote appears to be the expression of resentment of the threatened white collar group. In other words, persons of ambiguous status who felt disadvantaged in this political situation expressed their resentment by objectively inaccurate identification with the working class and a vote for Wallace's protest candidacy. Such tendencies are similar to the support rightist movements have gained historically from displaced middle class groups.[21]

Class consciousness does not automatically result in class polarization. Its effects depend on political factors, the parties and candidates, as well as on the voters' class positions. While congruence in status increases the likelihood of class division in the balloting, this potential can only be realized in an appropriate context, such as the election of 1964, and will be unfulfilled in elections in which class is less salient, such as 1968 and 1972.

The direct influence of social class on the vote, then, is limited and variable. Ballot choice is not determined by economic position alone, not even among those aware of the existence of classes nor those who are unambiguous about their own positions. Perceptions of the political world alter the impact of class factors, modify that impact from one campaign to another, and even reverse the expected results. The path from third base to home plate is not straight, but requires a long detour through first—the territory of the responsive voter.

SOURCES OF CONFLICT

While the total electorate is generally unpolarized along class lines, these divisions are not completely absent, and the potential for class politics does exist in certain groups. We may now examine the degree of class consciousness and status voting in particular social groups.

In regard to class consciousness, there is very little difference among demographic categories. Contrary to expectations that class awareness would be more common among the middle class,[22] the slim 2 percent distinction between occupational strata with respect to awareness fails to achieve statistical significance in 1972. Similarly, there is no variation between the races or sexes. Awareness of class is greater among persons raised in a large metropolis, those living outside of rural areas, Catholics, and college graduates. However, the margins between groups are slight in all of these comparisons.

At one time, class awareness was related to a demographic factor—historical generation. When persons endure intense experiences in youth, the experiences may affect all of their later lives. Therefore, when class awareness was found to be particularly high among persons born early in the twentieth century, this awareness was attributed to the fact that these persons were "in their twenties and thirties during the depths of the Great Depression, a generation long assumed to have been strongly affected by economic events."[23] We can reexamine this assumed relationship by comparing class consciousness in generational cohorts across the series of elections from 1952 to 1972. The Depression group can be followed as it ages further and can also be measured against those born at a later time, when economic problems were less prominent.

This examination does not show the Depression generation[24] as consistently most conscious of class. Although past relationships held in 1960, for example, in 1968 and 1972 this cohort was less aware of status positions than younger groups. As the group has aged, it has become less aware of class position—unless its most class-conscious members have died more frequently. An alternative explanation may be found in the life cycle. The data are not all of a piece, but they show that class consciousness does tend to be concentrated among the middle-aged, whatever the time of birth and political maturity. This pattern suggests that class awareness is a function of aging itself. As persons reach this stage of life, their occupational niche has become essentially permanent, their income and life-style largely secure, and therefore, their consciousness of class structure less ambiguous. Younger or older persons' positions are less settled, or more threatened, and their awareness of social stratification is similarly subject to change.

Demographic characteristics also may affect the direct relationship between class and the vote. A class-conscious age group would be expected, for instance, to show a greater correlation between occupation and presidential choice. Prior to 1960, for example, the Depression generation exhibited the highest degree of class polarization in its vote, when compared to other cohorts. Having passed through the sufferings of the 1930s, the group knew about social conflicts and expressed them in elections. In this relationship, as well, there has been a change. From 1960, as detailed in Table 3.3, the relative polarization within the cohorts maturing during the Depression varies considerably. While these voters are usually among the most divided along class lines, they do not maintain this position consistently.[25]

The variation in class polarization of these groups again underlines the

TABLE 3.3 / CORRELATIONS OF OCCUPATION AND VOTE, BY AGE COHORTS*

Years of Birth	Election Year					
	1952	1956	1960	1964	1968	1972
1887-1896	.26	.12	-.15	—	—	—
Depression Generations						
1897-1906	.31	.15	.03	.34	.15	.17
1907-1916	.32	.11	.30	.19	.18	.11
1917-1926	.13	.09	.11	.20	.23	.11
1927-1936	—	—	.13	.20	.07	.03
1937-1946	—	—	—	—	.04	.02

*Entries are the tau-b correlations between occupation and presidential vote, with entries deleted for cohorts with small numbers of respondents.

importance of the particular election and the responsiveness of voters, whatever their age, to differing circumstances. In 1952, with echoes of the New Deal issues still audible, the Depression generations were split more along occupational lines than other cohorts. Four years later, with these issues muted, their class fissures were barely visible. By 1960, a novel pattern is evident, which can be explained as a response to the distinct stimuli of the Kennedy-Nixon contest.

In 1960, there is a decided difference between the two age cohorts that were maturing during the Depression. Among those relatively older, there is virtually no effect of class on the vote. The probable explanation for its absence is the importance of religion in this campaign. The shaping of the contemporary party system came not only through the economic influences felt during the Depression and the New Deal, but also through the earlier exercise of Protestant hegemony in the Republican party and the rise of self-conscious Catholic ethnic groups to prominence in the Democratic party. When Catholicism became a critical factor in 1960, it brought an emphasis on religious affiliation of voters that was particularly salient to voters who entered politics during and before the 1920s—the time of Al Smith, the politicalization of urban ethnics, and the spread of nativist movements such as the Ku Klux Klan. For those whose first participation in politics came somewhat later, class factors had submerged ethnic influences, and class polarization remained high. To these voters in 1960, John Kennedy's religion was less critical than his class appeal.[26]

The 1964 election was free of religious division. Instead, the campaign was almost a renewed referendum on the New Deal itself, as Barry Goldwater appeared to threaten the legislative and social reforms of the earlier period. Such an apparent threat was most relevant to those who had begun their political lives during the economic crisis, the two Depression cohorts. Consequently, they reacted quite clearly to the class character of the issues. In 1968 and 1972, as the relevance of the issues debated in 1964 declined, the level of class voting in these groups also resumed the previous downward trend.

More generally, the level of social conflict in any particular generation depends on a combination of past and present, both the political circumstances of the time at which it enters the electorate and the relevant stimuli it receives periodically. The Depression generations began voting when class stimuli were plentiful. Accordingly, their initial and later ballots evidence relatively great polarization. Other generations have entered politics when there were fewer class-related stimuli. While their polarization may increase somewhat with age, the absolute level will be lower. Nevertheless, a potential for status alignments remains in all generations, since party identification retains a class basis.[27] The realization of this potential depends on the emphasis given to salient issues of economics.[28]

The possibility of a class politics can also be glimpsed in examining regional patterns of class voting, particularly in the South.[29] Before the 1960s little polarization existed in the region. Given the preoccupation of the area with the race question, conflicts associated with economic position were subordinated, resolved within the Democratic party, or suppressed by the dominant "merchant-planter-lawyer" class.[30] In 1960, for example, while class differences were quite evident nationally, they were statistically insignificant in the southern and border states.

In recent years, the accumulation of large social changes and immediate political developments have made class relevant to southern politics. As the region has industrialized, its social structure has been modernized as well. The emigration of blacks has reduced white fears of racial domination, while substantial immigration into the region has led to greater emphasis on economic development. Two-party competition has broken the monopolistic hold of the Democrats, and the parties' stances in Dixie are now analogous to those in the North, the Republicans directing their appeals largely to white collar groups, and the Democrats seeking votes of both blacks and whites of lower incomes. A century after the end of Reconstruction, the South is rejoining the nation politically.[31] Status polarization is higher in the South than the rest of the nation in both 1964 and 1968, and equivalent in the two regions in 1972. The trend is particularly notable since it occurred during elections in which racial issues were raised either implicitly or explicitly. Despite the historical sensitivity of the region to the question of race, the South was substantially influenced by class factors in these contests. In 1968, the effect remains evident even with the complication of a three-way race for president including a southern favorite, as well as in the pure two-party balloting for Congress. Thus, the New Deal economic basis of politics, after considerable delay, has crossed the Mason-Dixon line.[32]

Voting trends within educational groupings also evidence a novel relationship. Usually, class and education cannot be separated because the two attributes are so closely associated that, for example, the Republican preferences of college graduates are equivalent to the Republican choices of those in professional and managerial occupations. In Table 3.4, the two factors are separated in an analysis of the 1972 vote. Rather than arranging the data simply by conventional occupational categories, we dichotomize occupations within each educational classification. The highest category among college graduates comprises only professional occupations, while among those of grade school education, the highest category includes all but unskilled workers. By changing categories in this way, we have sufficient cases to make comparisons within each educational stratum.

The results are quite different from those of past elections, when the Republican percentage of the vote regularly rose up the educational and vocational ladder. Looking at the total percentages, the greatest Democratic vote comes at the extremes: the professionals and less skilled man-

TABLE 3.4 / CLASS VOTING BY EDUCATION, 1972*

	Education					
Occupation	Grade School	High School	Some College	College Graduate	Total	(N)
Professional	33.3	28.1	30.2	45.0 (160)	38.0	(294)
			28.1 (174)			
Managerial	22.7	22.5	25.6	28.9	24.7	(234)
	38.8 (103)	27.1 (199)				
Clerical, Sales	45.5	32.1	42.9	31.3	36.8	(198)
				33.3 (96)		
			40.6 (236)			
Skilled Worker	43.8	24.6	31.1	16.7	30.6	(290)
		35.0 (305)				
Other Manual	44.7 (85)	42.9	50.7	61.5	45.6	(342)
Total	41.5	31.9	35.3	40.6		
(N)	(188)	(504)	(410)	(256)		
Dichotomized Index of Class Voting	6	8	12	−12		

*Each entry is the Democratic percentage of the presidential vote among persons in the particular occupational group and of the indicated educational level. Class voting indexes are calculated within columns, by comparing dichotomized occupational groups. Numbers in parentheses are the number of cases on which each associated percentage is based.

ual workers, the most and the least educated. Republican support is highest in the middle groups: persons of moderate education and in the jobs of moderate status.

Comparison of the dichotomized occupations within educational strata shows that the largest differences occur among persons of moderate education. Traditional class politics of the "haves" and "have-nots" is greatest among those who have a high school education or only limited exposure to college. There is less class differentiation among those with the least schooling and a strong reversal of the expected relationship among the college graduates. Professionals with a college education actually show greater Democratic support than those of the same education but lower status, who traditionally would be expected to endorse the "left" party.

These results may be peculiar to the circumstances of the 1972 election. Even alone, however, they imply the emergence of a "top-bottom" alliance, a coalition of the highly privileged and the underprivileged, in opposition to those in more traditional occupations and with moderate social advantages. Traditional class divisions persist in the latter groups, while newer loyalties affect the votes of the more highly educated. A large proportion of high status persons are not following their presumed class interest and voting Republican, but are instead joining in the Democratic party with the least educated in the least prestigious jobs.

Whether derided as "limousine liberals" or evaluated as "reform

Democrats,"[33] the unique voting behavior of high status voters in 1972 may presage both a permanent shift in the class basis of American politics and the substitution of new alliances. As habitual party allegiances have weakened, traditional class loyalties may also be altered. The transformations of American society, wrenchingly evident in recent years, may have permanent effect. If so, "political front lines would be drawn in entirely new places; the trenches which so clearly marked the boundaries between the parties under the order established in the 1930s would rapidly become deserted and useless."[34]

The variable, and diminishing, incidence of class voting is further evidenced if we examine a political factor, the strength of partisanship. Since the character of the contemporary parties was formed amid economic crisis, persons who are more devoted to the parties should be more receptive to class influences, and the level of polarization should increase with the strength of identification. This relationship was clearly evident in 1952, when strong identifiers (of either party) showed a correlation of .42 between subjective status and their vote, while the association dwindled to insignificance among Independents.[35]

The relationship continued to be evident in 1960 and 1964, when the class basis of the parties was manifested. In 1968 and 1972, with social divisions de-emphasized in the campaign, party loyalty has less impact. Taking the regions separately, northern class voting remains highest among strong identifiers, but the correlation has dropped in 1968 to .20, and virtually disappears in 1972, at .08.

In the South, a different pattern again demonstrates the delayed development of class politics in the region.[36] Through 1968, polarization is most apparent among persons who are only weakly identified as Democrats or Republicans, and is diminished among those either strongly loyal or completely autonomous. As political development lagged in the South, persons of strong loyalties clung to affinities developed in earlier periods or around different issues. By 1972, however, the Southern pattern had become congruent with the rest of the nation. Class influence is most evident among the strong identifiers, even though low in all groups. This result further argues that party loyalties in the region are becoming fixed along the economic lines previously dominant in the rest of the nation.

Taken as a whole, the analysis of class voting among different groups provides additional reasons for rejecting the dependent profile of the electorate. Social polarization is not generally prevalent, nor is it inherent in any particular generation, region, or educational group. Even class awareness and strong party identification do not always stimulate division. In their reactions to class factors, as to other stimuli, the voters react to the given circumstances of the times and do not necessarily reflect fixed characteristics in their behavior.

There is but one consistent conclusion that appears in the varied relationships between social class and the vote: the vital importance of the electoral context.[37] When the parties, the candidates, and the events of the campaign emphasize class, the salience of social position will be evident. Such was the case in 1948, when the parties were still preserved in the mold of the New Deal, when the candidates personally represented conflicting social origins and interests, and when the critical issues involved control of the economy. Many of these characteristics were evident again in 1960 and particularly in 1964, when Barry Goldwater challenged and Lyndon Johnson defended the welfare state.

In presidential elections, however, class factors are not always stressed. Judgments on the quality of the individual nominees or on foreign policy issues are often decisive. Since these judgments are not inherently class-based, no consistent social polarization is likely in such contests. The absence of these judgments in 1956 accounts for the slight class difference in that election. By 1972, economic issues were subordinated, as the election turned on questions such as Vietnam and the abilities of the particular nominees; consequently, status polarization disappears. While economic issues were neglected, the voters did respond to the stimuli of the times.

THE POLITICS OF CLASS VOTING

On our conceptual baseball diamond, we have found that most of the play occurs around first base, or the area of political perceptions. Given the limited impact of both fixed characteristics (second base) and class consciousness (third base), we must therefore turn to a more specific examination of the political factors and perceptions that are located at first base, beginning with party loyalty, or partisanship. Partisanship may actually be a surrogate for class division. While little use is made of the direct path between fixed characteristics and the vote, in the overall play political loyalty may provide an indirect route. Class differences could effect differences in partisanship, and partisanship could in turn determine the vote.

As we have previously seen, there is some truth to the common class-related descriptions of the parties, the Democrats winning more support among blue collar groups and the Republicans winning more among the white collars. The relationship between occupation and partisanship has persisted since the New Deal, and represents the basic—but not deep—cleavage of the contemporary party system.[38]

However, these associations have weakened recently. By 1972, class factors provide a very limited explanation of partisanship. The relationship is particularly weak if we use self-identification as the measure of status. If occupation is used as the measure of status, the division of the parties has been more stable, largely because of different developments within and outside of the South. Below the Mason-Dixon line, the relationship of occupation and partisanship was not significant in 1960, but it is now equivalent to the relationship found in the rest of the nation. Outside of the region, the underlying class loyalties have been attenuated. Taking the nation as a whole, the two trends have virtually offset one another, at least until 1972.

While some occupational polarization remains as a result of these countervailing movements, the link between class and partisanship is slack. The other part of the relationship, between partisanship and the vote

TABLE 3.5 / OCCUPATION AND PARTY IDENTIFICATION, BY REGION, 1960-72*

	Democrat	Independent	Republican	(N)
	South			
1960				
Manual	62.8	23.0	14.2	(226)
Nonmanual	62.8	19.3	17.9	(207)
		Tau = .01		
1964				
Manual	74.0	16.9	9.1	(154)
Nonmanual	61.1	24.3	14.6	(144)
		Tau = .13		
1968				
Manual	60.4	26.6	13.1	(222)
Nonmanual	44.3	44.3	11.4	(167)
		Tau = .12		
1972				
Manual	52.0	31.9	16.2	(433)
Nonmanual	43.6	31.5	24.8	(298)
		Tau = .10		
	Non-South			
1960				
Manual	46.4	30.3	23.2	(534)
Nonmanual	30.5	27.4	42.1	(390)
		Tau = .19		
1964				
Manual	53.1	27.6	19.4	(439)
Nonmanual	38.9	26.9	34.1	(375)
		Tau = .16		
1968				
Manual	47.2	30.6	22.1	(447)
Nonmanual	32.4	31.0	36.6	(432)
		Tau = .17		
1972				
Manual	43.0	37.8	19.2	(762)
Nonmanual	29.8	39.3	30.9	(766)
		Tau = .15		

*Percentages add horizontally by rows to 100 percent, except for rounding errors.

itself, has also weakened. Party loyalty remains a vital political factor, but it neither is determined by class nor itself determines the vote. Political perceptions merit independent analysis. In this game, first base is intrinsically interesting, not only a relay point.

The importance of economics in political choice is found directly, in the voters' stands on vital questions. What citizens believe about economic issues does have impact, and considerably more than their categorical memberships. The vote is influenced by two such sets of attitudes: first, it is related to the voters' positions on relevant issues, issues that concern the social costs and benefits incurred by different strata; second, it is related to the differences voters see between the parties on these issues. To show these connections, two indexes have been constructed, which are described below.

The first measure, an opinion index on issues related to class, combines preferences on three issues: government support of medical care, a guarantee of full employment, and either federal aid to education (for 1960 to 1968) or progressive taxation (in 1972). Since medical aid, employment guarantees, education support, and progressive taxation are generally considered to benefit deprived social groups, favorable opinions on these redistributive questions[39] are considered "liberal" and the opposites "conservative."[40]

The second index measures the voter's perception of party differences on the three issues, as well as the expected effect of the election on his personal financial situation. On each question, the respondent declares which party, or neither, is more favorable to the particular program or more likely to improve his own economic position. The combined index indicates the relative party difference voters perceive on class-related issues.[41]

Although these two sets of opinions relate to class matters, the indexes are typically independent of social class. There is some tendency, but surprisingly slight in recent years, for opinions on these questions to follow class lines. Those who identify with the working class are more likely than their opposites to support the liberal position. In 1960 and 1964, these correlations are substantial, although not overwhelming (tau = .23 in both years), but the relationship dwindles considerably in 1968 and 1972 (.13 in 1968 and .04 in 1972). Since these social-cost issues, if any, are particularly salient to class, we would expect much greater correlations if opinions were a direct, deterministic response to social position. However, this relationship is no different among those who are class conscious. Rather, the general effect of class awareness appears to be an increase in support of liberal governmental policy among both self-identified workers and the middle class.

Perception of party differences is entirely independent of class. Whether of blue collar or white collar occupations, whether identified with workers or middle class, the respondents agree that the Democrats are more likely to support liberal policies and to improve their personal financial situation. Such perceptions are increased among those who are aware of class positions, particularly within the middle class. The Democratic identification with these policies is evident in all of the four elections, but the pattern becomes considerably clearer after 1960, as we will elaborate in Chapter 8.

Opinions and party perceptions provide a better explanation for party loyalty than social status does. Those who hold liberal positions on the issues also tend to be Democrats, and the relationship remains at approximately the same level within categories of social class. Loyalty to the parties is similarly associated with perception of party positions. Those who view the Democrats as more supportive of liberal positions tend to identify with that party.

These relationships cannot be dismissed as partisan rationalizations, resulting from loyalists mechanically adopting their party's position and declaring their party is in favor of good things. The relationships have changed over time, which would not be possible if voters were permanently determined by their initial loyalties. Moreover, voters' characterizations of the parties have altered in the direction of greater agreement among the electorate. If only rationalization were involved, we would expect many Republicans to view the GOP as supportive of these positions, at levels comparable to those of Democrats. Such is not the case, for partisans of both camps, regardless of their own opinions, tend to see the Democrats as more liberal. In fact, more Republicans acknowledge the Democratic position on the liberal end of the spectrum than claim this place for their own party.

Most vitally, there is an independent relationship between the voters' ballots, and their policy views and evaluation of party stands. This relationship is largely independent of social class and is distinct as well from pure party loyalty. Liberal voters express their opinions in a Democratic vote, even when class issues are muted as in 1972 (tau = .31), and still more when the issues are overt as in 1964 (tau = .41). Similarly, when liberal voters see the Democrats as supporting liberal positions, they are quite likely to vote for them.[42]

The importance of these voter beliefs can be seen if we combine them with the earlier measures of class position. When we control for class, the relationship between beliefs and the vote is virtually unchanged, thereby demonstrating that the original relationship is real, not spurious. On the other hand, if we control for opinion, there is little relationship left between class and the vote. Table 3.6 illustrates the relationship for the election of 1968, in which class was of moderate salience. Within each stratum, correlations of opinion to the vote remain above .30. When opinion is controlled, however, the correlation between class and the vote

TABLE 3.6 / POLITICAL OPINIONS, SOCIAL CLASS, AND DEMOCRATIC VOTE, 1968*

	Working Class Identification	Middle Class Identification
Opinion on Class Issues		
Liberal	62.6	55.5
	(198)	(173)
Moderate	42.7	35.7
	(178)	(168)
Conservative	18.5	18.5
	(124)	(151)
Perception of Party Differences		
Democrats More Liberal	67.9	59.9
	(196)	(187)
Democrats Slightly Liberal	33.5	26.6
	(242)	(233)
No Difference or Republicans Liberal	14.5	4.2
	(62)	(72)
Total	44.6	37.4
	(500)	(492)

*Each cell entry is percentage voting Democratic among those with given views and class identification. Number in parenthesis is the base for calculation of the percentage.

declines almost to insignificance. The same pattern is found in the effect of perceived party differences.

The effect of opinions and of perception of party differences clearly is increased polarization in the balloting. That these voter beliefs lead in a partisan direction is also clear. When persons become aware of party differences on the three social-cost issues, they overwhelmingly agree on the liberal direction of the Democrats and the conservative thrust of the Republicans, then follow these perceptions in their votes. The ballot is not influenced solely by class issues, and much of the electorate is unaffected at all by such issues. But when they do see the relevance of the parties to their opinions, the voters follow through. The clearest associations with the vote are not those of class and other deterministic factors. Instead, it is autonomous beliefs on social questions that are vital to democratic decisions.

The controlled effects of all class-factor variables can be assessed by contrasting the elections of 1960 and 1972, the beginning and end of a continuous trend. For this purpose, we perform two multiple regressions, with the presidential vote as the dependent variable. First, we include the two indexes (opinion on class issues, perception of party differences), the measures of class, and various demographic variables. Second, we add the factor of party identification in a separate analysis, to discover how much difference it makes on its own.

When party identification is excluded, the opinion on class issues and perception of party differences are the most important variables. The relationship between these indexes and the vote is genuine, holding even when all of the other social factors are controlled. These latter factors, to the contrary, have little impact on their own.

Upon adding the variable of party identification (Table 3.7), this factor immediately becomes most important in explaining the vote. This result is certainly in keeping with expectations that the vote is grounded in persistent loyalties. However, party identification does not eliminate the other relationships. Because of the overlap of partisanship with the opinion variables, their own independent explanatory power drops somewhat, but their value remains highly significant. While an important share of the vote is related to partisanship, it is not a sufficient explanation. The voter's position on important questions, and his perception of party differences on these questions, also affects his vote. We cannot understand the American electorate as responding only to its loyalties. Certainly the election is not determined by inchoate sociological drives, for these fixed factors have little stable impact. Insofar as they are important, they are largely incorporated within party identification.

A note of caution is necessary, however, in accepting these conclusions. Demographic influences such as class may have indirect as well as direct effects, but the former influences are minimized by the technique of multiple regression. Therefore, we must keep in mind the possibility that class affects the vote indirectly, by influencing opinion, which in turn influences the vote.[43] Another problem may arise from the reciprocal effects of independent and dependent variables. In the procedure used here, we view vote as the dependent variable, affected by class, opinion, and the other independent variables. It is also possible that the vote itself affects some of these variables. A person choosing to vote for Kennedy or McGovern on other grounds, for example, may change his opinion on an issue to conform to that of the Democratic candidate. Since our primary interest lies in explaining the vote, we are justified in using it as the dependent variable, so long as we recognize that we have made an important limiting assumption.[44]

As in the previous chapter, the bottom three rows indicate the amount of explained variance. The first of these rows, Total R^2, is the percentage of the variance in the vote which can be explained by all of the independent variables together. The second row is the proportion which is due to partisanship uniquely, when it is held back as the last variable in the regression. This proportion probably represents a purely traditional loyalty. The final row is the maximum proportion which may be attributed to partisanship. This figure results when partisanship is introduced first in

TABLE 3.7 / CONTRASTING IMPACT OF CLASS FACTORS ON VOTING,
1960 AND 1972
(Beta Weights, Multiple Regression of Republican Presidential Vote)*

	All Voters		South		Non-South	
	1960	**1972**	**1960**	**1972**	**1960**	**1972**
Party Identification	.45	.37	.42	.32	.47	.41
Opinion on Class Issues	.13	.18	.28	.13	.08	.16
Perception of Party						
Differences	.21	.08	.24	.02	.19	.11
Class Identification	.02	−.02	−.04	−.13	.03	.04
Occupation	−.03	.00	−.11	−.03	−.02	.01
Class Awareness	.02	.03	.10	−.05	.01	.09
Education	.06	.00	.04	.08	.08	−.03
Age	.04	.06	.06	.06	.03	.06
Religion	.20	−.03	.08	.00	.23	−.08
Race	.08	.21	.01	.42	.12	.14
(N)	(933)	(609)	(261)	(172)	(672)	(437)
Total R²	.546	.337	.432	.412	.613	.343
Unique R², Partisanship	.143	.110	.119	.088	.126	.128
R², Partisanship as						
First Variable	.423	.224	.304	.188	.506	.245

*Positive coefficients show that the Republican vote is independently related to Republican party identification, conservative opinion on class issues, perception of the Republican party as liberal on these issues, middle class self-identification, white collar occupation, absence of class awareness, higher education, greater age, Protestant religious affiliation, and white racial membership. Negative coefficients show that Democratic vote is dependent on these characteristics.

the regression, and thereby gets "credit" for all of the overlap between partisanship and the other independent variables.

The 1960 and 1972 elections are in marked contrast to each other. In 1960, partisanship is dominant. When introduced first, party identification alone accounts for over three-fourths of the explained variance in the vote. As between the two indexes, it is the one tied more closely to partisanship and more susceptible of rationalization—the perception of party differences—that has the greater impact. In 1972, the total degree of explained vote has dropped considerably. Even within this limited proportion, the share that could conceivably be attributed to partisanship has decreased. Conversely, opinion on the issues has waxed in its impact, while the perception of party differences has diminished weight, reflecting the consensus of the electorate on the relative liberalism of the Democrats. The changing rankings of demographic factors also show the variability of the electorate. Religion is vital in 1960, when the first Catholic president is elected, but race has become vital in 1972, when issues of color are emphasized.

Separate analyses by region show the particular change in the South. The total proportion of the vote that can be explained in 1972 is larger below than above the Mason-Dixon line. Traditional partisanship has decreased rapidly in this region, and there is a significant effect of opinion on class issues, which is considerably greater than that of perceived party differences. Changes in the independent effect of occupation and education are in the direction of a class politics.

The development of such alignments, however, is now only a potentiality. Racial divisions are still predominant in the South and closely correspond to divisions of opinion, just as the influence of the racial variable dominates the multiple regression. When this variable is removed statistically, the independent effect of class factors increases greatly, and among whites opinions on economic issues become almost as decisive as party identification. Regrettably, it is not as simple to remove the effect of race from history and minds.

Greater southern orientation to the problems of class remains possible. There is a strong strain of populist attitudes which persists in southern politics and which has been reflected from time to time in political movements, even across racial lines.[45] Through most of the region's history, as in 1972, this strain has been subordinated by racial questions, but economic grievances remain to be argued. "There is heavy support for economic liberalism in the working class and in the lower-middle class in the South,"[46] which was evident both in the votes for Democrats and for George Wallace. If race issues become moderated—unfortunately an unlikely prospect—or if their impact becomes less distinctly southern —which is quite probable—Dixie is as likely to evidence class voting alignments as the rest of the nation.

THE FUTURE OF CLASS POLITICS

The future character of class voting is dimly visible in viewing past behavior. Although social class is a prevalent fact of life, it need not determine the vote. The electors respond differently to varying influences in changing contexts. Ballot choices of manual and white collar workers do not divide sharply, and their differences in the voting booth have declined. Contrary to Marxian expectations, class differences do not increase among those conscious of social stratification. While class awareness does affect political perceptions, its partisan effect is not necessarily increased political differentiation, but often increased support for the Democrats or for a third party.

Class voting is not a constant feature of American politics, but a variable. It has been neither steady nor steadily declining, but episodic. The variation is not consistently related to fixed characteristics, such as historical generation, region, education, and partisan tenacity. Rather, the electoral context itself is of critical importance. Particular factors become important when they are made salient by a given campaign. In all elections, the opinions and perceptions of the voters have a significant impact that is increasing, while the direct effects of social status and traditional partisanship decline.

On the basis of these findings, two alternative developments in American class politics can be predicted. One possible trend is the complete disappearance of status polarization. We have seen the gradual loss of the Depression generations from the electorate, the diminishing associations of class and the vote, the inconsistent effects of class consciousness, the fading impact of traditional party loyalties based on economic divisions, and the development of noneconomic interests and alliances. Extrapolated only a few years into the future, these tendencies would result in a politics completely independent of social stratification.

Such politics would be in keeping with many of the larger developments in the United States, summarily described as the emergence of a postindustrial society. With the development of advanced technology and occupational structures, "it becomes increasingly difficult for labor conflict to polarize society along a single class-conflict dimension."[47] Economic life comes to be based on the possession of theoretical knowledge, not on resources and machine power. Work changes from a contest against nature to an interpersonal relationship, and service and bureaucratic occupations replace agriculture and manufacturing. Class structure is no longer a division of manual and white collar groups, but a complex arrangement of factory technicians, routinized clerks, diverse professionals, and multiple layers of managers. Without a clear class structure, politics cannot be structured along class lines. The contest for power becomes essentially irrelevant, as "government over persons is replaced by the administration of things."[48]

A contrary trend can also be predicted. In the data of this chapter, there are many indications that class differences remain a potential basis for American politics. Status polarization is significant in the presidential vote in 1960 and 1964, as well as in congressional balloting in all years, and is particularly evident among those of congruent status. As an underlying basis of party identification, occupation still remains evident; and its importance to partisanship and the vote has actually grown in the South, previously unaffected by such conflict. Furthermore, voters do see differences between the parties on class issues and tend to relate these perceptions and their own opinions on economic issues to their votes.

While it is certainly true that changes have occurred in the American class structure, this does not necessarily mean that there is no strong foundation for class politics. A basis exists so long as there are notable differences in power and status. "It is quite true that the composition of the elite is changing; it does not follow that the new elite will show greater reluctance to exercise social command than its predecessor. Indeed, its technical competence may increase its sense of legitimacy."[49] The result would be not the ending of class differences, but rather their mutation. "The increasing competence of those in intermediate positions in the new class system, then, may be matched by the increasing ability of those above them to command; the relative gap may remain the same."[50]

Class politics may reappear in the United States, but it is likely to be different from the direct clash of blue collars and white collars. The true lines of conflict may well be located higher in the social structure, for on many fundamental issues "the biggest 'break' in class structure is not between manuals and nonmanuals but rather is between the lower-middle and upper-middle groups."[51] Despite divergent voting, common opinions can provide seeds for the growth of political movements unifying the working and lower middle classes. This potential is further suggested by the data on the effect of class awareness and class congruence. Such class consciousness does not split the two basic occupational groups, but tends to make both of them more favorable to redistributive policies, more aware of party differences on such issues, and more supportive of the Democratic party.

For the further development of class politics in the United States, organizational structures and leadership will be needed. A major reason for the relatively low level of social polarization in America has been the absence of appropriate organizations, such as a politically oriented union movement or a continuing social democratic party.[52] The common opinions of diverse classes and their common perceptions of the liberalism of the Democratic party might stimulate such organization. Leadership is another prerequisite for class politics, which may be provided by those persons of higher education and status who voted against their presumed class interest in 1972 and who have "also revealed a wide range of attitudes many of which would not be consonant with the view of class position forcing the development of a narrow and very self-interested world view."[53]

Ultimately, the relevance of class to the vote will depend on whether events make it relevant and whether the parties develop the opportunities it provides. Much of the discontent in the United States today is based on justified economic grievances, such as dissatisfaction with the job environment, unequal access to opportunity for a fuller life, perceived favoritism by government on behalf of special interests, and the mounting cost of living.[54]

Should predictions be realized of permanent inflation or a severe depression, the present potential for class politics in America may be realized as well. It awaits the initiatives of parties and politicians. It is for political leaders publicly to debate issues involving distribution of the national wealth, and for the parties to offer alternatives on these questions. For their part, the voters do hold opinions, perceive the parties, and choose responsively. A class politics is possible, even desirable, but not inevitable.

THE IMPACT OF SOCIAL CLASS: FINDINGS

1. The influence of social class on the vote varies with electoral context.

   1a. Class voting has never been high in recent presidential elections.

   1b. Contrary to expectations, these influences have not disappeared completely.

2. Class polarization in voting is less evident among voters aware of social class.

   2a. Awareness of social class increases the Democratic vote among both the working class and middle class.

3. Class voting is greater among persons with congruent subjective and objective class identifications.

4. Awareness of social class is relatively constant in all population groups.

   4a. Contrary to past findings, class awareness is not consistently higher among persons maturing in the Great Depression.

5. Generational differences in class voting vary with the electoral context.

   5a. The "Depression generations" are not always distinctive in their class voting.

6. Class polarization is now equally evident in the South and the rest of the nation.

7. There is an emerging voting alliance within the Democratic Party of persons from the highest and lowest educational and occupational strata.

8. Class voting is no longer related to the strength of partisanship.

9. Opinion on class-relevant issues is highly related to voting choice.

   9a. This relationship is evident even within social classes.

10. Perceptions of the parties' positions on class-relevant issues are highly related to voting choice.

    10a. These perceptions are independent of social class.

    10b. This relationship is evident even with class controlled.

11. Opinions and perceptions are more closely related to the vote than social class itself.

    11a. The importance of opinion on class-related issues is greater in 1972 than in 1960.

CHAPTER 4

SEX, VOTING, AND WAR

Sex is obvious. Unlike the abstract characteristics of social class, to be a woman or a man is a permanent and distinctive identity. If behavior is determined, the causal agent may well be found in the chromosomes that fix individual gender. "Biology is destiny," decreed Freud, and his dictum might apply to politics as much as psychology. Probably from the days of Lesbos and Sparta, discussion of female participation in government has implicitly assumed that the matter of their sex would have some unique effects on political participants.

The argument over female suffrage itself was based on a deterministic assumption that women's participation in balloting would make a substantive difference. The more optimistic advocates of equality in the voting booth expected it would "abolish poverty, protect family life, and raise educational cultural standards; an international society made up of nations in which women had the suffrage would not tolerate war."[1] Concerning the first presidential election in which women fully participated, Democrats "hoped that women voters in 1920 would save the party from electoral defeat on the issue of the League of Nations."[2] In the contemporary United States, the major parties maintain distinct women's sections in their oganizations, draft platform planks specifically addressed to women, and tailor their campaigns to attract female votes.

Contrary to these great expectations, women's participation in the vote has had quite limited substantive impact. Despite biological differences between the two sexes, virtually all investigations show no political differences between men and women that can be attributed to the factor of sex itself. "With few exceptions, opinion patterns have been associated with

67

the same social and demographic factors among both sexes."[3] In the vote itself, "if we take a large variety of other social characteristics into account, there are no residual differences in partisanship between men and women."[4]

There are some limited exceptions to the lack of sexual differentiation in politics, and we will investigate two of the outstanding differences in this chapter. Yet, at the outset, it is important to realize that these are exceptions. Even on questions directly related to sex distinctions, differences between men and women are neither large nor consistent. For example, as recently as 1969, men were more willing than women to vote for a female candidate for president, while a 1972 poll shows women more accepting of a nominee of their own sex. In both cases, the difference between the two groups was 9 percent; this limited and inconsistent margin hardly provides evidence of sexual conflict.[5]

Political differences between men and women have been limited because necessary conditions for such differences have been absent. The most important prerequisite of political distinctiveness is "an economic division of labor or a physical separation or a social differentiation in the population such that people of unlike characteristics are affected in different ways by a single political policy . . . . It would be difficult in contemporary America, for example, to maintain strong voting differences by sex, because there are few policy issues persisting over a period of time that affect men and women differently."[6] Given the absence of this condition, the sexes have been quite similar politically.

In the 1970s, however, the situation may have changed. Sexual differentiation in politics is possible as a result of the women's liberation movement; its causal antecedents, such as the changed occupational structure and the spread of effective contraceptives; and the rise of sex-related issues, such as job discrimination, abortion, and child care. Therefore, one observer predicts: "For the elections of the 1970's female voters and activists will differ from male groups primarily because of their link to the developing women's liberation. For the first time we are witnessing on the American scene a woman's movement which is self-interested, coming into consciousness along with new racial, ethnic, religious and student groups."[7]

The full development of political divisions between the sexes remains to be seen; it hardly seems likely that these differences will reach the level of racial conflict or even class polarization in the United States because social separation is unlikely to be very great. Biology certainly will continue to bring men and women together physically. The economic division of labor between the sexes is narrowing, not increasing, as women leave the drudgeries of housework for schools and for jobs similar to those of men. The sexes are not segregating themselves, but coming together—in sports, colleges, on the job, and in their leisure.

Although new issues have arisen that might form the basis of a sexual politics, positions on these issues do not correlate very highly with gender. Even on an issue like abortion, the only difference is a slight tendency for men to favor the practice more than women. A more general opinion is that on "women's place," but there is virtually no sex difference on a seven-point scale that ranges from "women and men should have an equal role" to "women's place is in the home."

Politically, then, "vive la difference!" is largely an empty slogan, for most attitudes are not sex-determined. As we have mentioned, though, there are some variations, and we will devote most of this chapter to two of them. The first is the relatively lower participation of women in the voting act. The second is sex difference on a small range of opinions relating to war and the use of force. For the most part, these sex differences reflect particular circumstances of the sexes and are subject to change in different situations. The portrait of the responsive voter can be drawn as either a man or a woman.

SEX AND VOTING TURNOUT

One of the few aspects of female electoral behavior to receive scholarly attention has been participation in voting itself. The most publicized struggles involving women in politics have been over the suffrage, and considerable notice has been given to the frequency with which they have exercised this power over the past half-century.

The consistent conclusion from this research has been that women participate less than men in the vote.[8] In the first American study of the subject, only a third of women were found to vote in the Chicago mayoral election of 1923, compared to twice as many men.[9] We can also see this relationship historically. National voting turnout dropped considerably in 1920, the first presidential election after passage of the 19th Amendment, and has never since reached the levels attained during the period of exclusively male suffrage. Surveys of individual voters have also substantiated this conclusion. Dealing with the decade of the 1950s, the authors of *The American Voter* found "the vote participation rate among women in our samples is consistently 10 percent below that of men as an over-all estimate."[10]

The primary psychological cause of these differences in turnout is to be found in sex role typings. Whether enforced by men and/or expressed by women, a significant proportion of female adults have believed that "politics is a man's business." In the early Chicago election, 13 percent of the females expressed such sentiments as "All our family troubles are caused by our women folks getting away from the ways of living in previous and former years."[11] Even in more contemporary periods, we find that women have less interest in politics, tend to define their roles in less political terms, believe that they are less efficacious politically, and feel less of a citizen's obligation to vote.[12]

We would expect lessened sex differences in turnout in recent years. The women's liberation movement is one indication that past sex typings are no longer widely accepted, and more general opinion data supports this supposition. Among both sexes there is increased acceptance of the idea of a woman as president and of female activity in politics generally.[13] Demographic change will further this trend. Reluctance to participate in politics has been concentrated among older women of lower education and of immigrant background.[14] As the sexes become equal in education and as new native-born generations mature, past role definitions will alter.

Nationally, these expectations have been largely fulfilled. A Census Bureau report on the 1972 presidential election found only the slightest difference in turnout between the sexes. While 73.1 percent of males were registered and 64.1 percent claimed an actual vote, the figures for females were very similar: 71.6 percent registered and 62.0 percent voting.[15] Even these small differences were eliminated among younger respondents, where women in fact tended marginally to outvote men. In the University of Michigan study, the sex differential remains somewhat higher, about 5 percent more of men voting. Even this difference, however, is only half of that observed in the 1950s.[16] In total participation, then, the nation has moved toward sexual equality at the ballot box.

This overall similarity may well disguise differences among subgroups. We can observe the changing effect of role definitions by concentrating on three demographic variables, which previously have been found to be related to lower female turnout: age, education, and region. Older, less educated, and southern women have been particularly unlikely to vote, as they were more likely to adhere to traditional conceptions of women's restricted political role. We would expect the sex differential in turnout to diminish as new generations enter politics, as the level of schooling increases among women, and as the cultural patterns of the nation diffuse through the more isolated South.

In Table 4.1, the voting turnout of men and women is compared within age, education, and regional groupings.[17] In 1972, in the North, the first two variables have only weak effects. While male turnout is still relatively higher among older voters and the less educated, large differences are found only when these two factors combine. A statistically significant difference in voting participation is found exclusively among persons who are 55 years or older and who also have no more than a grade school education. In contrast to this group are the younger and more educated persons, where a slight feminine lead is found. In the North, we may conclude that women have been largely liberated in regard to electoral participation.[18]

TABLE 4.1 / SEX DIFFERENCES IN VOTING TURNOUT, 1972*

Age	Non-South Education				South (White)** Education			
	Grade School	High School	College	Average	Grade School	High School	College	Average
Less than 35	4.4	− 8.4	− 5.6	− 2.8	−15.1ₐ	11.9	6.4	11.6
	(14)	(205)	(305)	(525)	(23)	(88)	(131)	(242)
45-54	9.0	4.7	− 0.1	3.2	20.6	22.4	− 5.8	9.5
	(56)	(228)	(254)	(538)	(35)	(76)	(63)	(174)
55 and Over	22.2	13.4	4.9	15.0	30.2	15.2	−27.5	7.2
	(177)	(161)	(105)	(443)	(80)	(73)	(53)	(207)
Average	16.3	3.4	− 2.1		19.8	16.0	− 5.9	
	(248)	(596)	(667)		(138)	(241)	(249)	

*The percentage in each cell is a subtraction of the proportion of women in the category voting for president from the same proportion among men. Positive percentages indicate greater male turnout; negative percentages indicate higher female turnout. The number in parenthesis refers to the number of cases.

**Previous and current restrictions on black voting in the South complicate historical as well as contemporary analysis of the independent effect of sex on turnout. Race must therefore be considered separately.

ₐThe small number of cases in this cell make the finding of greater female voting in this group of no significance.

In the South, sex differences in turnout remain. Disparities exist particularly among older and less educated persons, as in the rest of the nation, but the differences tend to be larger. Among the two lower educational strata, we find a growing sex effect on turnout as we pass from younger to older age groups. There also is an independent effect of education, with more equal voting rates evident as we climb the educational ladder. The southern woman with a college education is quite unusual. She participates more in 1972 than a comparable man, and also, relative to males, votes more than her northern sister.[19]

There evidently has been some movement toward equality in voting between the sexes. A particularly dramatic change has occurred among those in the South with only grade school education. When this group was largely aged 35-54 (in the 1950s) there was a 53 percent sex disparity in voting rates; in 1972 the disparity of the group over 55 is reduced to 30 percent. Since we are dealing in the South only with white voters, this change cannot be due to legal innovations such as the civil rights legislation. The cause is more probably found in general modifications in social and political attitudes.

While disparities have lessened throughout the nation, a regional discrepancy remains. The areal difference in turnout can be found in all of the elections of the past two decades. In the North, women are actually outvoting men by 1962, while men continue their predominance in the South up to the present. When we further subdivide the northern samples, there is no consistent pattern of male or female advantage in turnout. Evidently the norm of participation has been diffused throughout the population. In the South, during all of this period, there is a consistent pattern: the highest sex difference is always found among those of grade school education, while male predominance is always lowest or absent among those who are college educated. The norm of political equality has reached especially those white southerners most exposed to the modern influences that pervade the other regions.

The distinctiveness of the South in female turnout is a descriptive fact. To explain this fact, we can pursue two lines of investigation. The first is to follow the apparent evidence of a distinctive regional culture, as we shall below. The second is to attempt to explain the South by analyzing other population characteristics that happen to be unusually frequent in the South. Level of education, for example, is closely related to voting turnout and to sexual equality. Regions with higher levels of education, such as the non-South, can be expected to evidence more sexual equality. The disparity in southern turnout might therefore be due only to its lower levels of education, not to any unique feature of the region as a cultural and geographic entity. However, the data already presented show that southern distinctiveness largely remains even with a control for education.

Another explanation of this distinctivness might be the more rural character of the South. Divergent sex roles and female abstention from politics are more characteristic of a rural society. Therefore, the lesser participation of southern women might be related to the residential patterns of the area.[20] Again, the data do not support this hypothesis. In 1972, men did outvote women in the rural areas of both the South and the rest of the nation, but the difference is the South was 15.4 percent, compared to 10.0 percent in the North.[21] The demographic features of the South do not provide a sufficient interpretation of the area's patterns of turnout.

Another indication of a true regional effect can be found by examining the effect of parental status on turnout. The most enduring sex role of women, of course, is that of mother. As women are held primarily responsible for child rearing, we might expect that this task would have some effect on voting participation. In fact, mothers do appear at the polls somewhat less frequently than either childless women or fathers, as the presence of children tends to emphasize differences in sex roles. In an early Chicago election, women were four times less likely than men to vote because they were "detained by a helpless member of the family," and this explanation was most commonly offered by females aged 30-39, the mothers of young children. Illustrative of this problem was "Mrs. Palek, aged thirty-eight, who said she had eight small children and had no time for voting. She added that if her husband voted and she took care of her children she was doing her duty for her country."[22]

Role differences in the care of children are complicated, however, by regional factors. The care of children has its greatest impact when the

TABLE 4.2 / SEX DIFFERENCES IN NONVOTING, BY PARENTAL STATUS AND REGION, 1968*

	North		South	
	Male	**Female**	**Male**	**Female**
Preschool Children	21.8	28.6	34.2	43.3
	(101)	(90)	(35)	(53)
School-Age Children Only	20.3	18.8	20.0	41.4
	(86)	(125)	(45)	(58)
No Children, or Over 18	27.9	16.0	22.1	41.5
	(215)	(256)	(104)	(135)

*The entry in each cell is the percentage of the group not voting for president in 1968. The number in parenthesis is the total number in the group.

youngest child is of a preschool age and requires the most attention. Among parents of such children, sex differences between the regions are virtually equal. Both northern and southern women vote about 8 percent less than men at this stage of the life cycle. When the children are older, however, areal effects become apparent. In the North, even when there are still school-age children in the home, women's turnout increases and becomes equal to that of men. When the children are past high school age, or there are no children, northern women actually outvote men. In the South, by contrast, women's turnout barely changes with the status of children. Since men do vote more as they age, the sexual differential in turnout increases.[23]

WOMEN AND SOUTHERN TRADITION

Rather than in demography, we must seek the cause of southern nonvoting of women in the distinctive attitudes of the region. Biology does not determine women's place in the home or out of the voting booth, but regional disparities in turnout can be attributed to contrasts between defined sex roles in the more modernized North and the more traditional white South. Both women and men below the Mason-Dixon line are more inclined to agree that women should stay out of politics. Moreover, in the South there is a noticeable sex difference. Only 47 percent of the area's men and 55 percent of its women favor more female political activity, while in other regions at least 55 percent of both sexes support such involvement. Only in the South, in addition, is a reduction in women's political role supported by even a tenth of the females.[24]

A regional effect is evident also when sex role definitions are compared directly to turnout. Regional differences in the behavior of men and women continue, whether they believe that women are fully equal or that they belong in the home. To show this effect, attitudes on "women's place" have been collapsed into three categories of egalitarian, moderate, and traditional role definitions. In Table 4.3, sex differences in turnout are presented within categories of these definitions and education. In the North, marked disparity in voting is seen only among the few grade school educated with traditional role definitions. In the South the effect of role prescriptions on turnout is evident among high school graduates as well as those with lesser education. Comparison between regions shows that southerners more frequently accept traditional role definitions, but that a regional difference is evident even within the other role categories. Unliberated southerners show more sex distinction in voting than their northern brothers and sisters who agree that women's place is in the home. Even southerners who speak for sexual equality do not evidence it as strongly as northerners in the voting booth. An important exception again is found among college graduates, where the southern woman is at least as strong as her northern sister in maintaining her active franchise.

Another index of traditional attitudes is found in the frequency of church attendance. The aphoristic description of women's role as "kinder, küche, kirche" illustrates the presumptive link between adherence to organized religion and a restricted female role. When we analyze voting by church attendance, we find the effect of religious observance different in the two regions. Outside of the South, there is no regular relationship with male or female predominance in turnout. Even among regular churchgoers with only a grade school education, women vote more frequently than men by 1968.

If religion was once restrictive of female political activity, northern women have been liberated from these bonds. In the South, by contrast, there is a definite effect of religious traditionalism, particularly among those whites of lower education. The quality of southern religion apparently has been more closely related to confining sex typings. It is not simply that churchgoing itself is more common in the South. The very nature of that traditional behavior is more inhibitive of female political activity.[25]

TABLE 4.3 / SEX DIFFERENCES IN TURNOUT, BY ROLE DEFINITIONS, 1972*

Education	Non-South Role Definitions			White South Role Definitions		
	Equality	Moderate	Traditional	Equality	Moderate	Traditional
Grade School	11.6	12.2	21.8	5.3	20.5	27.5
	(83)	(66)	(99)	(48)	(22)	(57)
High School	7.6	0.5	0.3	19.5	32.5	11.2
	(253)	(162)	(181)	(84)	(49)	(96)
College	− 4.1	0.4	1.8	− 0.1	−16.5	− 5.7
	(395)	(138)	(134)	(130)	(54)	(59)
Total	2.8	6.5	8.1	5.8	8.0	12.2
	(731)	(287)	(414)	(262)	(125)	(212)

*The form of this table is similar to that of Table 4.1.

We must conclude that the South has a more traditional culture, which defines the sex role of women in such a manner that they are less likely to participate in voting than their regional brothers or their sisters elsewhere. More than in other areas of the nation, the southern woman has been placed on a pedestal above the mundane world of conflict and politics. This attitude has persisted in the region from the antebellum era, when women's separate place became symbolic of southern virtue.

She was the South's Palladium, this Southern woman—the shield-bearing Athena gleaming whitely in the clouds, the standard for its rallying, the mystic symbol of its nationality in face of the foe. She was the lily-pure maid of Astolat and the hunting goddess of the Boeotian hill. And—she was the pitiful Mother of God.[26]

This role provided a protected, but dependent, position for the southern white woman and also promoted "yet more precious notions of modesty and decorous behavior for the Southern female to live up to."[27] In political activity, these ideals served to reduce women's participation. That effect continues, albeit with lessened impact, to the present.

We can further illustrate this effect of southern tradition by comparing two groups of southerners. More traditional attitudes would be expected among those who have lived most of their lives in the South, and therefore have been most fully exposed to the political culture of the region. Liberation would be more likely among women who have immigrated after childhood. To examine this hypothesis, we compare turnout rates among southern whites who have lived in their present state at least since the age of ten and those who grew up elsewhere.[28]

The data confirm the hypothesis fully. In both 1968 and 1972, there is a sharp sex difference in turnout among those who have remained in the same state since the age of ten. Turnout of men is 14 to 20 percentage points higher than among women. Among the mobile voters, however, there is virtually no sex difference. The effect of static residence is notable in the South—but not in the rest of the nation.

While the number of cases is small, these differentials also tend to remain when we control for age and education, factors that might be disguised as geographical mobility. A further indication of the effect of continued contact with southern tradition is evidenced when we control for sex role definitions. Whatever their characterization of "women's place," long-term southern residents show more of a sex difference in turnout. Thus, long-term residents who believe women's place is in the home evidence this belief in an 18.3 percent turnout differential. Migrants with the same traditional view, however, show a mere 1.8 percent difference in their vote. Traditional southern-bred women stay at home even on election day. Traditional migrants venture outside at least once a year.

The controlled effect of the sex-related variables on turnout can be measured through the technique of multiple regression. Such analysis leads to the unoriginal conclusion that men and women voters are considerably different—even in the factors that bear on voting. For both sexes there is a large effect of education, and its weight is increased among women in 1972. But females are additionally affected by region and the presence of young children in the household, while these factors do not consistently correlate with male turnout. These special influences on women are clearly reflections of role differences, for southern tradition and the duties of parenthood have served to limit women's turnout in that region. By 1972, however, the disparities are reduced considerably. The effect of education now becomes predominant for both sexes; children equally affect men and women; and the differential effect of region is reduced to a marked degree.[29]

This detailed analysis has shown a definite, but diminishing, effect of sex roles on turnout. To a limited extent, the suffragettes' hopes for equal participation of men and women in the political process have been unfulfilled. However, the gap is slight and the trends are clearly toward closing that gap completely. Those demographic characteristics associated with equality in the voting booth are ever more prevalent. The increase of education, movement away from rural areas, and passing of generations continue. Even the cultural gap of southern tradition appears to be fading. Among college-educated southerners in 1972, women voted more frequently than men, and this was true even of long-term residents. Higher education is one means by which modern conceptions of women's place are replacing the southern chivalric myths. Migration is another such means, with new residents of the South carrying new conceptions of women's political equality in their baggage.

Sex, the basic biological fact, does not determine voting turnout. At least in this aspect of their lives, men and women do not depend on their bodies. Appearing at the polls instead is related to the views they hold of their proper place in society, and the conditioning effects of their circumstances. The trends in America are toward reduced differences in these conditioning factors and toward greater equality between the sexes in their ability to react to the events and issues of their times. The responsive voters will soon be unidentifiable by their genders.

THE POLITICS OF THE SEXES

Does sex really matter in voting? Once in the voting booth, do women act differently from men? Deterministic descriptions of women as the "gentler sex" predict their political views on the basis of inherent characteristics. Responsive women, like responsive men, on the other hand, would not have predestined attitudes, but would react to the stimuli of their times. For the remainder of this chapter, we will consider variations in the opinions and electoral behavior of the sexes.

The earliest European study of female voting found that women were more likely to support bourgeois over socialist parties, and to reject both left and right-wing extremists in favor of clerical and moderate parties.[30] Given these findings, gross generalizations about inherent female conservatism have been accepted.[31] However, these studies were conducted in the early period of woman suffrage, when participation among the working class was restricted. It is quite possible that the supposed conservative character of the "weaker sex" was really a reflection of the class interests of the bourgeois women who voted.[32]

Among Americans, there is no evidence of a more conservative character among women—but some slight indication of the opposite. In party identification, in the more distant period of 1952, there was a slight tendency for more women than men to be Republicans (29.8% identifying with the GOP, compared to 25.8% of the males). By 1968, the marginal sex difference had shifted toward the Democrats (48.4% of the women identifying with the more liberal party, compared to 43.0% of the men, while similar proportions of each sex considered themselves Republicans). The Democratic leanings of women further developed in 1972, as seen in Table 4.4.

The sex difference in identification is located in particular groups. Most importantly, women under the age of thirty are far more likely than men to be Democrats, by proportions of 38.7 percent to 23.7 percent. This sexual disparity existed in 1968 as well, but became even more exaggerated in 1972. Young males do not compensate by disproportionate support of the Republicans, but rather by an Independent posture. In the other age groups, a substantial sex difference is found among those over sixty, where women are more likely than men to be Republicans. Only in that passing generation is the alleged conservatism of women evident.

In the vote, American women have not evidenced any special fondness for conservative or Republican candidates. Any early tendencies in this direction could be explained by the disproportionate frequency of voting among wealthier and white women. By 1952, contrary to the stereotypes of the time, women did not fall prey to the glamorous appeal of General Dwight Eisenhower,[33] nor, until 1972, did their votes differ appreciably from those of men in any other presidential election.

TABLE 4.4 / PARTY IDENTIFICATION BY SEX, 1972*

	Male	Female
Strong Democrat	15.5	14.7
Weak Democrat	22.0	29.1
Independent	39.4	31.9
Weak Republican	13.2	13.4
Strong Republican	9.9	10.9
(N)	(1152)	(1507)

*Percentages add vertically by columns to 100 percent.

In 1968, Nixon drew virtually the same vote from men (37.9%) and women (37.1%), while Humphrey's slightly greater appeal to women (32.9%) than men (31.0%) is statistically insignificant.[34] A marked sex difference was evident in support of Governor Wallace, however, with nearly twice as many men voting for him (12.1%) as against (6.3%). The lower female support for Wallace cannot be explained by regional factors, even though his vote was concentrated in the South, where women vote less than men, nor by any other demographic influence.

In 1972, for the first time in available survey research, a significant sex difference was found in the two-party vote, as 7 percent more of men voted for Richard Nixon. The difference between the sexes was particularly important among the youngest voters. Reflecting their Democratic partisanship, women below 30 preferred McGovern by a 12 percent margin and actually gave him a majority of their vote. Further analysis indicates that the senator's advantage was concentrated among white northern women with a college education. This is the youth vote that McGovern strategists had expected to provide the core of his electoral majority.[35] The strategy was half effective, reaching particularly the female members of the new generation.

Women and men voted differently in 1972. This difference could not be predetermined, for it is contrary to the alleged conservatism of females. In contrast to the past, women in 1972 were more closely identified than men with a liberal party and voted in greater proportions for a liberal candidate. They were responding here not to biological necessity, but to the policy issues of the time.

War policy has been most significant in recent times, and the fact of war relates to the fact of sexual difference in the vote. From the time of Aristophanes to the torment of Vietnam, women have been viewed as more pacific. Defending his continued intervention in Southeast Asia, President Johnson insisted that he would not take a weak, womanly position; and, as Halberstam has pointed out, "the advocates of force were by the very nature of Johnson's personality taken more seriously, the doubters were seen by their very doubts as being lesser men."[36] Opinion data support this common belief that women have been more opposed to war. As American soldiers applied brutal force in Vietnam, these views became critical to the 1968 and 1972 voting choices.

From the beginning, women were more opposed than men to the American intervention in Southeast Asia. In 1968, over two-thirds of women regarded U.S. involvement as a mistake, compared to somewhat more than half of the men. While men were more active on the issue, the feminine population registered greater opposition[37] when asked its preferences on a seven-point Vietnam Action Scale ranging from withdrawal to the use of unlimited force. In both 1968 and 1972, as seen in Table 4.5, women are more dovish, although the difference between the sexes

TABLE 4.5 / VIETNAM ACTION SCALE BY SEX, 1968 AND 1972*

Scale Position	Male		Female	
	1968	1972	1968	1972
1. Withdrawal	11.8	18.4	15.4	23.4
2.	6.7	9.0	9.9	10.4
3.	6.5	13.9	9.4	13.3
4.	26.3	24.4	33.0	25.5
5.	11.2	13.0	10.3	11.4
6.	12.0	7.0	7.0	5.7
7. All Force	25.5	14.3	15.1	10.2
(N)	(552)	(1018)	(690)	(1260)

*Percentages add vertically by columns to 100 percent, except for rounding errors.

narrowed between the two elections. The proportion of male hawks in 1972 drops to the level of females in 1968. In the interim, however, women became even more opposed to the use of force.[38] Yet, there is no male predominance in the emphasis given to the intervention question by the two sexes. Among both men and women in 1968, 44 percent consider the issue the most important issue or very important in influencing their vote. By 1972, more women consider the war as an important issue than men, and more women (49% to 44%) give first priority to ending the war.[39]

Women's more pacific views are persistent. The degree of sex-association, however, varies with political circumstances. In 1968, gender is a major influence upon views about Vietnam, while party loyalty is of no assistance in understanding these attitudes. By 1972, the independent effect of sex is considerably reduced, and partisanship becomes the best predictor of opinion on the war. In the intervening four years, as detailed later in Table 4.7, an issue that caused a social division separating men and women was transformed in great part to a political issue distinguishing Democrats and Republicans.

The immediate cause of this change was the transfer of power and responsibility for the war from Lyndon Johnson to Richard Nixon. The doves could now concentrate in the Democratic party. The different views of the sexes could thereby be absorbed into the system of party competition. Deterministic factors, such as gender, influence opinion when political alternatives are incoherent. Their influence lessens when the parties provide an opportunity for responsive voters to express their views politically.

The sex difference on the use of force explains the sex difference in political choice. The effects of gender and opinion on the vote are specified in Table 4.6, which compares the ballots of those less or more interested in Vietnam in 1968 and those of all electors in 1972. Among the less interested voters in 1968, whether men or women, there is little relationship between opinion and vote. Among the more interested voters, a significant relationship is found, but at about the same level for both sexes. However, a small sex difference does remain, with even hawkish women being less ready to support George Wallace. In the simpler policy choice of 1972, the relationship of Vietnam positions and the vote is unusually high for both sexes. Men and women taking dovish views give similar majorities to McGovern, while the only (statistically insignificant) sex difference is the marginal tendency of women to support the less aggressive candidate. As will be elaborated in Chapter 9, the relationship of opinion on Vietnam to the vote also remains when partisanship is controlled.

Because women are more opposed to war, they will also vote more for candidates whom they believe to be opposed to war. The greater feminine vote for McGovern in 1972 is a direct result of this association. Like males,

TABLE 4.6 / OPINION ON VIETNAM AND VOTE, BY SEX, 1968 AND 1972*

	Humphrey, 1968 McGovern, 1972	Nixon 1968-72	Wallace 1968	(N)
	Men			
1968—Less Interest				
Doves	35.3	52.9	11.8	(34)
Hawks	44.6	45.8	9.6	(83)
(Gamma)	(.09)			
1968—More Interest				
Doves	51.7	43.1	5.2	(58)
Hawks	27.9	45.0	27.1	(129)
(Gamma)	(.42)			
1972				
Doves	56.3	43.7		(272)
Hawks	11.7	88.3		(239)
(Gamma)	(.62)			
	Women			
1968—Less Interest				
Doves	49.3	46.5	4.2	(71)
Hawks	35.5	59.7	4.8	(62)
(Gamma)	(.12)			
1968—More Interest				
Doves	54.7	43.4	1.9	(106)
Hawks	28.6	53.3	18.1	(105)
(Gamma)	(.40)			
1972				
Doves	57.4	42.6		(371)
Hawks	15.7	84.3		(235)
(Gamma)	(.55)			

*Percentages add horizontally by rows to 100 percent. "Doves" are those at positions 1-3 on Vietnam Action Scale; "Hawks," those at positions 5-7.

females saw the South Dakotan as holding a dovish position on Vietnam. Because more women were themselves doves, more of them voted for McGovern. Women's vote is not a direct, dependent consequence of their femininity, but of politically responsive views women hold.

WOMEN AND FORCE

Sex differences on Vietnam are a rare instance of distinctiveness between the opinions of men and women. Previous research has not found consistent sex differences on most issues of public policy, such as economic regulation, foreign aid, or civil rights. While women have shown some inclination to concentrate on local and reformist matters, they have generally been less interested in political issues, rather than distinctive.[40] One historic issue that did divide the sexes was prohibition. In elections from Illinois to Scandinavia, women were consistently found to be more favorable than men toward banning the bottle.[41] For this reason, woman suffrage was often favored by prohibitionists and opposed by liquor interests.[42] As one female opponent of both prohibition and woman suffrage is reported to have complained: "her husband got drunk on moonshine and beat her so she left him. She blames woman suffrage for this and for all other political evils."[43]

Of greatest contemporary significance is the persistent sexual difference on war. After World War II, men and women largely agreed on foreign policy issues, except that females were less likely to have an opinion at all and were also more likely to take "idealistic" or "internationalist" attitudes, such as a preference for action by the United Nations, rather than military means, to achieve national security.[44] More generally,

differences between the sexes have pertained to attitudes on the use of military force and the implementation of policies regarded as risking U.S. involvement in war. Females were more likely to view our entry into the two world wars and the Korea and Vietnam conflicts as a mistake than were males. Women have been more likely to support U.S. withdrawals from wars already entered into and to be less receptive to the idea of "peacetime" conscription. . . . Support for the defense establishment, military aid, and collective security arrangements has been less as well among the fair sex.[45]

These general sex differences were specifically evident in regard to the American intervention in Korea from 1950 to 1953. Women were consistently more dovish on this first Asian war, although they were also less willing to express an opinion. "Women generally are less favorable to escalation than men, but only slightly more opposed to it; and women are less opposed to withdrawal than men, but only slightly more in favor of it."[46] Responding to the election survey of 1952, in the middle of the Korean conflict, women were significantly less inclined than men to believe the United States had been correct in intervening in the conflict (gamma = .26). In regard to future policy, almost two-thirds of females preferred the relatively dovish alternatives of withdrawal or negotiation, while close to half of the males were more hawkish, favoring the use of additional force (gamma = .22). Even today, after both Korea and Vietnam, the contrast between the sexes continues concerning use of force. When Congress passed the War Powers Resolution in 1973, inhibiting the use of military force by the president, 85 percent of women favored the act, compared to 76 percent of the men.[47]

Tenaciously, women raise their voices against war. Perhaps women are indeed the "gentler sex," and inevitably take a more humanitarian and more moral position. Undoubtedly some husbands and Elizabethan historians would dispute this global characterization. Nevertheless, there *is* a persistent sex distinction on one aspect of social policy, the use of force. Beyond the issue of war, there are other indications that women consistently are less willing to employ coercion in the settlement of group conflicts. To that extent, women may be entitled to credit as more humanitarian than men.

Race issues are illustrative of the character of women's humanitarian attitudes. Favoring programs to aid minorities certainly would be considered the humanitarian position, but women do not consistently show stronger support for such programs than men. Thus, in 1972, more women than men (39% to 32%) favored spending for poverty programs, but men were more willing (by 28% to 22%) to spend money to aid cities, and there was no sex difference in attitudes toward welfare spending.[48] In the 1972 election survey, women were slightly more favorable to school integration and government guarantee of equal public accommodations, but slightly more in favor of housing and social segregation—yet none of these relationships were statistically significant.

When the use of force is involved in civil rights, sex again does make a difference. To assess these attitudes, an Urban Unrest Scale has been established suggesting alternative means of dealing with the problem, ranging from "solve the problems of poverty" to "use all available force." In both 1968 and 1972, women were more likely to express the less aggressive opinions, and in both years almost twice as many females as males are at the very softest point. Between the two elections, both sexes moved toward more liberal positions, but the difference between them remained.[49] Overall, by 1972, a slim majority of men tended toward social solutions, while almost two-thirds of women approved of these gentler methods.

Men and women saw the issue differently, but they viewed the candidates similarly. To both sexes, Humphrey, as well as McGovern, seemed inclined to deal with urban unrest through solving the problems of poverty, and this evaluation was shared by persons on both sides of the issue.

George Wallace was also perceived quite distinctly, no fewer than five of every six voters seeking him at the forceful end of the scale. Distortion of the candidate's position occurred only in assessments of Richard Nixon, who was seen by liberals of both sexes as advocating social solutions and by hardliners as favoring the use of force. The former president alone came close to meeting the traditional political formula of seeming to be "all things to all men"—and all women.[50]

Candidate perceptions were sufficiently distinct on the issue to permit a direct effect on the presidential vote. In 1968, the association between opinion and vote is apparent even among those less interested in the issue, and becomes quite pronounced when we consider those more interested. Among all voters in 1972, there remains a substantial correlation (.38 for men, .34 for women) between position on this issue and the vote, although it is less robust than the effect of Vietnam. Once their opinions are taken into account, however, women do not differ from men in the vote. Among those advocating peaceful solutions, 56 percent of the men and 58 percent of the women voted for Humphrey in 1968. Four years later, McGovern received the support of 43 percent of these liberal males and 48 percent of the liberal females.

In all of these cases, there is a slight but consistent inclination on the part of women to take the less hard alternative. Thus, women who favor the use of force still are less willing than men to support Wallace in 1968 or Nixon in 1968 and 1972. On both Vietnam and urban unrest, women advocate the use of force less than men and are also less likely to carry through on their forceful convictions in voting for candidates perceived as taking a more militant position.

Other data reinforce the evidence of a sex distinction in behavior related to differential readiness to employ force. For example, women tend to be more favorable to strict gun control than men.[51] Another example is found in the 1972 issue of campus unrest and the use of force in quelling college disturbances. While women do not favor students more than men do, they are less willing to use force to repress campus unrest (51.8% of women, compared to 59.3% of men). There is a high correlation between position on this issue and the vote. McGovern wins the vote of 65 percent of the relatively few men and 71 percent of the small number of women favoring students, while Nixon wins 80 percent of the men compared to 73 percent of the women advocating the use of force. Again, we find the pattern of women being somewhat more inclined to support the gentler candidate, with men more consistently inclined to back the perceived advocate of force.

The factor of sex has a consistent influence on political opinion, but the effect changes with political circumstances. The variation is revealed by regression analysis of the two vital issues in the elections of 1968 and 1972: Vietnam and urban unrest. In regard to urban unrest, sex is an important

TABLE 4.7 / SEX AND OPINION ON THE USE OF FORCE
(Beta Weights, Multiple Regression)*

Variable	Vietnam 1968	Vietnam 1972	Urban Unrest 1968	Urban Unrest 1972
Party Identification	.00	.19	.11	.07
Sex	.17	.08	.12	.14
Education	−.06	−.02	−.12	−.05
Age	−.03	.04	.03	.18
Race	.16	.14	.26	.14
Region	.09	.12	.10	.13

*Positive coefficients indicate that approval of the use of force is dependent on Republican party identification, male sex, higher education, greater age, white race, and southern residence.

predictor of opinion in both years, and in 1972 it is more important than party identification and as important as the critical variable of race. Opinion on Vietnam is related to sex in 1968 but, as we have seen, becomes a more partisan issue in 1972.

Political developments explain these contrary movements. Between the two presidential contests and with the decrease of civil disorders, the urban issue became less salient. Opinions were therefore less tied to the political world, and political cues such as partisanship were made less relevant to opinion, while basic social influences such as sex could become more influential. The Vietnam issue remained salient in 1972 and was more closely related to party feelings, which came to substitute for underlying social memberships.

Women and men respond to the electoral environment. While women are indeed gentler in their approach to national problems, their compassion cannot always find an appropriate political expression. In such cases, opinions will be particularly related to the fixed characteristic of gender. When the parties present programs relevant to the opinions of women and men, however, biological determinism is replaced by political responsiveness.

THE FUTURE OF SEXUAL POLITICS

The contemporary tremors in the established terrain of America may change its political landscape. One possible result of present upheavals would be a sexual politics, with men and women facing each other across partisan fissures. The analyses in this chapter provide little reason, however, to anticipate such a future. There are few issues that are primarily related to a person's gender, and opinions on such matters as job discrimination actually do not polarize men and women. Nor is social segregation between the sexes likely as long as hormones do their pleasant work.

The one long-standing behavioral difference between the sexes—in voting turnout—is likely to be totally eliminated very soon. A lag is evident only in limited populations where traditional restraints on female participation continue. These restraints will be removed shortly and cannot stand against the impact of the education of women, the eased burdens of motherhood, and the diffusion of egalitarian norms.

In regard to opinions and voting, we have found relatively few differences between the sexes. In 1972, women showed greater support of the Democratic party and candidate, but this difference can largely be explained by their greater opposition to the Vietnam war. The permanent construction of sexual alignments partially depends on the future salience of issues involving war and force, as well as on the sources of women's greater reluctance to employ coercion to settle social conflict. Alternative speculations are available to comprehend these variations by sex. Deterministic theories find them inherent and unchanging, while cultural theories allow more autonomy to contemporary men and women.

One deterministic theory finds biological origins for sex differences. Recent anthropological research has pointed to the inheritance not only of physical features, but also of learned human behavior. Through the processes of natural selection, people have evolved with certain characteristic behaviors that enabled them to survive the many dangers of the race's history. It is possible that these characteristics necessary for survival included a relative aggressiveness on the part of men and a relative aversion to force on the part of women. For most of their time on earth, humans were hunting and migratory animals. A division of labor was efficient, in which one group hunted for food and defended the group, while another group attended the young and helpless, and maintained domestic life. Since women bore the children, theirs became the latter role, increasing their concern for survival of the group and their reluctance to risk lives in war. Women who were adapted to a nonaggressive role would survive longer and reproduce in greater numbers. For men, aggressive qualities would serve better in the hunt and defense, and forceful men therefore would be favored in the evolutionary struggle. Over the long period of human existence, these differential characteristics could become fastened onto the very germ plasms of the species.[52]

Inherently, it is impossible to test this theory, since we have no relevant records of the preliterate history of man and obviously cannot conduct controlled experiments. Nor can we refute it by noting that the human race is no longer primarily a hunting species. The "civilized" life of man has been very short, less than one percent of the species' time on the planet. If certain behavioral characteristics were imprinted in the genes of primitive man, they would still affect our responses today.

The principal difficulty with this theory for social science is its deterministic and static quality. If behavior is greatly affected by inherited characteristics, we cannot expect significant changes in this behavior in a short period of years, or indeed for the imaginable future. We must become passive in regard to the control of our fate and any changes in our predestined lives. On the microscopic level of changes in opinion, deterministic theories do not explain the shifts that occurred in support of the Vietnam war from 1968 to 1972. Clearly, genetic transformations do not account for the increased dovishness of men or for the narrowing of the sex difference in this period.

A second theory, relying on the effect of childhood socialization, is also deterministic, but allows for greater change. According to this theory, differences in adult political behavior are related to the sexes' divergent experiences in childhood. For example, Gorer argues that American boys are compelled to demonstrate their masculinity by forceful behavior. "To prove to himself, and to the world that he is a real 'he-man' (the reduplication of the term is itself suggestive) the little boy has to be more strident, shout and boast more, call more attention to himself than his sister need."[53] Therefore, we should expect more aggressive behavior and attitudes among these boys grown to men.

The more common argument today is that of the women's liberation movement, which emphasizes the socialization of girls, rather than boys. Sex differences exist not because boys are socialized to be aggressive, but because girls are taught to be submissive.[54] Girls are kept from rough play as children, and are expected to be passive and restrained. The models they are presented with are those of a politically neuter housewife or, in the occupational world, of women in less competitive or more humanitarian activities, such as nursing and teaching. These influences in the girl's immediate environment of home and school are then reinforced in the mass media.[55]

We cannot consider these arguments in any detail here, but at least two doubts about them must be raised. First, it has not been demonstrated that socialization does produce the stated differences in boys and girls, in relation to politics itself. While we have overwhelming evidence on sex stereotypes in textbooks, the media, and other sources, there is not corresponding evidence that these influences produce differential attitudes when children are considered as potential citizens. That girls are personally less aggressive than boys does not necessarily mean they are taught to disapprove of the use of force by others, such as adult males. Furthermore, while there is no specific finding that children are different in their attitudes on the use of force in politics, girls tend if anything to have more positive affect toward the wielders of authoritative force, such as presidents and policemen.[56]

A second point is more vital. Whatever the differences in the socialization of children, the connection has not been made between these experiences and mature attitudes. In fact, it is no more than an unverified hypothesis that the political actions of men and women are directly determined by their childhood influences. Recent research has cast in doubt the influence of even the most salient political attitude learned in childhood, identification with a political party; and other research has found almost no differences between boys and girls in political interest, affect, and activity.[57] The alleged ties between early learning and adult opinion are tendentious.

These arguments approach absurdity in Gorer's examples, or when the Vietnam war is virtually attributed to sex standards that "force" men "into the continued pursuit of policies associated with aggressiveness, determination and presumed bravery after these policies have proven fruitless and damaging to the nation and the world."[58] Such explanations cannot account for behavior and particularly fail to explain changes in male opinion. To argue that men support the use of force in Vietnam because boys play with wooden rifles is not political science, but only cocktail party rambling.

Rather than being determined by evolution or in childhood, sex differences on public issues may be related to contemporary attitudes and role definitions. Although boys and girls are raised to be different, these expectations can change fairly quickly, as has been occurring recently in the United States. As the prescribed roles of men and women alter, their positions on other questions may also change, including their views on the use of force. One limited finding along this line suggests that if women become "more assertive so that they can compete in a male-oriented society, a correlative result may be to make them more hawkish on war and foreign policy."[59]

Our data provides a better test of the effect of sex role definitions. In Table 4.8 the difference between men and women on the use of force remains evident among the liberated and unliberated alike. Moreover, on the questions of both Vietnam and urban unrest, feminists who hold egalitarian views are still more opposed to the use of force than those who accept their place in the home. Similarly, egalitarian males also are more opposed to the use of force. The two issues are clearly related, but women especially continue to show a reluctance to use force to settle conflicts. Thus, feminism does not mean severity, since females generally do favor milder policies.

Women's persistent opposition to the use of force can be politically relevant. When issues of war and social coercion are raised, the truly gentler sex is particularly likely to be on the side of pacific settlement. Political leaders therefore have an available constituency in women, one that is increasing in size and relative participation. If candidates and parties offer less aggressive policies, they are likely to hear an augmented response from the feminine section of the collective popular voice.

The source of women's more moderate temperament cannot be located deterministically in their genes or their unconscious. It is more likely to be

TABLE 4.8 / SEX ROLE DEFINITIONS AND THE USE OF FORCE*

| | Sex Role Definitions | | | | | |
| | Equality | | Moderate | | Traditional | |
Policy Attitude	Men	Women	Men	Women	Men	Women
Vietnam						
Doves	45.8	54.5	35.0	39.0	34.2	41.2
Moderates	22.2	23.3	33.9	31.1	23.6	25.8
Hawks	31.9	22.2	31.1	29.9	42.3	33.1
(N)	(504)	(589)	(180)	(264)	(284)	(357)
	G = −.18		G = −.05		G = −.15	
Urban Unrest						
Solve Problems	58.7	67.8	54.7	61.0	45.5	62.1
Moderates	16.0	13.9	17.3	18.0	24.1	13.7
Force	25.4	18.4	28.0	21.0	30.4	24.2
(N)	(213)	(267)	(75)	(100)	(112)	(153)
	G = −.18		G = −.13		G = −.24	

*Percentages add vertically by columns to 100 percent, except for rounding errors. The moderate opinion is position 4 on the scales of women's equality, Vietnam, and urban unrest, with positions 1-3 and 5-7 collapsed into the other two categories.

found in their contemporary lives as mothers and wives, lives grounded in biological inheritance but conditioned by social norms. While men plan abstract strategies, women worry about the safety of individuals they love. While men praise fallen heroes, women weep at the deaths of sons and husbands. We cannot fully explain this difference between the sexes, but we can respect it. For those seeking more peaceful solutions to the problems of society, this quality is worthy of preservation among women and of development among men.

SEX, VOTING, AND WAR: FINDINGS

1. On almost all political issues, including women's rights, there is no significant difference between the sexes.
2. Women's participation in voting is now essentially equivalent to that of white men.
   2a. Lower female participation is evident only among older and less educated white Southerners.
   2b. But the sex difference in the South is not due to the demographic character of the region.
3. Female voting is depressed by responsibilities for the care of young children.
   3a. But the sex disparity in Southern turnout is independent of this factor.
4. Lower female voting in the South is a manifestation of a regional culture.

    4a. Unlike life-long residents of the region, migrants to the South show no sex difference in voting participation.

5. In contrast to the past, women recently show greater support for the Democrats than do men.

6. Women consistently opposed the Vietnam war more often than men.

    6a. These opinions explain the recent Democratic vote of women.

7. Women are generally more opposed to the use of force than men, whatever the social context.

    7a. Females are less inclined to use force to deal with urban unrest.

    7b. But there is no sex difference on other "humanitarian" issues.

8. Greater female opposition to the use of force exists among both "liberated" and "traditional" groups.

CHAPTER 5

THE NEW POLITICAL GENERATIONS

Aside from sex, the most apparent human characteristic is age. Inevitably, often unwillingly, we pass from childhood to maturity to senility. These changes are not only biological, for behavior is different at different ages. Shakespeare poetically described seven ages of man, contrasting the young soldier,

Full of strange oaths, and bearded like the pard,
Jealous in honor, sudden and quick in quarrel,

to the middle-aged judge,

In fair round belly with good capon lined,
With eyes severe and beard of formal cut,
Full of wise saws and modern instances.[1]

Political response also changes with age. Youthful enthusiasm changes to seasoned skepticism; children's crusades often give way to middle-aged strolls.

Age is significant for an entire society as well, whose dynamics can often be traced to "demographic metabolism," the replacement of one generation by another. Social renewal is typically related to such transformations, for "the potential for change is concentrated in the cohorts of young adults who are old enough to participate directly in the movements impelled by change, but not old enough to have become committed to an occupation, a residence, a family of procreation or a way of life."[2] The pace of politics quickens when "the torch has passed to a new generation," with new ideas and its own novel experiences.

The impact of age is particularly vital in current American politics. With the enfranchisement of 18-year-olds in the presidential election of 1972, potentially 25 million new voters were added to the electorate. This expansion of the American political universe is far greater than the previous inclusions of the propertyless, or blacks, or even those women added to the rolls in 1920. Projecting into the near future, the impact of young people will grow. Because of high birth rates in the period after World War II, coupled with limited population growth earlier and later, these new citizens will constitute a continually increasing proportion of the electorate.

By 1980, two of every five voters will be persons too young to have participated in the election of John Kennedy.[3] The entrance of a new group of voters often brings a new politics as well, as westward expansion led to the Jacksonian period in American history and the participation of the immigrant generations led to the New Deal. The initiation of this sizable young generation presents the quantitative possibility of another epochal change in the American political order.

The change may be qualitative as well. Contemporary youth is not only large in numbers, but has been shaped by unique circumstances. It was born after the advent of atomic weapons, was educated and attended by the novel medium of television, has developed sexually and morally with the dissemination of birth control pills, is entertained by the new rhythms of rock and soul music, and is trained for an economy of affluence. Even in a period of social stability, these influences alone might make this generation distinctive. Yet the period from 1960 was politically wrenching as well. As the children of the postwar "baby boom" began to obtain a civic consciousness, they were rapidly subject to the racial revolution, the agony of Vietnam, and the assassination of the particular political leaders with the greatest appeal to youth.

As the newest members of the polity, relatively free of tradition, young persons should be particularly sensitive to the disturbances of the period. As the very trustworthiness and stability of American institutions were disputed, those newly eligible to vote were likely to ask questions most persistently. While internal and external violence saddened all Americans, its likely effects would be even greater on the generation that pressed the triggers and caught the bullets. Responsiveness to the times is evident among all voters, but may be evident first among those who are unlimited by habits of political thought.

Concurrent with these political events, a recognizable "youth culture" has developed in the nation. Some of its characteristics, such as manner of dress, are not inherently of political significance, while others are only of marginal relevance here, such as the widespread violation of marijuana statutes. The pertinent question in this discussion is the political distinctiveness of recent entrants to the electorate. Some observers have argued that the new generation is qualitatively different—that its members are more interested, more knowledgeable, and more idealistic than their predecessors. Evaluating the vanguard of the generation, one observer predicts they "will be tough, articulate leaders and social, cultural, and political agents in the coming years. Community by community, they will be providing much of the public cut and thrust both substantively and tactically. Their interests will generally be less in winning immediate elections than in relentlessly pressing for a fundamental recasting of values and direction."[4] Other writers agree youth is distinctive, yet politically conservative.[5]

Because of their numbers and their potentially novel character, the new voters merit intensive examination. Such inquiry also relates to the general theoretical concerns of this book. To examine the effect of age is again to assess the dependent portrait of the voter. If individuals' political behavior largely reflects their demographic characteristics, the relationship should be seen in the impact of age, an irreversible characteristic. Must youth be rebellious, the middle-aged complacent, and the elderly nostalgic? Or do voters respond differently to different circumstances, not because of their biological age, but because the times change?

In this analysis, we will concentrate, first, on the behavior of the voters newly enfranchised in 1972; second, on the "middle-aged" groups of voters then aged 25 to 35.[6] The effects of social change should be most evident in the entering members of the polity. Their distinctiveness does not need to be proven—it is evident from rock concerts to protest marches. For the long run, the important question is whether their behavior is but a deterministic reflection of their own lean years, or a more lasting response to the nation's recent ones.

THE YOUTH OF 1972

In the most apparent political ways, the new 1972 voters are clearly different, but the causes of their distinctiveness are not self-evident. Compared to their elders, they are weaker in their party loyalty, but more inclined to express a Democratic or Independent preference and to vote for George McGovern. This youthful distinctiveness in the vote persists when partisanship is controlled, as in Table 5.1. New Democrats are truer in their partisan faith. While four out of five of the group voted for McGovern, barely half of the party's identifiers over 35 were faithful.

The new voters also show a different ideological position. More than twice as many consider themselves liberal than conservative, while a plurality of the older groups are of moderate and conservative ideologies. This difference holds even controlling for party allegiance. Fresh Democrats are more liberal than older Democrats, and the relatively few young Republicans are more liberal than the elders of the GOP.

An immediate conclusion from these data could be that postadolescence provides an explanation, since it is common folklore that young

TABLE 5.1 / AGE DIFFERENCES IN VOTE AND IDEOLOGY, BY PARTISANSHIP, 1972*

	Vote in 1972			Ideology			
	Nixon	McGovern	(N)	Liberal	Moderate	Conservative	(N)
Democrats							
Age 18-24	20.9	79.1	(86)	44.7	43.6	11.7	(94)
Age 25-35	38.8	61.2	(121)	40.3	36.1	23.5	(119)
Age Over 35	46.6	53.4	(436)	27.2	42.3	30.5	(371)
Independents							
Age 18-24	59.0	41.0	(78)	48.3	31.4	20.3	(118)
Age 25-35	60.8	39.2	(143)	30.7	33.1	36.1	(166)
Age Over 35	71.5	28.5	(253)	20.5	41.5	38.0	(258)
Republicans							
Age 18-24	94.6	5.4	(37)	28.9	31.6	39.5	(38)
Age 25-35	92.0	8.0	(87)	11.4	35.2	53.4	(88)
Age Over 35	94.0	6.0	(332)	8.5	32.0	59.4	(281)
Total							
Age 18-24	49.3	50.7	(201)	43:5	35.6	20.9	(253)
Age 25-35	61.0	39.0	(351)	28.9	34.7	36.3	(377)
Age Over 35	68.2	31.8	(1021)	19.5	39.0	41.4	(912)

*Percentages add horizontally by rows to 100 percent, except for rounding errors. Liberals are those at positions 1-3 on the self-identification scale; moderates, at position 4; and conservatives, at positions 5-7.

people display their immaturity by being Democrats and liberals, but become more sensible when they "settle down." It is also possible that new voters are Democrats and liberals because of more permanent influences, because the leaders and issues of their time have created lasting allegiances and beliefs.[7]

The data provide some reason for seeing the youth of 1972 as unique in its attachments, and not necessarily fickle. Particularly to the point is its higher consistency between Democratic partisanship and voting. This tendency has not been evident previously among the young and may indicate distinct behavior. If we glance back at earlier elections, there is no age difference in partisan consistency. In 1968, 70 percent of both young and old Democrats selected Humphrey, and in 1964 89 percent of both partisan age groups supported Johnson. There appears to be something different about the new voters of 1972.

The youth of 1972 had two defining characteristics: it was young, and it was young in the particular time of 1972. Each characteristic may have its own consequences, as the behavior of an age group may be affected by either of two distinct factors: the age itself, and its historical generation.[8] The first factor is that of the age itself, or the different place a group holds in the life cycle. Regardless of external circumstances, persons 20 years old are always different from those 40 or 60. Their biological and psychological development are different, and their places in the occupational structure vary. In the United States today, 20-year-olds are unlikely to have family responsibilities; more mature adults are in the midst of these problems; while the elderly have separated from their children. Since humans are affected deeply by their life-cycle experiences, we must expect their political views to be affected as well. As the sardonic comment has it, "A conservative is a socialist with a wife and two children." The liberal, Democratic views of contemporary youth may only reflect its inexperience.

The other factor related to age is generation in a historical sense. All adults are 20 years old sometime, but they reach this age at different dates and are subject to different influences of the times. Almost every parent has begun an argument with his child saying, "When I was your age . . .," and later wondered why this point was not persuasive. The reason is that each generational cohort is a different generation, living in a particular period, even though the biological and psychological characteristics of age itself hardly change. "Each cohort has a distinctive composition and character reflecting the circumstances of its unique organization and history."[9] Present youth has received a different political education. Growing up in the Depression is not equivalent to growing up amid racial disorder; the military draft to fight in Vietnam is not the same as the draft to fight Nazism. These unique events, not maturation, may be the source of contemporary youth's Democratic and liberal leanings.

In comparing age groups, the effects of the life cycle must be separated from the effects of generational experience. The importance of the distinction is evident in research on the relationship between age and partisanship. An influential study in 1962 found that older persons were more likely to be Republicans; it argued that aging itself led to greater conservatism and therefore to greater attachment to the GOP.[10] The defect in this analysis was that generational influences were not considered. Older persons in the study also were those who had entered politics before the New Deal, a time when the nation was predominantly loyal to the Republicans. Their party loyalty reflected their early upbringing, not their later conservatism. To correct this defect, each age cohort should be examined separately and followed over time. Using this technique, the alleged relationship disappears, and actually "there are more decreases in Republicanism with age than there are increases."[11] Further analysis, as well as that presented in Table 2.4 above, "provide[s] no evidence for any form of the aging-Republicanism thesis."[12] Consequently, the new voters of 1972 may well continue to be Democrats and liberals in the future.

For a more general analysis, we can turn to the pioneering theories of Erik Erikson, who describes youth as a distinct psychological as well as physical state. According to Erikson, the age of 18 approximately marks the end of the period of adolescence, in which the chief psychological process is that of identity formation. The diverse experiences of an individual's life are integrated in this period so that the personality constitutes a relatively stable whole as a sexual, occupational, and emotional being.[13] With the lowering of the voting age, political citizenship comes now as the individual completes the formation of his psychological identity. Characteristics of the adolescent period are carried forward into early adulthood and are likely to show themselves in political activity also.[14] One typical form of adolescent behavior is strong commitment to peer groups, along with the abandonment of parental restraints and values, as young persons seek "the achievement of a sense of free choice as the very result of ritual regimentation."[15] We would therefore expect the young to act differently from older persons.

Erikson's theory leads us to expect a particular style of politics on the part of postadolescents, a more clearly ideological politics. Ideology itself becomes a means of integrating the personality, of incorporating impersonal and personal experiences, and a means of expressing the "idealism" of the age group. Ideologies "thus channel the forceful earnestness, the sincere asceticism, and the eager indignation of youth toward that social frontier where the struggle between conservatism and radicalism is most alive."[16] The devotion to idealistic ideology is not accidental, but closely related to personality development. "From the middle of the second decade, the capacity to think and the power to imagine reach beyond the persons and personalities in which youth can immerse itself so deeply. Youth loves and hates in people what they 'stand for' and chooses them for a significant encounter involving issues that often, indeed, are bigger than you and I."[17] On the basis of Eriksonian theory, we would expect new voters to be more concerned with issues than older generations and to evidence that concern more in their ballot choices. Moralistic attitudes seem to be the particular contribution of adolescence to political thinking.[18]

These inherent characteristics of youth have been reinforced by the particular events of recent times. The formal tendency of the young to differentiate themselves from their elders has been accelerated in America by the rapidity and unchallenged character of social change. Generations learn less from each other because the circumstances facing each generation are so different. "The wisdom and skills of the fathers can no longer be transmitted to sons with any assurance that they will be appropriate for them; truth must often be created by children as learned from parents."[19]

The distinctiveness of age groups has also been reinforced by residential segregation. Young people increasingly live exclusively among themselves, decreasingly in touch with their elders. Burgeoning college campuses, a substantial military establishment, urban "singles" neighborhoods, and scattered communes all provide social support for any unique characteristics. As youth becomes spatially isolated, so do other generations, with nuclear families populating suburban housing tracts and the elderly congregating in "golden age" retirement communities.

Youth's common emphasis on issues, particularly moral issues, also has been further stimulated in contemporary times. The 1972 generation is better prepared to deal with issue dimensions of politics because of its greater educational achievement, with the proportion of young Americans attending college close to double that of older generations. Youth's receptivity to issues became particularly salient when attention was focused in the 1960s on questions of racial equality and the Vietnam war. On these questions, debate was conducted in terms of social justice and the legitimacy of force, in the absolutist and moralistic language of particular appeal to the young. By contrast, the dominant issues in previous times were economic ones, involving relatively bargainable decisions on the distribution of wealth and government services. The nature of the times up to 1972 therefore supplemented the inherent ideological proclivities of the young.

The expected characteristics of young persons recently have been reinforced by particular circumstances. However, the forms in which the qualities of youth are expressed are not fixed. Youth can distinguish itself by traveling to unexplored continents or by hallucinatory trips. It can express its moralism by active participation in politics or by a withdrawal from all evil. Being young, above all else, means that multiple alternatives are available. Psychology determines no more than a disposition to respond; political and social circumstances remain influential in the specific direction of youthful choices. "Most political thinking results from a combination of genetic-maturational and politically related environmental factors."[20]

We are left with the problem of distinguishing between the effects of the life cycle and those of unique historical experiences. The present liberal, Democratic, or Independent affinities of youth have very different implications for the future if they are only temporary manifestations of a stage in the life cycle. Ultimately, the question will be answered after future elections. If the new voters continue to show distinctive characteristics, we will have a true generational difference. If the new voters become less unique over time, life-cycle influences will be predominant.

Even at present, however, there are some means tentatively to distinguish between these two effects. Two techniques can be employed. One is comparison over time, matching youth in 1972 with youth in earlier elections. Life-cycle effects would produce similarities between the two groups. A second technique is following cohorts of persons born at the same time through successive elections, as we have already done in Chapters 2 and 3. Life-cycle effects would be revealed by changes in the cohort's behavior through the years.

Still another test is available through static analysis of the 1972 survey results. The new voters of 1972 can be compared to the age group most similar to them, those aged 25 to 35, who came to political maturity in the 1960s. If life-cycle influences are predominant, those aged 25-35 would be different from the youngest group. Having already passed through the prime of youth, being more established in families and jobs, this "middle-aged" group would be more like the truly older generation. The group that first voted in the 1960s would have expressed its immature feelings earlier—in the 1964 and 1968 presidential contests, and would now be more traditional.

In the following sections, these various comparisons are applied in analysis of the new generation's political activity, citizen attitudes, issue positions, and vote. The general finding is that contemporary youth is responding to its times, and is not determined by its chronological age.

The new generations have entered politics in times perilous for the nation. Some of the attitudes formed in this period carry further dangers for American democracy, such as widespread cynicism among the young. Other attitudes may lead to a renewal of the nation's political life. Their new ideas, their concern for peace and the socially deprived, and their questioning of habitual practices, convey hope for the future of American politics.

THE YOUNG POLITICAL ACTIVISTS

Much rhetoric has been heard about the unusual concerns and knowl-edgeability of the new voters. Given the rising level of education, we might expect increased political awareness on their part. On the other hand, their generational experiences might lead to less political interest, and many observers have commented on the alienation from American poli-tics of the youth of 1960s and 1970s.[21] Withdrawal, rather than involve-ment, might be the response of this cohort, particularly among college students. Evidence of disaffection has been plentiful on the campuses—in the spread of radical loyalties, the occasional resort to violence, wide-spread opposition to the Vietnam war and the draft, outrage over racial inequality and academic misgovernance, and condemnations of tradi-tional authorities from policemen to presidents.

The data of Table 5.2 certainly do not show the new generation of voters to be more knowledgeable than older groups. On five purely factual questions, the youngest group is generally less informed than the oldest group. Among those with some college training, there is virtually no difference between the age groups. Age and education are alternative sources of political information. As individuals gain experience as citi-zens, they also acquire basic facts. The young, with less experience, can obtain this same information through formal agencies of instruction, such as the colleges.

Neither do the young appear to be more interested in electoral politics.

TABLE 5.2 / AGE AND POLITICAL AWARENESS, BY EDUCATION, 1972*

	No College Education			Some College Education		
	18-24	25-35	Over 35	18-24	25-35	Over 35
Accurate Factual Knowledge						
Limit on Presidential Term	83.3	86.1	89.6	95.4	97.9	90.5
Length of Senator's Term	36.5	35.0	39.7	59.6	50.6	54.4
Length of Congressman's Term	56.8	56.7	51.9	68.0	59.5	67.2
House Majority Party Before Election	63.3	81.6	92.0	85.2	95.3	91.6
House Majority Party After Election	71.7	80.5	87.5	78.0	85.2	83.3
Electoral Political Activity						
Have Voted	46.9	61.5	72.0	81.0	85.5	89.5
Concern About Election Outcome	45.9	59.7	61.6	64.7	65.0	74.2
Give Money to Parties	4.3	4.0	6.3	13.7	18.0	26.8
Strong Partisanship	13.0	15.5	32.5	15.6	16.8	28.7
Believe in Duty to Vote	36.3	48.9	56.7	39.6	57.0	65.9
General Political Activity						
Perceive Lack of Power	48.1	46.4	47.9	30.9	24.8	18.8
Find Politics Confusing	80.1	84.7	80.5	59.9	59.4	52.6
Talk to Others	27.7	25.4	25.1	52.7	46.6	42.0
Write to Public Officials	11.7	18.7	21.5	32.9	43.4	48.9
Vote on All Ballot Referenda	55.2	62.6	66.5	75.7	81.6	82.5
High General Interest in Politics	14.9	23.1	33.9	42.5	52.9	58.2
(N)	(236)	(380)	(1260)	(162)	(230)	(389)

*Entries are the percentage of each age and educational group with the designated knowledge, attitude, or behavior.

On each of five measures, the new generation is less active and concerned, votes less, and is less committed to the duty to vote in all elections. Frequent popular assertions about the rise of a new and politically involved generation are not borne out by the facts. Moreover, the same age difference is evident even when we examine only the group with some college education, in which political activity among the young has been most evident. Although education increases electoral involvement in every age group, the age difference remains. On these measures, age rather than education appears to be the most important influence.[22]

In examining general or nonelectoral political activity, some significant differences are found. The prevalent pattern is the greater significance of education than age. Whether young or old, the college group believes itself more able to cope with politics and shows its subjective competence by such activities as writing to public officials, voting on referenda, and talking about elections. Differences between age groups are far less than those between categories of schooling.

Within this overall pattern, the youngest college-educated group has some distinctive marks. While it engages in more political discussion than its elders, it has less belief in its political efficacy and is more likely to be confused by the world of politics. This same group shows slight acceptance of the duty to vote or concern over the election outcome. These data conform better to the common portrait of the alienated college student, who does care about social problems but finds normal politics an ineffective means to accomplish his goals. Such feelings could derive from the generational influences upon the new voters, which have heightened political involvement generally, while frustrating electoral goals.

The pattern of responses from the college-educated group aged 25-35 in 1972 supports this view also. From 1968 to 1972, this cohort increased its relative political involvement substantially, eliminating or closing most of the previous age gaps in voting turnout, letter writing to public officials, general interest, and political discussion. At the same time, feelings of inefficacy and confusion continue to be relatively more evident in this cohort. The bare statistics suggest a living reality of this group as college students learning about politics during the 1960s. They see possibilities of change with such leaders as Martin Luther King or Robert Kennedy. They attend rallies and write their congressmen, as the civics texts urge. Then they see their leaders assassinated before television cameras and their peers slain before their eyes. For such persons, political effort understandably results in public frustration.

The case for generational influences is strengthened if we look backward to the 1960 election. In that contest, the candidacies of two young and apparently able nominees increased the activity of college-educated youth. They felt greater personal efficacy than their elders and the same degree of interest in the campaign. Despite the presumed apathy of the age group, they were more likely to be strong partisans than other electors and actually voted 8 percent more frequently. The initial enthusiasm of the college-educated youth of 1960 continued in later years, with the cohort persistently more active than older persons in later elections. By contrast, the college-educated youth of 1968, entering the voting booth after the searing experiences of the decade, are less involved initially than their elders and remain relatively disaffected after four more years.

A different dimension of political involvement relates to substantive issues. While activity regarding policy generally is not closely associated with age, there are some notable differences in the generations' concern with policy questions. Such concern involves two elements: holding an opinion of one's own and being aware of the positions of the party candidates. The new voters of 1972 are not distinctive in the frequency with which they hold opinions themselves. Although the newly enfranchised are more likely to take positions than the oldest group, they do not differ in this respect from the cohort aged 25-35.

The larger differences relating to age occur in the knowledge of the candidates' stands in 1972. The new voters are far more aware than the oldest voters of the positions of both nominees and are also relatively more familiar with those positions than the 1960s cohort. To be sure, education generally increases such knowledge. Still, the same results are evident when we control for education. With or without college training, the young claim to know both candidates' position more commonly than those close to them in age, as well as more frequently than those more advanced in years. Moreover, this greater familiarity with the candidates appears to be a particular generational hallmark of the new voters, not a result of either their youth or education.

In 1968, the cohort aged 25-35 did not show greater awareness than their elders of the candidates' positions on the critical issues of urban unrest and Vietnam, and the youngest voters of that time did not consider these issues unusually important in their vote. The lack of an age difference concerning issues in 1968 held within educational strata as well. Events in the following four years, however, had an effect on consciousness, making the middle-aged more familiar with the nominees and especially making the newest voters aware of politcans' issue stands.

The youthful understanding of the candidates' positions applies to most particular questions. Only on matters of social welfare, such as health insurance, is the oldest group equally informed. The familiarity of the new voters, however, is evident on most other issues, including matters involving the youth culture, civil rights, and urban problems. It is not only evident on topics particularly salient to young, such as marijuana usage. On that matter, 86 percent of new voters with a college background are aware of the nominees' stand, compared to 76 percent of the middle-aged and 63 percent of the older respondents. The familiarity of new voters extends to issues that lack distinctive impact on their lives, such as urban unrest. On this question, 87 percent of the college-educated youngest group knows both candidates' views, compared to 78 percent of the middle-aged cohort and 70 percent of the oldest voters. In the group without college training, the age differences are smaller, but still clear and in the same direction. This awareness of issues cannot be explained as a reflection of simple self-interest, but is instead the result of a generally greater stress by the young on policy matters.[23]

The new voters, then, are not clearly more knowledgeable nor more concerned about electoral politics than their elders. While they have somewhat greater familiarity with the candidates' issue positions, this knowledge does not always contribute to their subjective feelings of competence and political efficacy. These combinations of attitudes have important implications for the future of American public life.

CITIZENSHIP AND YOUTH

In a healthy democracy, there is broad popular participation in public activities, in discussion about politics as well as in the voting act itself. If these activites are meaningful, they will be based on the citizen's belief that he can be effective, that—to use the wording of the relevant survey question—"people like me have political power." Among contemporary youth, responses to questions concerning such belief suggest a decline in the well-being of the American political system, and its need for renewal by the young.

In general, as would be expected, persons who believe in their own political efficacy engage in more discussion about an election and vote more often. This relationship is particularly evident among older and more educated people. Among those who are both young and educated, however, feelings of efficacy are not associated with political conversation or turnout. Even while they continue to talk and to vote, the younger members of the college group feel less efficacious than the older members of the group.

A related measure concerns personal acceptance of the normative duty of a citizen to vote, even if he does not care about the outcome of an election. As is logical, persons with a higher sense of citizen duty enter the voting booth more frequently. But the effect of citizen duty is less among young collegians. While those of more limited education increase their turnout rate from 38 percent to 61 percent when they accept a duty to vote, the participation of college youth rises less strikingly—from 77 percent to 86 percent. This high rate of turnout stems more from the educational level of these voters than from their acceptance of the norms of the system.

The distinctiveness of this young college-educated group can be seen more fully if we combine these two measures, subjective feelings of efficacy and personal acceptance of citizen duty to vote. By cross-tabulating the responses, we classify the electors into groups that have quite different perspectives on their role in government. Four categories result:

1. Those who feel no duty to vote and who believe they have no political power—the alienated;
2. Those who feel no duty to vote even though they believe they do have influence in government—the skeptics;
3. Those who express a duty to vote, even while they believe themselves to be powerless—the ritualists; and
4. Those who both believe in the duty to vote and view themselves as efficacious—the model citizens.

The validity of these categories is evidenced by actual voting behavior in 1972. The alienated show the lowest rate of turnout, below half, while 85 percent of the model citizens came to the polls. At an intermediate position are the ritualists and skeptics, who ballot in equal proportions. Among the young college-educated, however, the skeptics are significantly less frequent at the polls than all but the fully alienated. While this new generation feels personally competent, it will not vote simply to perform a civic duty. Its vote must be earned by parties which speak to the basic issues and which offer attractive candidates.

The ideal of democracy, whatever the reality, is best represented by model citizens, persons who are politically competent (at least in their own minds) and who are ready to participate in the basic act of democratic politics, voting. Even if not ideal, at least the appearance of democracy can persist with the support of the ritualists of the third category.[24] Estrangement from the existing system is most evident in persons in the first two groups. The potential for system change, whether for good or ill, is particularly located among the skeptics, believing themselves effective, but not feeling bound to follow traditional practices.

The last groups appear to be growing rapidly, providing sources of instability and innovation in the general system. In Table 5.3, the potential for system change is most evident among the new voters with some college education. Among the oldest persons with some college education, model citizens predominate, with over half of the group accepting the duty to vote and believing themselves effective. By contrast, the educated young—the "leaders of tomorrow" as commencement addresses have it—are most likely to be skeptics. Similar differences are evident among postadolescents off campus, but to a considerably lesser degree. These persons are more likely to be fully alienated, and therefore relatively quiescent.

College-educated youth thus appears to constitute a different political force, relatively confident about its ability in politics, but rejecting one of the basic political forms. This combination of attitudes leads to new forms of political expression, sometimes beneficial and sometimes disruptive. In the electorate in recent years generally, there has been a decrease in perceived efficacy and a turn to new forms of action.[25] The college-educated young have also turned to sit-ins, demonstrations, marches, and violence. However, their adoption of these methods is not necessarily

TABLE 5.3 / AGE, EDUCATION, AND POLITICAL EFFICACY, 1972*

	Alienated	Skeptics	Ritualists	Citizens	(N)
Some College Education					
Age 18-24	21.4	39.0	10.1	29.6	(159)
Age 25-35	12.7	30.1	12.2	45.0	(229)
Age Over 35	7.6	26.4	11.2	54.7	(382)
No College Education					
Age 18-24	33.0	30.5	15.0	21.4	(233)
Age 25-35	25.5	25.5	21.2	27.9	(373)
Age Over 35	23.1	20.1	24.4	32.4	(1240)
Total	21.0	24.7	19.3	35.0	(2616)

*Percentages add horizontally by rows to 100 percent, except for rounding errors. See text for definitions of categories.

based on feelings of inefficacy. Their mood is one of anger, rather than despair.

From analysis of responses in 1972 alone, we cannot distinguish between age and generational differences with respect to the question of political efficacy. The apparent disaffection of the new voters may be due only to the characteristic differentiation of the young. Being skeptical and disdainful of the political system is in keeping with the common callow rejection of adult institutions. On the other hand, the middle-aged group partially shares these attitudes. There is some reason to suspect, then, that the unique events of the 1960s stimulated these responses, not only the inherent rebelliousness of young persons.

Data from the 1960 election provide further evidence of a generational effect. In the Kennedy-Nixon contest, youthful attitudes were highly supportive. Among college-educated youth through thirty years of age, the largest proportion—nearly half—were model citizens. Almost as many were skeptics, but the proportions of inefficacious ritualists or alienated persons was very small. Moreover, these supportive beliefs largely persisted through the trials of the decade. Twelve years later, in 1972, the distribution of attitudes among this group of voters (now aged 33-42) showed half as many skeptics, a growth in the proportion of model citizens, and a total array very similar to that of the older generation. It appears that youth can support the political system if its character at the time the young reach political maturity deserves support.

Voter attitudes over the years are also related to their view of the political system. From 1964 to 1972, respondents repeatedly were asked to assess both their personal civic competence and to judge the benevolence of the government, whether it is "run for the benefit of all the people or for a few big interests." The paired questions fuse two distinct elements in the linkage of citizens to the government. Feelings of personal civic competence refer to "the individual's sense of his own fundamental capacities," while judging the benevolence of the government refers to the character of the government's response and to "perception of properties of the political system as it stands at a point in time."[26] Over time, the linkage has weakened considerably, with voters increasingly emphasizing the failures of government, rather than their personal deficiencies as citizens.

When the two questions are combined, four categories again result, with differing implications for the total system:

1. Those who both feel personally competent and believe government is altruistic—the supporters;
2. Those who think government works for all, even though they feel personally incompetent—the trustful;
3. Those who combine confidence in their own ability with the opinion that government acts for special interests—the cynics; and

4. Those who both feel personally incompetent and believe that government serves only a few—the subjectively oppressed.

The polity is most stable when its members are supporters, although the system can also be sustained by trustful participants. Cynics are a destabilizing element, and the most estranged group is that of the subjectively oppressed.

In 1964, when these questions were first asked, supporters predominated in the electorate, as well as in all age and educational groups. Cynics, the second largest element, were outnumbered by 3-1. Even in 1968, the predominance of supporters remained at 2-1. By 1972, however, there was a plurality of cynics in the population. General confidence in politicians' responsiveness had been sharply reduced, while assessments of personal competence held steady after 1968. Justifiably, citizens blamed not themselves but their government for the failures of war in Vietnam, declining social programs, corruption, and the abuse of power.

Changed attitudes were particularly marked among the younger and more educated voters. Following a single cohort over time shows how it reacts to the events of the time, even as it grows older. When persons who

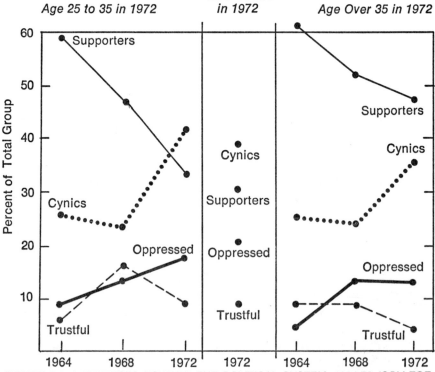

FIGURE 5.1 / ATTITUDES TOWARD THE POLITICAL SYSTEM, 1964-72 (COLLEGE-EDUCATED, BY AGE COHORTS)

reached the ages of 25 to 35 in 1972 first began voting in large numbers eight years earlier (at ages 18 to 27), their attitudes were much like those of their elders. As pictured in Figure 5.1,[27] later events had a particular impact on the college-educated members of this group. The proportion of supporters was nearly halved, while the proportion of cynics rose to 41 percent. The same trends were evident in the older voters (over 35) with a college background, but were considerably less extensive. By 1972, the middle-aged (25 to 35) resembled the new voters, not the older group. Positive attitudes were also declining among the noncollege group, but among these persons, the movement was toward similarity of attitudes, not the generational division evident in the college-educated.

From 1964 to 1972, the college-educated members of the 25-35 cohort experienced college and advanced in years. Their alienation from the government increased and an age split opened between them and the older generation. Those who had not attended college, on the other hand, came to resemble the older generation. Maturation did not necessarily lead to conservatism or to reconciliation between cohorts. To the contrary, the experiences of the period pushed a significant group in the opposite direction—away from the attitudes of older persons and away from generalized support of the political system.

The negative attitudes of youth in 1972 are not inherent in the life cycle. While young people are particularly impressionable, the impressions they receive of politics need not be negative. It is the character of politics at the time they reach political maturity that is critical in determining whether new voters will support or reject that politics.

Since the 1972 election, opinion polls have evidenced a continued decline of public confidence in government. The distance between the college and noncollege groups has been reduced, but both groups now show less supportive attitudes. Illustratively, only 19 percent of college youth believe "patriotism is a very important value," and only two of every five noncollege young persons share the opinion.[28] The Watergate revelations of crime, illegal contributions, and abuse of power; the forced resignation of a vice-president and the resignation under fire of a president have surely reinforced these feelings of cynicism and distrust. The potential for increased instability and for renewal of American politics both exist in the attitudes of today's young people. A different kind of politics, inside and outside the voting booth, is likely to follow. The character of this politics is suggested by the attitudes of youth on contemporary issues.

ISSUES OF THE GENERATIONS

Contemporary youth defines itself as liberal. On specific issues as well, today's young persons have attitudes consistent with conventional meanings of liberalism, in favor both of greater individual freedom and of government action to further social justice. Generational divisions are greatest on "cultural" issues such as women's rights, legalization of marijuana, and campus protest; and these divisions remain evident on questions of Vietnam withdrawal and civil rights. On economic programs, however, age differences are not significant.[29] The middle-aged group's opinion generally lies between that of the younger and older groups. On cultural issues, however, it is much closer to that of the older group, pointing to an identifiable generation gap.

If we separate the age groups by degree of education, as in Table 5.4, a strong generational difference becomes clear among the college-educated. Young persons with campus experience are quite distinct from the oldest age group on such contemporary issues as Vietnam, marijuana, student unrest, civil rights, and abortion, as well as in general ideology.

Indications of a distinct generational impact are strengthened in examining the middle-aged group. When they are college-educated, these persons are more similar to the new voters than to the older citizens. The unique historical events of the 1960s and 1970s were likely to have affected them, as well as their younger peers. Student protests on Vietnam, for example, would emotionally reach not only those still on campus, but recent alumni. Consequently, support for withdrawal from the war among the college-educated middle-aged resembles that of the newly enfranchised college students. Among those without college training, these effects are less apparent. On Vietnam, as on other issues, the noncollege middle-aged are closer to their elders.

The distinctiveness of the new college-educated generations is demon-

TABLE 5.4 / ISSUE POSITIONS, BY AGE AND EDUCATION, 1972*

	No College Education			Some College Education		
	18-24	25-35	Over 35	18-24	25-35	Over 35
Job Guarantee	36.7	27.4	34.5	34.9	31.8	24.2
Progressive Taxation	49.0	48.1	43.9	45.6	39.6	46.8
Health Insurance	47.6	39.7	46.7	50.0	45.0	43.3
Vietnam	50.0	43.5	41.2	65.4	54.0	37.5
Legal Marijuana	32.3	15.2	8.8	65.8	45.5	28.6
Campus Unrest	29.2	15.0	13.7	51.2	31.9	22.1
Rights of Accused	45.1	37.0	27.4	54.0	43.0	37.8
Aid to Minorities	43.9	32.1	27.6	48.9	46.1	34.6
School Busing	11.6	5.1	6.6	20.4	17.2	10.8
Urban Unrest	78.3	64.5	52.9	73.3	65.7	55.3
Abortion	43.5	42.7	31.3	68.6	57.8	53.7
Women's Equality	51.6	43.3	41.1	70.2	65.0	58.0
General Ideology	28.3	20.3	17.5	57.1	39.4	23.9

*Cell entries are percentages of each group favoring the "liberal" position, as defined in text. Number of cases varies with each question, but proportions are similar to those in Tables 5.2 and 5.3.

strated further by cohort analysis of the middle-aged group. Comparisons can be made between the responses of those who were aged 25-35 in 1972, and older voters, as well as of their peers in 1968 (then aged 21-31, and older). These comparisons, detailed in Table 5.5, show considerable change by the group with some college education on the most salient issues, and in the direction of the views of emergent youth.

On Vietnam in 1968, the younger cohort was much like its elders, and those without college education were actually more hawkish.[30] In the following four years, opinion generally became more dovish, but the swing was greater among those with some college education; and a considerable gap opened between that group and the older generation. The same trend is evident on the issue of urban unrest, although education is less evident as an influence and a preference for social solutions developed in the youth of both educational strata. Since this issue was raised not only in the classroom but in ghetto streets, it affected all young people.

On other issues, the uniqueness of the college-educated is again apparent. On the civil rights issues of fair employment and school integration, those with no college education show no age difference by 1972, and on the economic issues of a government job guarantee and medical care they have become actually more conservative than older persons. On the economic questions, but not on civil rights, the college-educated also tend

TABLE 5.5 / COHORT CHANGE IN OPINIONS, 1968-72*

	No College Education		Some College Education	
	1968	1972	1968	1972
Vietnam				
Age 25-35 in 1972	24.8	43.5	33.9	54.0
Over 35 in 1972	30.9	41.2	30.0	37.5
Urban Unrest				
Age 25-35 in 1972	39.7	64.5	47.4	65.7
Over 35 in 1972	40.7	52.9	39.6	55.3
School Integration				
Age 25-35 in 1972	54.3	43.3	51.6	52.6
Over 35 in 1972	43.8	41.0	47.5	44.2
Fair Employment				
Age 25-35 in 1972	50.3	51.8	51.8	58.2
Over 35 in 1972	44.8	50.0	50.2	56.9
Job Guarantee				
Age 25-35 in 1972	44.2	36.8	42.2	40.2
Over 35 in 1972	42.0	44.6	29.9	32.6
Medical Care				
Age 25-35 in 1972	64.7	47.7	58.7	51.1
Over 35 in 1972	72.0	54.5	50.9	50.6

*Cell entries are percentages of group favoring "liberal" position, as defined in text.

toward the position of older persons. These trends provide some support for the belief that people become more economically conservative as their developing wealth makes them wary of government spending. On the unique issues of the period, however—race and Vietnam—a generational influence persists. Affected by the experiences of the time, the middle-aged persons with some college education did not become indifferent to social causes, but more distinctively supportive of liberal positions.

To be a liberal, however, is obviously a vague identification. No coherent philosophical theory unites the liberal who favors abortion with the liberal who advocates government guarantees of medical care, or unites the self-defined conservatives who oppose these policies.[31] To specify the belief systems of the voters, attitudes on particular questions can be correlated with self-placement on the scale of general ideology, ranging from "liberal" to "conservative." Such analysis reveals the ambiguity of ideology and its different meanings to the generations. A young conservative or a young liberal is substantively different from a middle-aged or older advocate of either ideology. "The war and cultural issues were much more systematically related to the liberal-conservative framework by younger respondents than by older individuals. The responses of the older age group in the general domain of social or economic issues were, however, more consistently related to the liberal-conservative scale than were their policy positions on the war or cultural issues."[32]

Among the young, ideology is most closely related to questions of Vietnam, of life-style (e.g., use of marijuana), or of civil rights (e.g., the means of coping with urban unrest). These associations evidence the distinctiveness and moralism of the young, as the theory of Erikson leads us to expect. A generational effect is also apparent. Contemporary youth can literally afford such an emphasis, because it has been historically unique in its financial security. As a cohort enjoying, until recently, relative affluence, it has been able to place more emphasis on noneconomic issues and on matters of individual freedom and rights.[33] Older persons have lacked such shelter. Raised in a threatening industrial economy, amid extensive poverty, their task of making a living necessarily took precedence. Having had less of the luxury and leisure that allow concentration on other issues, they have defined their ideology in relation to primary needs.[34] A continued weakening of the American economy may lead to a new emphasis on economic problems by all generations.

The new values of the young are further indicated by independent research on American beliefs. From 1968 to 1971, persons in their twenties and thirties—the two younger generations of interest here—increasingly emphasized nonmaterial and personal goals. "The findings suggest that this sub-group of adult Americans may be undergoing more extensive value changes than any other segment: toward a lesser emphasis on tradition and religion; toward greater concerns with racial and sexual egalitarianism, ecology, peace, and peace of mind."[35]

Generational differences can be further analyzed through factor analysis, presented in the Appendix to this chapter. The most important findings of this procedure is that the underlying ideas of the three age groups are considerably different. The unifying elements in the beliefs of the youngest voters concern questions of life-style and the Vietnam war. For the oldest group, by contrast, the two most important factors both concern questions of social justice with the first element apparently based primarily on racial issues and the second more closely related to economic matters.

These different emphases are also evident in the generations' definition of their ideology. A young liberal is one who favors more individual freedom for smokers of pot, women, and the criminally accused; increased educational opportunity for minorities; and withdrawal from Vietnam. To the older person, liberalism means government aid for integration, welfare, jobs, and health. Opinions on life-style and individual freedom are not an important part of his liberalism or conservatism.

These different meanings of liberalism might possibly be dismissed as a reflection of age alone. An emphasis on personal freedom is not surprising in the young, and may diminish with the assumption of greater responsibilities. Conversely, these beliefs may continue to affect the beliefs of the new voters of 1972, even when they must worry more about jobs and medical care. Whatever the inherent tendencies of young persons toward individualism and moralism, the times in which they have been shaped politically have made these issues deeply relevant. Their attitudes on these issues are not isolated opinions, but have been partially encapsulated into a generalized ideology. The particular issues of marijuana or women's equality may lessen in salience, but the general problems of individualism and social justice will surely remain. To these questions, the overall ideology of the newest generation will continue to suggest answers.

The structure of attitudes among the middle-aged group provides another indication of a persistent generational effect. While it gives priority to social justice, this group, too, displays a "life-style" factor in its political attitudes. The emphasis on personal freedom, then, does not seem to be simply a response of unattached youth, but also of those somewhat older persons who have been particularly affected by recent events.

The analysis points to the existence of divergent belief systems in the electorate, which parallel two distinct ideological traditions. Although both have been called "liberalism," their content is sharply different. An emphasis on individual freedom is the older meaning of the term. Liberty, according to John Stuart Mill and the Manchester economists, is best promoted by restricting the power of the government. In its newer meaning, the emphasis of the term is on increasing opportunities for individual development. For such theorists as T. H. Green and John Dewey, freedom is often promoted by government intervention in social and economic life.[36] Both of these traditions have been strong in the United States, and both have claimed to be the true "liberal" creed as recently as the presidential competition of Franklin Roosevelt and Herbert Hoover.[37]

The divergent meanings of liberalism in political theory are matched among contemporary voters by the differing structures of opinions. The practical consequence is that political alliances across generational lines will be difficult to establish. Although the young are relatively "liberal" by their own description, this label reads differently for them than for older liberals. Hubert Humphrey is a likely hero to the more mature group, but Eugene McCarthy is more appealing to liberal youth. These divergences are even greater among political activists, further inhibiting a united ideological coalition.[38] Generational divisions are not simply reflections of age, which will pass with the years. They represent different philosophies, based on different experiences, voiced by different leaders.

Generations are shaped in the crucible of their early political experiences and can be remolded when past fires are rekindled. The older generations entered politics at times when economic issues were dominant. Such class-related questions can become relevant in particular elections, as we have shown in Chapter 3. The newer generations have begun to cast ballots at a time when issues of equality, war, and life-style are emphasized. These matters, too, may become as irrelevant as the once-fierce debate over the Tennessee Valley Authority. If these questions become voiced again, however, there will be a ready audience in the newer political generations.

A NEW POLITICS?

If the new political generations are to affect American politics lastingly, they must evidence their differences at the ballot box itself. In 1972, the new voters provided unique support for the Democratic party and candidate, and provided a distinctly liberal addition to the voting public. Even more significant in the long run may be the character of their general beliefs and the greater importance of those beliefs, compared to partisan loyalty, in their votes. The newer voters are moving American elections toward new issues and a greater stress on public policy.

Vietnam provides the most obvious illustration of the influence of issues. It was the single most important question in 1972 and was directly relevant to the new voters, who faced at least disrupted lives and at most death itself. They not only supported withdrawal from the Asian war more than other citizens did, but evidenced this view more consistently in their vote. Two-thirds of the young doves voted for McGovern, compared to 57 percent of the middle-aged and 54 percent of the older group with the same policy position. Among the middle-aged, ballot choice varied with education. Those without college training voted like the older group, while those with it behaved more like the newly enfranchised. Again, there is an indication of a generational influence—the college antiwar movement—which would have its greatest impact on those who recently had been at the scene of the protests.

The impact of the Vietnam issue on the young is evident even when examined in relation to party identification. Young Democrats who tended toward advocacy of withdrawal were virtually unanimous in their vote for McGovern, while a quarter of the older voters chose Nixon, even though they were both Democrats and doves. At the other extreme, the few young voters who were neither Democrats nor doves were somewhat more likely to vote for Nixon than the older voters. Where conflict between partisanship and Vietnam preference existed, the young consistently resolved the psychological dispute by selecting the Democratic candidate, suggesting other influences toward a McGovern ballot.

The distinctive importance of issues to youth is revealed in separate multiple regressions of the vote within each age group. Partisanship and general ideology are included in the analysis in Table 5.6, as well as four particular issues. Constituting the most important questions from different sets of public policies, the four issues are Vietnam, government guarantee of full employment, school busing, and legalization of marijuana.[39]

Among the new voters, there is little independent effect of cultural issues, as represented by support for the legalization of marijuana. Although the direct correlation between position on this issue and presidential choice is relatively high, its influence is of no significance when compared to the other issues. The youth culture is not the source of differential voting in 1972, although its effect may be partially included in the generalized measure of liberalism.

TABLE 5.6 / SOURCES OF THE PRESIDENTIAL VOTE, BY AGE, 1972
(Beta Weights, Multiple Regression of Republican Vote)*

	Age 18-24	Age 25-35	Age Over 35
Party Identification	.30	.26	.30
Vietnam	.29	.31	.20
School Busing	.13	.12	.22
Job Guarantee	.15	.11	.15
Legalization of Marijuana	.03	.07	.01
General Ideology	.30	.13	.17
(N)	(75)	(125)	(320)
Total R^2	.578	.422	.504
Unique R^2, Partisanship	.069	.135	.145
R^2, Partisanship as First Variable	.287	.195	.234

*Positive coefficients show that the Republican vote is dependent on Republican partisanship and a conservative position on the particular issues or general ideology.

The true distinctiveness of the young, as seen in Table 5.6, is in the relative impact on them of issues and partisanship. Although party loyalty continues to have an influence, it is no more important among the newly enfranchised than Vietnam attitudes or general ideology, as measured by the beta weights. Party loyalty unrelated to any of the issues (the unique R^2) can explain a mere 7 percent of the ballot choices. In contrast, over half the vote of youth can be explained simply on the basis of the ideology and issues included in the regression. This figure is simply calculated as the difference between the total R^2 and that which can be explained uniquely by partisanship.

Party is of greater importance to the two older groups. Among those aged 25-35, loyalty to Democrats and Republicans is rivaled in impact only by Vietnam. Less than 30 percent of the variance in its vote may be attributed to all of the issues, as measured by the difference between the total R^2 and the unique R^2 provided by partisanship.

In the over 35 age group, a multitude of causal factors exist. The overwhelming issue for the group is school busing (athough the concentration of opinion and vote at the extremes makes this conclusion statistically dubious). Party is clearly very important, uniquely accounting for over a seventh of the explained variance. Even when partisanship is held back as the last variable, all of the issues together only account for slightly more than a third of this generation's vote.

The multiple regressions summarized in the table show the effect of both youth as an age group and the generational influences to which it has been subjected. The greater receptivity to ideology characteristic of the postadolescent is evident, as is the differentiation from the partisan traditions of his parents. The impact of historical events is evident in the impact of the Vietnam issue. The middle-aged group also evidences this generational influence in its responsiveness to the Vietnam issue, which arose to prominence during the earliest years of its electoral participation. In 1968, this issue was of relatively little impact on the vote of the entire electorate.[40] As the issue became defined by the choice of candidates in 1972, the middle-aged voters were most open to its influence, particularly those with higher education.[41]

In the influences on their vote, as in their ideology and attitudes toward the political system, new generations are different. Their uniqueness, however, is neither explicable not determined by their chronological age. Youth as a stage in the life cycle is likely to be marked by distinctiveness and an ideological emphasis, but these developmental characteristics can be variously shaped by the social environment. While moral absolutism may be a common characteristic of the young, there is a vast difference in expressing it by working on an Israeli kibbutz or registering voters in Mississippi, as against bombing laboratories or reviling policemen. As a generation comes of age, the political world along with biological facts influences its responses.

Youth is particularly subject to these social influences, but aging does not necessitate rigidity. The more mature persons we have analyzed, aged 25-35 in 1972, also have been affected by recent events. They have not inexorably become more conservative, but have often come closer to the attitudes of the youngest group. Even those past the "advanced" age of 35 evidence considerable change in attitudes, although the movement tends to be slower. Voters are not determined by their age, sex, or class. In all groups, there is considerable responsiveness to political stimuli.

New generations, bringing new ideas developed amid the stresses of their initial years, will increasingly influence the total character of the nation. Their weight in the electorate was enlarged in 1972 by constitutional amendment and will be further swollen by maturation of the babies of the postwar period. If there is to be a new politics born in America, contemporary youth will be its parents.

The oncoming generations are concerned about politics, and knowledgeable about candidates and their policy positions, but they are relatively uninterested in electoral activities and cynical toward government. Reflecting the moralism of youth, they are prone to be ideological, but their beliefs are defined differently from the traditional bread-and-butter issues of distributive bargaining. Although tending to be Democratic or Independent, the young rely in their vote less on partisanship than on their liberalism and their issue concerns.

The distinctive characteristics of these voters can be largely explained as the result of their unique generational experiences. The influences and effects of these experiences are most marked among the presumptive future elites, those who have had some college education and who are particularly notable for their dissatisfaction. Because of these experiences, preserved in memory and ideology, the new generations can be expected to act differently from their elders even as they mature and settle down to more conventional lives. It appears likely that while "almost all young people will eventually be *in* the system . . . a relatively large number of them will never be *for* the system."[42]

There is indeed a generation gap in American politics, particularly among the more educated. The young are not only less mature, but different—in their partisanship, their ideology, and particularly in their dissatisfaction. The likely resultant clash between age groups need not be unhealthy, even if it is destabilizing. If conflict is restricted, "a flexible society benefits from [it] because such behavior, by helping to create and modify norms, assures its continuance under changed conditions."[43] However, the total system may be endangered if conflict becomes extensive and challenges underlying legitimacy. There are some signs of such extensive rejection in today's youth.

The qualities of the new generations and its trained elites should give pause to any who observe smugly or with relief the decline of campus unrest and street demonstrations. Outward manifestations of protest and alienation may diminish, for a shorter or longer period. Yet the experiences that have shaped the new generations and those who speak for them, and the social needs they address, cannot be erased from their personalities or from national history. The brutality of Vietnam, the cruelties of racism, the corruption of a president, the separatism of the youth culture have stimulated new loyalties and new attitudes. These characteristics may serve the nation well as the new generations grow in influence and move toward leadership. They may also subvert American democracy, for they include cynicism, quiescence, and privatism. Future responses of the young, like those of their elders, await future stimuli. The character of parties and politicians ultimately will determine the political effect of contemporary youth on the United States.

THE NEW POLITICAL GENERATIONS: FINDINGS

1. Youthful voters in 1972 are distinct in their political preferences.
   1a. These new voters tend to be Democrats or Independents voting for McGovern.
   1b. They are more likely than older persons to be ideological liberals, regardless of party.
2. Contemporary youth is no more informed or politically active than older groups.
3. By 1972, however, young voters were more aware of candidate positions on issues.
4. Expressions of inefficacy and avoidance of politics are recently characteristic of the educated young.
5. Young voters tend to reject a citizen duty to vote and tend to consider themselves without political influence.
   5a. Among educated youth, the duty to vote is rejected even though the group is subjectively efficacious.
   5b. These attitudes are only recently characteristic of the young, not inherent.
6. Cynicism toward government has grown considerably in the past decade.
   6a. This development is particularly evident among educated youth.
7. Generational differences exist on most issues, with younger persons taking a more "liberal" position.
   7a. The greatest differences exist on questions of "culture" and "life style."
   7b. Differences are particularly evident among the college-educated.
8. The age groups also differ in the content of their ideologies.
   8a. To youth, the most central issues in 1972 are those of life style and Vietnam.

    8b. Older voters define their ideology in racial and economic terms.
9. The vote of age groups in 1972 is influenced by different issues.
    9a. Younger voters are particularly affected by Vietnam, but less influenced by school busing.
10. The new voters are little affected by partisanship, and more influenced by policy issues.

APPENDIX TO CHAPTER 5

In factor analysis, we seek underlying dimensions that tie together the responses to a series of questions. The basic data are the correlations between variables. This technique enables us "to see whether some underlying pattern of relationships exists such that the data may be 'rearranged' or 'reduced' to a smaller set of *factors* or *components* that may be taken as *source variables* accounting for the observed interrelationships in the data."[44]

For each of the age groups, a separate factor analysis was undertaken to extract three orthogonal factors, independent of one another. In Table 5.7, the listed coefficients indicate the "loading," or importance, of each issue on the underlying factor. Given these loadings, the factor is assigned a convenient label. Each factor is then correlated, in a multiple regression equation, with the general scale of liberalism and conservatism. The latter step indicates the degree to which each underlying factor defines liberalism and shows the contrasts in basic ideology among the generations.[45]

If we look at the new voters of 1972, the most important factor is one particularly associated with such policies as the legalization of marijuana, school busing, women's equality, and the rights of persons accused of crime. An appropriate name for this all-embracing factor might be "life-style." The second most important factor has highest loading on attitudes concerning Vietnam. The third factor shows the greatest relationship to issues of both economics and civil rights, and might be labeled "social justice."

In like fashion, we can see that the most important factors for the oldest group concern economic and racial attitudes. Among the middle-aged, social justice is the most important element, but there is also a significant secondary factor relating to "life-style." Although not the predominant element in its thinking, this factor still has a significant impact and is related at a moderate level to positions on the general scale of ideology.

The bottom rows in Table 5.7 are the results of regressing the liberalism scale upon the three factors. The greater beta weights and correlations of the first factors show that they are particularly associated with the ideology of each generation, and that the content of liberalism and conservatism differs among the age groups. It should be noted, however, that these results also are dependent on the order in which variables are introduced in the regression procedure.

TABLE 5.7 / FACTOR ANALYSIS OF ISSUE POSITIONS, BY AGE, 1972*

	Age 18-24			Age 25-35		
	Loadings				Loadings	
	Factor 1 ("Life-Style")	Factor 2 ("Vietnam")	Factor 3 ("Social Justice")	Factor 1 ("Social Justice")	Factor 2 ("Life-Style")	Factor 3 ("Economics")
Vietnam	.262	.855	.075	.378	.275	.025
Job Guarantee	−.039	.360	.337	.543	.041	.340
Progressive Taxation	−.058	.012	.353	.305	−.093	.312
Legalized Marijuana	.844	.085	−.130	.128	.721	.039
School Busing	.561	−.032	.750	.545	.304	.141
Health Insurance	.186	.466	−.020	.079	.221	.626
Women's Equality	.497	.162	.034	.249	.443	.178
Rights of Accused	.449	.151	.056	.472	.214	.089
Aid to Minorities	.383	.226	.327	.720	.199	.122
Percent of Variance	59.7	21.7	18.6	71.3	16.9	11.8
		N = 96			N = 166	
Relationship to Liberalism Scale:						
Beta Weight	.52	.18	.06	.38	.28	−.03
r	.49	.10	.09	.42	.35	.09
		R = .53			R = .50	

*The loadings in the upper half of this table indicate the association of the individual issue variables with the underlying factors. In the bottom part of the table, these factors become independent variables explaining position on the liberalism scale. The beta weights show the effect of each factor on liberalism, r is the direct correlation of each factor with liberalism, and R is the total correlation of the three factors.

	Age Over 35		
	Loadings		
	Factor 1 ("Race")	Factor 2 ("Economics")	Factor 3 ("Life-Style")
Vietnam	.389	.225	.177
Job Guarantee	.370	.487	−.037
Progressive Taxation	.037	.284	.102
Legalized Marijuana	.195	.153	.585
School Busing	.568	.240	.111
Health Insurance	.228	.526	.127
Women's Equality	.106	.069	.410
Rights of Accused	.480	.040	.292
Aid to Minorities	.571	.200	.178
Percent of Variance	75.1	15.7	9.2
		N = 396	
Relationship to Liberalism Scale:			
Beta Weight	.40	.12	−.04
r	.41	.07	.20
		R = .43	

CHAPTER 6

BLACK AND WHITE ASUNDER

Class warfare is muted in the United States, even in the demilitarized zone of the voting booth. The "generation gap" and the "battle of the sexes" have been found in previous chapters to be limited conflicts. There is one American social division, however, that is sharp and persistent: the racial strife between blacks and whites.

The conflict has been the principal threat to America's survival throughout its history. Like a protagonist in a classical drama, the United States has been marred by a fatal flaw, its inability to reconcile two races. Even amidst the happiness of the early Republic, Tocqueville saw the clash of color as leading inevitably to American tragedy. "These two races are fastened to each other without intermingling; and they are alike unable to separate entirely or to combine. . . . All intermediate measures seem to me likely to terminate, and that shortly, in the most horrible of civil wars and perhaps in the extirpation of one or the other of the two races."[1]

Tocqueville's prediction was soon verified, as the basic issue of human freedom led to the bloodiest of America's wars. Yet, the racial issue itself was unresolved by the Civil War and continued to fester. Eventually, blacks despaired. "For the black man in America the only solution is complete separation from the white man," declared Malcolm X. "The only way the black people caught up in this society can be saved is not to integrate into this corrupt society, but to separate from it, to a land of our own, where we can reform ourselves, lift up our moral standards, and try to be godly."[2]

By the 1960s, the tragedy was written once again in blood. Across the

117

continent—from Newark in the East, to Detroit in the Midwest, and to Watts on the Pacific coast—the chasm between the races was demonstrated in hundreds of ghetto revolts and urban pillagings. From 1965 to 1968, civil disorder affected virtually every American city.[3] A new civil war threatened, not between regions, but between the races.

In classic tragedy, the actions of the characters are predetermined by their original characteristics. The United States has seemed fated by its original adoption of slavery to undergo torment and self-destruction. In electoral analysis, the influence of original characteristics is the mark of the dependent voter. The effect of race on American political life is therefore a critical test of the portrait of the dependent voter. If demographic features cause political response directly, the effects certainly will be obvious when the voters are analyzed in relation to their ineradicable color. Perhaps more than in the case of any other feature, reliance on race may be an accurate cue to rational and beneficial action. It surely makes sense for blacks to vote cohesively when confronting racist policies.

The responsive voter, too, will be affected by his racial membership, but the effect will not be complete and unchanging. It will vary with circumstances and in response to the cues provided by national leaders. When racial issues are foremost, unity among blacks and whites is likely. At such times the two portraits of the voter will be alike. At other times, when racial questions are less evident, the two portraits will differ, with the responsive voter emphasizing the particular questions of the particular election.

Racial conflict in the United States has varied greatly in its focus, in the groups involved, and in its mode of expression. In this chapter we will concentrate on the issues of racial integration. We will be particularly concerned with the effect of these issues on blacks and whites as distinct groups, and with differences between the races expressed in electoral opinions and behavior from 1960 to 1972. Since racial concerns affected all American lives during this period, however, we cannot ignore nonelectoral opinions and activities. Blacks and whites expressed choices not only in their votes, but also in their protests, alienation, economics, and deaths.[4]

THE DEVELOPMENT OF RACIAL POLITICS

The problem of race has been present in America since the first sad slave ship docked in Virginia in 1609, but its immediate salience has varied considerably. Even when ignored or repressed, though, the issue has remained. Like "a fireball in the night," it has been disregarded only at the nation's peril, bringing a later and more extensive conflagration. There has been a historical pattern of attention and negligence concerning this problem. Evident in such times as Reconstruction, the pattern can also be seen in recent years. The reactions of the voters have varied with these changing emphases.

In 1960, the first election under consideration in this chapter, race was not a central issue. There was little difference in the platforms of the two candidates, and both Nixon and Kennedy were then regarded as moderate liberals. Four years later, race was of major importance, and a clear choice was presented to the electorate. Lyndon Johnson assumed leadership of the national effort for racial integration and achieved a strong civil rights law. In opposition, Barry Goldwater won the Republican nomination after voting against the civil rights law and received his firmest support from nascent southern segregationist politicians.

By 1968, racial concerns had assumed dramatic priority, spurring George Wallace's third-party candidacy. Democratic identification with civil rights was reinforced when President Johnson adopted the movement's slogan, "We shall overcome," and the party nominated Hubert Humphrey. The new Republican emphasis on southern white support continued with the nomination of Richard Nixon, who promised a slowdown of federal efforts toward abolition of the dual school system.[5] In 1972, race received less attention. The Nixon administration ignored most black demands and instead moved to relieve white fears of job quotas or forced school busing. George McGovern supported, but did not stress, civil rights programs. After a brief period of concern, national attention again had turned away from the conflicts of color.

The voters responded to these initiatives of the parties and their candidates both in behavior and in underlying opinions. Among the important developments of these years was the heightening of political consciousness in the black community. As issues central to their lives were placed on the American agenda, blacks came to be more fully involved in the nation's governing processes. The new black political awareness is evident in electoral activity. One indication is attachment to the political parties. In the Eisenhower era, more than a quarter of blacks found the political world irrelevant and could not identify with either the Republicans or Democrats, or even as Independents. But by the end of the 1960s, such "apolitical" blacks had virtually disappeared.[6] Indeed, blacks surpassed whites in their partisan commitment. As may be recalled from Table 2.3, while others have been slowly abandoning strong loyalty or even nominal identification with the major parties, blacks have turned in large proportions toward the Democrats. As Kennedy, Johnson, and Humphrey made campaign commitments to their cause, blacks became correspondingly devoted to the party, while a lessened advocacy by McGovern brought a decreased racial identification with the Democrats in 1972.

Blacks have become participants in politics, as well as partisans. Until 1960, their activity was inhibited not only by relative poverty, but by additional factors such as the absence of pertinent organizations. As a result, black involvement in politics was below even the limited level that would be expected of a deprived group.[7] Currently, "rather than the average black being an underparticipator, we find that he participates in politics somewhat more than we would expect given his level of education, income, and occupation, and more than the white of similar status."[8]

The major reason for this change has been the development of group consciousness among blacks. The greater involvement of the race in elections and community activities is directly related to an awareness of group identity. Blacks who are consciously identified with their race not only participate as fully as whites in politics, but actually are far more involved. This increased activity points to "the potency of symbols such as Black Power and the need to create cohesion among blacks as a step toward full participation in society."[9]

The most obvious measure of change has been in voting turnout. From 1960 to 1972, white participation in elections declined steadily, while blacks entered the voting booths in increasing numbers. The change is particularly striking in the South. Where whites once voted almost twice as frequently as the minority race, the disparity was virtually eliminated by 1972, as can be seen in Table 6.1.[10]

Two factors have been critical in the growth of black turnout: the series of national civil rights laws, and the prodding efforts of black organizations to bring voters to registration offices and polling places. Five recent civil rights laws have undermined the defenses of southern racism, providing successively for court tests of registration practices, judicial examiners, the abolition of such discriminatory practices as literacy tests, the appointment of federal registrars, and the eventual suspension of biased state election statutes.

Black organizations created mass pressure for these laws by conducting registration campaigns, by bringing a quarter of a million citizens to the 1963 March on Washington, and by leading nonviolent resistance to segregation and discrimination throughout the South. Perhaps for the first time, and hopefully not for the last, blacks came to share in the promises of the American political system. "One had only to hear in the mass meetings of the Negro movement in the South the expression of the fundamentals of American democracy, the loving reiteration of the words ('All men *are* created equal . . . AMEN . . . and *do* have inalienable rights . . . YES YES'), to understand how new life was breathed into old truths, and how the truths became alive in the people, giving them strength and courage."[11] Hope, effort, and sometimes the sacrifice of life, yielded a considerable growth in black voting registration, from only 35 percent of the race's southern population before 1965 to 57 percent within three years. Over half of the group had registered in every southern state by 1968, representing as much as a tenfold increase in Mississippi.[12]

Black participation in the electoral system is now quantitatively comparable to that of whites. The racial similarity can be further seen by examining the influences upon voting turnout, using the technique of multiple regression. In the 1960 election, these causal factors were different for each race. Black participation was substantially affected by residence in the South and by psychological feelings of inefficacy. Whites, on the other hand, were little affected by these factors, with their turnout most influenced by education and by their interest in the particular contest.

Over time, the races have become more similar in the variables affecting turnout. Region no longer has a marked impact on the participation of blacks in voting, nor do feelings of efficacy have a distinct effect. In fact, in 1968, such feelings are important only in their effect on the turnout of whites. In general, the races now vote or abstain for parallel reasons, particularly their relative education and their concern over the outcome of the specific election.

TABLE 6.1 / POLITICAL ACTIVITY, BY RACE AND EDUCATION, 1960-72*

	Whites				Blacks			
	1960	1964	1968	1972	1960	1964	1968	1972
Attempt to Influence Others	34.8	32.4	33.2	31.7	22.2	32.6	32.4	31.5
College	43.7	52.2	43.6	44.9	47.4	46.0	44.8	60.5
High School	34.8	28.8	30.8	28.5	27.6	34.2	32.2	27.0
Grade School	27.4	19.0	20.0	18.0	12.5	28.5	30.8	19.4
Financial Contributions								
to Parties	11.9	11.2	9.2[a]	10.6	9.2	5.9	4.4[a]	8.8
College	19.8	23.1	16.3	21.3	5.3	12.2	10.0	20.9
High School	11.5	9.3	5.9	6.7	20.7	7.0	5.9	8.1
Grade School	6.2	2.1	6.8	2.8	1.4	3.1	0.0	1.6
Follow Politics Closely	21.1	31.0	34.7	37.4	20.4	29.7	20.3	28.8
College	30.0	47.8	51.1	53.4	31.6	48.0	40.0	48.8
High School	19.5	28.6	30.7	32.0	25.9	30.4	16.1	27.0
Grade School	16.6	18.3	20.8	24.9	14.1	23.6	19.2	18.0
Voted for President	82.0	79.6	77.1	73.8	53.3	67.8	66.5	64.7
South	73.1	71.1	68.1	63.4	39.0	55.8	61.5	60.9
North	86.1	82.8	80.8	78.5	70.0	83.6	73.0	71.1
College	91.1	87.3	84.8	87.0	73.7	100.0	80.0	86.0
High School	83.2	79.5	79.7	70.9	60.3	69.0	62.5	62.9
Grade School	72.3	71.5	59.8	59.4	39.4	56.9	68.4	53.2
Write Letters	—	18.4	21.7	28.6	—	5.5	5.8	14.4
College	—	33.9	39.6	45.2	—	26.0	16.7	32.6
High School	—	15.2	16.1	24.5	—	3.8	6.0	11.7
Grade School	—	8.6	9.2	11.5	—	1.2	1.3	6.5
Care Great Deal/								
Much About Election	69.3	68.8	59.3	61.5	47.8	84.6	75.5	69.3
College	77.0	76.8	64.2	68.7	82.6	80.8	61.7	75.9
High School	70.2	70.1	59.2	60.0	40.9	88.1	78.6	68.8
Grade School	61.4	56.8	52.5	53.8	45.5	82.5	76.4	64.6
Total (N)	(1764)	(1399)	(1388)	(2397)	(172)	(422)	(265)	(267)

*Entries are the percentages evidencing the designated attitude or behavior.
[a]The 1968 question on contributions is not comparable to that asked in the other years.

The growth of black consciousness is evident as well in other measures of political activity, as detailed in Table 6.1. While white involvement has remained relatively constant, there has been a marked increase in black attempts to influence the votes of their peers, attention paid to politics, concern about election outcomes, financial contributions to the parties, and frequency of writing letters to public officials. Long excluded from the many forms of American politics, blacks have come not only to vote, but to participate in all political activities.

The development of black political activity displays a responsiveness to the stimuli of the general political environment. Involvement is not a constant determined by race, but varies with external encouragement. The greatest growth came in 1964, when the combination of governmental support, racial organization, and the clear choice between national candidates stimulated a quantum change in black participation in electoral politics. The change of that year is particularly notable because it affected all educational strata of the black population. Not only the college-educated elite, but relatively unschooled ghetto residents and dirt farmers were politicized by the events and personalities of the time.

With the frustration of some of the high hopes of 1964, there has been a reduction in the political involvement of less-educated blacks. The leaders and emotional foci of the racial revolution, Martin Luther King and Robert Kennedy, were assassinated within two months of each other in 1968. With the presidential choice confined to the racism of Wallace, the antagonism of Nixon, and the conventional liberalism of Humphrey, black campaign activity declined.[13] The slighting of racial interests in the subsequent Nixon administration and the vacillation of McGovern contributed to a further decline in political activity in 1972 among less-educated blacks.

Among those blacks with a college education, however, continued political interest is evident, and by 1972 elite members of the race were as, or even more, active than comparable whites on most measures. They showed greater concern about the outcome of the election, and were more likely to evidence that concern in attempts to influence the votes of others. These data suggest that a coherent black political leadership is forming among the better-trained persons in the community, which will be able to mobilize mass support for racial goals.

Similar developments are evident elsewhere on the political scene. A Black Congressional Caucus has been formed, consisting of seventeen national representatives, which is disposed to use its voting power as a bloc to secure legislation favorable to its constituents. National organizations, such as the Conference of Black Elected Officials, meet regularly and are served by an independent research organization, the Joint Center for Political Studies. The likely result of these developments is an articulated political structure within the black community, with elected officials in the leadership positions, an attentive public of persons with higher education providing advice, and underlying support by the mass public of black citizens.[14]

The existence of such a political structure is a necessary precondition for the remediation of the grievances of the black community and is entirely consistent with the practices of American democracy. With a developed structure for black political action paralleling the established organization among white voters, two politically well-organized races will soon exist together in the United States. It is not inherently impossible that two different racial groups can live peacefully in the same nation. When those groups differ on fundamental questions of policy, however, and even question the worth of the political system itself, conflict may become unavoidable. The evidence of such fundamental polarization and alienation, unfortunately, abounds.

AMERICAN ALIENATION

The American political system, like any other, depends for its stability on an underlying popular trust that is unaffected by particular events. Governments and leaders inevitably make mistakes, but they are easily forgiven in a stable polity, where "diffuse support provides a reservoir upon which a system typically draws in times of crisis, such as depressions, wars, and internecine conflicts."[15] In recent years, this foundation of the political system has been eroded, with decay particularly evident in the period leading up to the 1972 election. More and more citizens believe that they have no power in or understanding of government, that politics is run only for the benefit of special interests, and that politicians are untrustworthy. Only in acknowledging a duty to vote do the electors evidence even ritual support of the political system. The corruption and immorality revealed since 1972, and the resignations of the only nationally elected officials, may increase these sentiments of alienation.

Dissatisfaction is evident in all subgroups of the population, but is particularly frequent, as seen in Chapter 5, among college-educated youth. The concentration of negative feelings among the likely future elites of the nation constitutes a distinct threat to American political stability. These sentiments are also more common among blacks—a substantial, self-conscious, and identifiable group. Their alienation therefore implies an additional challenge to the maintenance of traditional politics.

Blacks surely have valid historical reasons to question the fairness and legitimacy of American government. Nevertheless, despite the experiences of slavery, discrimination, and injustice, their hostility toward the political system has not been manifestly high. In 1964, a year of hope for blacks, their support of the system was approximately the same as that of whites—and even higher on some measures, as seen in Table 6.2. Gov-

TABLE 6.2 / POLITICAL EFFICACY, BY RACE AND EDUCATION, 1960-72*

	Whites				Blacks			
	1960	1964	1968	1972	1960	1964	1968	1972
"People like me have power"	73.8	70.8	59.6	60.3	61.0	66.4	48.0	53.0
Some College	88.5	84.4	75.4	77.6	70.8	88.2	69.0	78.2
High School	74.9	73.2	59.6	57.1	74.2	77.1	47.0	50.7
Grade School Only	59.8	51.1	36.5	41.7	45.9	49.4	41.9	37.7
"Politics not complicated"	42.2	32.9	30.1	26.7	35.0	30.3	20.9	18.9
Some College	59.8	56.4	48.9	44.5	58.3	68.6	44.8	34.5
High School	40.8	30.2	26.1	22.3	45.9	32.9	19.1	16.4
Grade School Only	30.4	13.5	12.1	10.7	18.1	17.8	14.7	11.6
"Duty to vote"	56.1	—	—	54.1	50.3	—	—	54.4
Some College	59.4	—	—	56.7	54.2	—	—	70.9
High School	59.5	—	—	53.3	60.7	—	—	49.3
Grade School Only	47.3	—	—	52.5	39.7	—	—	51.5
"Government for benefit of all"	—	68.9	54.3	43.0	—	71.6	68.1	26.2
Some College	—	68.1	61.9	48.0	—	78.3	77.8	29.3
High School	—	71.9	54.0	42.5	—	69.2	71.8	22.0
Grade School Only	—	62.4	42.9	35.0	—	73.2	59.7	32.7
"Trust government most of time"	—	77.8	62.7	56.6	—	75.7	59.0	32.5
Some College	—	80.4	65.7	63.6	—	83.7	58.6	32.6
High School	—	80.3	64.9	56.3	—	72.4	57.9	31.5
Grade School Only	—	68.1	52.6	44.9	—	75.5	60.3	33.9

*Entries are percentages agreeing with each statement in the given group.

ernmental programs in support of civil rights, and the symbolic identification of national leaders with the integrationist movement, apparently encouraged blacks to believe in the equity and trustworthiness of the political system.

Race does not predetermine political alienation; such feelings develop in response to political events. After 1964, the national commitment to civil rights lessened, and blacks reacted by withdrawing their trust in government. These years brought the diversion of social resources to the war in Vietnam, an increase in white resistance to integration in the North, the election of hostile "law-and-order" mayors, and the election of a federal executive unfriendly to school or housing integration. The decline in the diffuse support of blacks is most striking during the first Nixon administration and is surely related to its "benign neglect" of civil rights. While other events also contributed to the decline of support, as reflected in white attitudes, blacks had special reasons to doubt the fairness and trustworthiness of government.

Since the survival of a political system is closely related to the attitudes of its potential elites, the college-educated are particularly important. In both of the racial communities, favorable attitudes in the past were most marked among more educated persons, thereby promoting political stability. Although this general tendency persists even in 1972, among blacks there are some indications of declining support within the vital group with campus experience. These college-educated persons have been particularly prone to changing and downgrading their evaluation of government. Similarly, young blacks especially condemn the character of the political system and reject traditional obligations such as the duty to vote.

These severe attitudes do not stem from subjective or personal inadequacies, for educated and young blacks are relatively confident of their own abilities. Rather, they reflect a censure of the political system. The precipitous decline in supportive opinions reflects a felt betrayal by the government of its promises of progress and equality. When national leaders legislated in 1964 to end discrimination, virtually all college-educated blacks felt confidence in the political institutions. When other leaders failed to enforce these laws, less than a third of the black elite maintained their faith.

Attitudes toward the political system can be further explicated by combining responses to the question on efficacy with that on the presumed fairness of government, in a manner similar to that employed in the last chapter on generational differences. Considerable destabilizing change is revealed by combining these responses. The four resulting categories are those of supportive, trustful, cynical, and oppressed participants. Over the past three elections, there has been considerable erosion in the underlying support given the political system. In both races by 1972,[16] supporters and the trustful together account for less than a majority of the population.

As pictured in Figure 6.1, the change has been particularly great in the black community. Over a majority are supporters in 1964, and the combined supporters and trustful predominate even in 1968. After four more years, however, neither support nor trust is much in evidence among blacks. Cynicism toward the political system is the most prevalent black reaction, and there is also a growing perception of oppression.

When educational level is considered, the races differ considerably. Among whites, the college-educated group has always shown the highest degree of support and the most favorable ratio of supporters to cynics, and this remains true even in 1972. In the past, the same relationship has been evident among blacks as well, with the ratio of supporters to cynics among the college-educated reaching as high as 8:1. In 1972, by contrast, cynicism is particularly evident in this leadership group.

These patterns again show that the source of critical black attitudes is not perceived personal inefficacy, but disdain of political institutions. The college group, which is the most active politically, also more often believes itself able to understand politics and to exercise power, but its activities are conducted in an increasingly critical mood. The same combination of activism, sense of personal efficacy, and cynicism toward the political system is evident among both younger black adults and adolescents.[17] This is a volatile mixture, leading not to disgusted withdrawal from politics, but to vigorous attempts to change intolerable conditions.

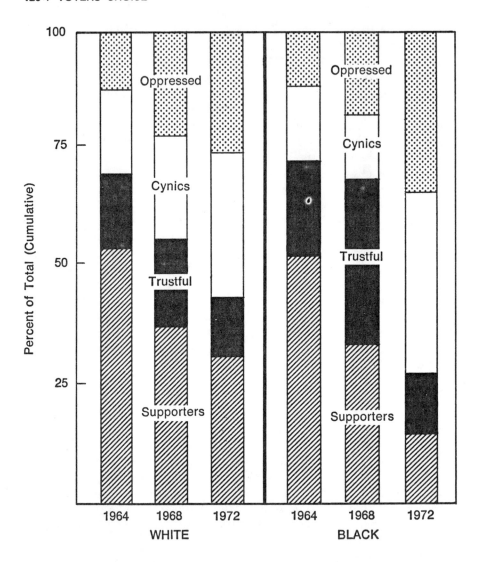

FIGURE 6.1 / RACIAL ATTITUDES TOWARD THE POLITICAL SYSTEM, 1964-72

The expression of racial discontent is increasingly likely to be through nonconventional methods, such as protests, civil disobedience, and mass demonstrations. Blacks have learned that they can be politically effective, if not at the ballot box, then in the streets. The wall of legalized segregation was little affected by voting, but began to crumble when blacks rode in the front seats of buses and sat at lunch counters reserved for whites. Civil rights bills buried in congressional committees were miraculously resurrected when marchers defied the police dogs of Birmingham and the state police blockading the highways at Selma.

Seeing the results of direct action, blacks have been particularly likely to favor these tactics, the differences between the races regarding such action increasing with the level of protest. In 1972, some two-thirds of blacks accept efforts to halt government through sit-ins and mass demonstrations, but only three of eight whites are even neutral toward such behavior. In both races, younger and more educated respondents are more permissive, but black tolerance is greater than that of whites in all groups.[18] As seen in Table 6.3, approval of protest is particularly high among minority youths, who have had the most personal experiences of the pains and prizes of protest.

Electoral and other modes of political activity are not necessarily opposed to one another, and politically active blacks are prone to use both kinds of techniques. Blacks who feel personally efficacious are more likely to vote and engage in campaign activities, yet also are more favorably disposed toward protest and demonstrations. By contrast, efficacious whites are likely to restrict themselves to electoral participation, finding protest less essential.

Support of protest, however, has varied with changing assessments of government, particularly among blacks. In 1968, direct action is more favored by those who vote, trust government, and see it as operating for the benefit of all. By 1972, the relationship is reversed. Protest has become

TABLE 6.3 / ATTITUDES TOWARD PROTEST ACTIVITIES, BY RACE AND GENERATION*

	1968		1972	
	Whites	**Blacks**	**Whites**	**Blacks**
Protest Marches	42.7	72.9	57.4	79.9
New Voters, 1972	—	—	82.3	90.0
The 1960s	56.6	83.0	69.5	90.9
Postwar	47.3	79.6	56.0	82.5
New Deal	38.8	67.3	47.2	˙56.1
Pre-New Deal	26.2	58.3	33.5	67.6
Civil Disobedience	35.6	61.6	54.1	71.4
New Voters, 1972	—	—	72.8	82.5
The 1960s	45.4	66.7	60.2	82.1
Postwar	36.0	69.2	52.9	71.9
New Deal	33.8	60.4	46.1	60.5
Pre-New Deal	25.9	45.9	40.6	47.1
Demonstrations	21.9	58.5	38.3	68.0
New Voters, 1972	—	—	53.6	85.0
The 1960s	34.0	73.5	41.0	69.2
Postwar	20.5	61.8	36.2	71.9
New Deal	17.9	46.2	34.5	61.0
Pre-New Deal	14.9	50.0	28.3	47.1

*Entries are the percentages of each group expressing either favorable or neutral attitudes to each activity. The generations are as defined in Chapter 2.

the approved method for those who refrain from voting and who mistrust government. Earlier, protest was based on hope: a fair government will respond when injustice is brought to its attention. More recently, protest has been based on despair: demonstrations are necessary to oppose an unfair government. When actions are based on these negative evaluations, the possibility of violent protest increases significantly. "Clearly, the foundation for the continued growth of unconventional activity, perhaps to the exclusion of some conventional behavior, and with a deepening of political distrust, now exists in the black community."[19] The negative stimuli of government have drawn a negative mass response. Since 1964 blacks have changed from a position of confidence in political institutions to positions of neutrality and alienation.[20] Resentments long submerged have become open.

Resort to unconventional politics and distrust of government is growing, not only among blacks but among whites, further increasing the possibilities of racial confrontation. In the brief period from 1968 to 1972, protest activity has drawn more support in both races, and in virtually every educational and generational category. A majority of whites is now prepared to permit some unconventional action short of actual disruption of government. This change in attitude is most marked among whites of middle age and of moderate education, the very "middle Americans" presumed to be opposed to protest.

White behavior has also changed, with more whites engaged in actual demonstrations. The purpose of their activities, however, is not parallel to that of blacks. When whites have marched and demonstrated, it has often been in regard to Vietnam or, more pertinently, in opposition to school busing or other actions to promote integration. Whites still do not favor protest to the same extent as blacks, but "it is reasonable to predict, nevertheless, that approval of protest activities will increase in the white community as time passes and increasingly, whites adjust to and imitate the techniques employed by blacks."[21]

A vicious cycle may be in progress, in which blacks and whites imitate each other's protests, each race legitimizing its actions by the opposing group's behavior. Black marches to gain construction jobs validate white construction workers' demonstrations to monopolize those positions; white protests against housing integration in suburban developments certify forceful exclusion of whites from all-black dormitories. Confrontation tactics are inherently conflictful and, when frequently employed, become ever more difficult to contain. As diffuse support lessens, political institutions are less trusted by both races to reach authoritative resolutions. Furthermore, the two races use these perilous tactics for different, opposing ends. With the policy objectives of blacks and whites markedly disparate, the American tragedy approaches a decisive climax.

THE ISSUES OF RACE

Racial polarization is the hallmark of recent American life. The division has been seen in confrontations on school and housing integration, etched in the blood of murders, smelled in the fires of urban destruction, shouted by ghetto rioters: "The man's got everything. I ain't got nothin'! Make Whitey run—that's the only way I get my kicks. They come down tonight, I gonna kill myself one of the fuckers!"[22]

In electoral opinion as well, events have moved the United States toward "two societies, one black, one white, separate and unequal."[23] This split has not been consistent or predetermined, but a response to the circumstances of the times. It is apparent in voting, party loyalty and evaluations, and policy issues, particularly questions of race.

In the 1950s, before racial matters moved to the top of the American agenda, voting already revealed a difference between the races. However, this difference was relatively moderate, with blacks in 1956 voting about 25 percent more heavily for the Democratic party than did whites, comparable to the pro-Democratic margin of union members contrasted to nonunionists. Moreover, if one took account of other social influences, there was less division on a racial basis than on that of union membership.[24]

The same limited difference was manifested in 1960, when the national black vote for John Kennedy exceeded white support by 23 percent. Racial and partisan differences were not yet mutually reinforcing. Since the 1960 contest, though, political behavior has become closely related to race. Black and white differences in the vote for president have grown to some 60 percent. In both 1968 and 1972, the ballots were "as sharply polarized along racial lines as at any time during American history," and were more distinct than class or other social cleavages in any democracy.[25] Moreover, these differences have become evident both within and outside the South, and even in periods of relative economic advancement for blacks. The races are not expressing a regional or class conflict in the voting booth, but a direct political clash.

The gap in voting behavior is founded on a growing differentiation in underlying party loyalty. The races have been moving away from each other in their basic partisanship, as well as in the actual ballots for president. Black Republicans have virtually disappeared since the evolution of the Goldwater "southern strategy" of 1964, while black votes have become crucially important to the Democratic party's success.[26] Whites, conversely, have reduced their commitment to the party of Roosevelt. In an earlier time, two authors warned that "The day some major element completely deserts one party in favor of the other, the stage will have been set for the kind of conflict that leads to actual civil war, and our parties will have failed to maintain our kind of consensus."[27] Unlike the period in which these words were written, today there are signs that such a crisis may be near.

Changes in general loyalties are paralleled by differing racial evaluations of the parties and candidates. By employing a series of open-ended questions, we can establish the voters' attitudes on various political dimensions.* Nine such dimensions have been established, relating to assessment of the individual candidates, the parties' performance in office, protection of group interests, and general philosophy, as well as issues. The issue dimensions include the parties' and candidates' positions on general domestic and foreign policy; the specific questions of race and public order; and, for 1968 and 1972, Vietnam.

Over the period from 1960 to 1972, racial evaluations of the parties and candidates have become sharply distinct, as shown by the sizable percentage differences in opinion summarized in Table 6.4. The partisan polarization of the two races is also indicated in this table, where the prevalence of positive coefficients shows that blacks consistently favor the Democrats more than whites do. Southern evaluations of McGovern, the top row in the table, are illustrative. In considering his personal characteristics, 33 percent of the region's blacks were pro-Democratic, finding more likable than objectionable personal characteristics in the South Dakotan. Only 8 percent of southern whites reached the same conclusion. There was, then, a 25 percent difference in racial judgments of the Democratic candidate in the South.

In the beginning of this time span, racial differences are restricted. Blacks are not consistently more supportive of the Democrats than whites in either region. In fact, southern whites are more favorable to Democrats than their black neighbors on six of eight contemporary dimensions. Northern blacks tend to have a more favorable image of the Democratic party, a reflection of the greater liberalism of blacks above the Mason-Dixon line. Even in the North, however, whites are more supportive than blacks when considering Kennedy's personal qualifications, or when assessing the parties' records in office or their foreign policies.

In the later years of this period, blacks have become decidedly more likely than whites to express favorable evaluations of the Democrats, and this racial difference is evident in both regions and on virtually every dimension. (The few small exceptions are due to the small number of nonneutral responses.) Consistent with their vote, blacks view the Democratic nominees more favorably and are comparatively unattracted by Goldwater and Nixon. The change over time is particularly notable in the last case, for whites were less friendly than blacks to Nixon, both nationally and in the South, when he first sought the presidency in 1960. When he

---

*The procedures used will be discussed more fully in Chapter 7.

TABLE 6.4 / RACIAL DIFFERENCES IN POLITICAL EVALUATIONS*

Evaluative Dimension	1960	1964	1968	1972
South				
Democratic Candidate	− 7.7	12.4	43.8	25.4
Republican Candidate	−18.0	0.4	22.9	17.0
Party Performance	− 8.2	16.0	29.3	6.7
Group Association	−15.1	12.3	40.3	28.6
General Philosophy	−12.6	8.4	13.3	− 2.5
Domestic Policy	11.2	8.1	36.0	33.4
Foreign Policy	− 9.7	1.6	3.9	6.1
Race and Public Order Policy	0.6	57.7	51.2	20.8
Vietnam Policy	—	—	4.1	16.9
Non-South				
Democratic Candidate	− 3.8	11.5	16.9	24.6
Republican Candidate	4.0	3.1	26.2	21.2
Party Performance	−33.1	19.4	20.9	0.5
Group Association	3.8	12.4	28.9	18.3
General Philosophy	5.1	4.0	10.3	7.3
Domestic Policy	21.7	16.6	15.0	24.2
Foreign Policy	− 9.3	− 4.5	− 0.4	− 1.3
Race and Public Order Policy	21.8	60.6	35.7	23.9
Vietnam Policy	—	—	8.4	10.6

*Cell entries represent the percentages of blacks expressing a pro-Democratic party attitude on the dimension, minus percentages of whites expressing the same attitude. A positive number shows that blacks are more favorable to the Democrats on this dimension; a negative number, that whites are more favorable. For the construction of the dimensions, see Chapter 7.

made his comeback, his appeal was to the whites, and he no longer attracted the minority community.

Changing evaluations of the parties and candidates are clearly related to the different political stimuli provided in these four campaigns. With race neither emphasized nor distinctive in the partisan programs of 1960, racial differences are limited. Blacks and whites first evidence consistent differences in 1964. Responding to the political stimuli, blacks are far more likely to praise Johnson, oppose Goldwater, and to favor the Democrats on grounds of civil rights. In 1972, racial differences on this particular dimension are somewhat reduced, paralleling its diminished emphasis in the campaign. But conflict remains on this and related dimensions, such as other issues of domestic policy and the parties' protection of nonracial groups. Considerably more often than whites, blacks are now drawn to the Democratic party because of its economic and social program, and because of its presumed concern for "the working man." At least for one race, class and race interests lead to a common partisan conclusion.

The split between blacks and whites also exists in opinions directly on policy issues and across the spectrum of political questions. On all issues, under any ideological definition, blacks take a liberal position, while whites are substantially more conservative. These differences are not only evident on matters related to race, such as means of dealing with urban unrest or aid to minority groups. On the economic issue of government guarantee of jobs, three-fourths of blacks are favorable, compared to only a quarter of whites. By 1972, some two-thirds of blacks leaned toward withdrawal from Vietnam, while the same position won support from about two out of five whites. Overall, the issue of progressive taxation is the only policy question on which the disparity between the races is as low as 10 percent.

The core of racial differences in politics is race itself. Black and white differences in the vote and party loyalty are founded on basic policy differences on group integration. The trend of opinion in recent years reveals a movement—perhaps too slight—toward resolution of racial differences on this issue and offers political leaders an opportunity further to close this gap.

Attitudinal differences on integration can be seen in Table 6.5 , which presents opinions on various form of integration. The inquiries on employment, schools, and public accommodations deal with the desirability of federal government action to promote civil rights. On housing, the respondent decides if "white people have a right to keep black people out of their neighborhoods," or if "black people have a right to live wherever they can afford." Finally, the respondent expresses his personal preference for "desegregation, strict segregation, or something in between." Aside from racial considerations, therefore, these items involve the desirability of government action or the legitimacy of restricting personal mobility.[28] Although different in their content, each of the items can be

TABLE 6.5 / ATTITUDES ON RACE ISSUES, 1960-72*

	Whites				Blacks			
	1960	1964	1968	1972	1960	1964	1968	1972
South								
Equal Employment	57.7	31.3	31.4	39.3	98.9	96.3	91.7	91.8
School Integration	24.3	23.8	23.8	26.5	60.0	83.2	92.2	82.4
Housing	—	37.8	52.0	66.8	—	97.2	98.6	100.0
Public Accommodations	—	24.5	36.0	55.1	—	94.0	97.9	94.0
Personal Preference	—	13.2	17.2	29.0	—	72.6	78.2	65.0
Combined Index	15.6	13.1	17.6	31.9	63.6	89.1	93.0	88.8
Non-South								
Equal Employment	73.7	41.9	41.2	47.5	96.1	90.1	85.7	89.7
School Integration	55.6	50.9	43.1	41.9	80.3	90.3	86.9	78.4
Housing	—	74.5	80.7	87.0	—	100.0	98.6	99.0
Public Accommodations	—	56.0	62.7	72.9	—	95.5	95.4	97.0
Personal Preference	—	32.6	38.9	42.7	—	84.4	79.2	72.6
Combined Index	48.8	40.3	38.8	42.6	77.5	96.3	92.8	89.5

*Entries are the percentages of each group supporting full integration on each question or, for the combined index, on all of the items.

compared over time. A similar comparison can be made to an index that combines answers to the five questions.[29]

During this period, there was an apparent decrease in support of integration by whites immediately after 1960, countered by a slow increase in the last few years in most areas. The initial precipitous drop is partially explicable by a 1964 change in the form and wording of the questions used.[30] Over the long two decades since the Supreme Court outlawed segregation, other researchers have found growing support of the concept of racial integration, and this trend has been most marked in formerly resistant groups, such as southerners and persons of lower education.[31]

Despite the long-term trend, there are countermovements. While the nation, including the South, approves of school integration as an abstract concept, it does not always favor real action toward this end. Far more persons will support the concept of integration than will support the federal action that is essential to achieve the goal.[32] As the issue has changed from one of nondiscrimination to one of positive action to promote integration, resistance has increased. In particular, as the school focus has altered from abolition of segregated schools in the South to the use of busing, district boundary changes, and other methods in the North, fewer persons have favored such policies. The reality of such resistance is evident in the 1964-72 trend, when the survey question was unaltered; and can be seen still more clearly in the series of local northern votes in opposition to school busing, the defeat of school board members advocating such policies, and direct violence by white parents.

Among whites, consequently, there is a discrepancy between theoretical and practical attitudes. "The tentative acceptance of the goals of black Americans, particularly for equal treatment by the law and for equal educational opportunities, coupled with a rejection of the means employed by action groups striving for equality of opportunity, has long characterized white attitudes."[33] They have opposed sit-ins, Freedom Rides, the March on Washington, and registration drives as means, even while approving the ends of equality in public accommodations, transportation, jobs, and voting. Decreases in white support of federal government action toward integration parallels these incongruities.

Blacks' opinions are quite different. Indeed, the disparity in the views of the two races suggests that they occupy two different political worlds. While whites present limited and incrementally increasing support of integration, blacks have consistently and overwhelmingly advocated such policies. Despite repeated rejection, they still want to join America. A decade ago, it seemed doubtful "whether a viable political system in the South will be possible, granted the extreme polarization of opinion, without one race being dominated by the other."[34] Today, the question remains, but now applies to the entire nation.

A slight trend away from integrationist sentiment is evident among northern blacks in 1968 and among blacks of both regions in 1972. Particularly in regard to school integration and their personal preferences, a significant number of blacks appear to be choosing racial solidarity over unity with whites. Such a position would be consistent with those "black power" arguments that have given priority to the separate development of homogeneous racial communities.[35] Discouraged by the repeated frustrations of integrationist efforts, a minority of blacks have turned away from this historic goal. In an irony of history, some blacks have begun to disdain racial interaction just as whites have begun to accept that policy. Combined with the growing cynicism within the black community and its distrust of government, the turn from integration points to a broad alienation from the general American community. As James Baldwin expresses this rejection, the Negro now asks, "Do I really *want* to be integrated into a burning house?"[36]

Potential conflict between the races is further affected by social class. Most blacks identify with the working class, but their attitudes on racial questions are distinct from the views of whites in the same economic group. Biracial political cooperation, through working class alliances, is hindered by these differences. As seen in Table 6.6, black and white laboring men remain as far apart in their attitudes today as in the recent past. Only in the middle class are there indications of greater agreement on integration, with white support rising as black advocacy falls.[37] The evaluations of the parties, detailed above, also show growing racial differences on class-related assessments.

These varying opinions reflect the differing interests of each group. To

TABLE 6.6 / RACIAL ATTITUDES BY CLASS IDENTIFICATION, 1964-72
(Combined Index of Five Questions)*

Self-Identification	Black	White	Race Difference
1964			
Working Class	91.9	33.7	58.2
Middle Class	93.8	31.7	62.1
Class Difference	− 1.9	2.0	
1968			
Working Class	92.0	29.6	62.4
Middle Class	95.0	36.3	58.7
Class Difference	− 3.0	− 6.7	
1972			
Working Class	90.5	33.4	57.1
Middle Class	81.4	44.8	36.6
Class Difference	9.1	−11.4	

*Entries are the percentages of each class, within race, that support full integration on all of the five questions. Class and race differences result from subtraction by columns or rows. Positive differences show greater support for integration by the working class or by blacks.

the black worker, integration in schools and jobs remains vital to his advancement, while the black middle class has more freedom to enjoy the presumed benefits of separatism and cultural development. In the other race, the white middle class feels less threatened by integration. It can be more liberal and advocate the integration of schools and neighborhoods—at least until policies are suggested that directly affect its own interests, such as the consolidation of urban and suburban school districts or interdistrict busing.

The white working class is most likely to feel adversely affected by integration. Typically, it is manual jobs that are reserved for minorities by government employment goals and quotas, as it is the schools of working class families that are involved in busing and other efforts to integrate across neighborhood lines. "With little equity but his mortgaged house and his union card, the white worker is especially resistant to integration efforts that appear to threaten his small stake in the world. . . . Many lower-class whites feel that an unholy alliance has grown up between the liberal Establishment and Negro militants to reshape American life at their expense."[38]

The resistance to integration by white workers has been attributed to inherent class characteristics, such as an authoritarian childhood or the pressures of technological obsolescence.[39] Such explanations are essentially demeaning, since they suggest that there is no current and valid source for concern by the white working class. In fact, the working class is not inherently segregationist. In 1964, no class difference was evident among whites on the issues of integration. More recent disparities would seem to reflect the feelings among the white working class of "personal anxiety concerning their own economic situation and serious doubts about political capabilities of the country to solve its internal problems."[40] Integration is opposed because any change is threatening in a time when workers' jobs and income are insecure, and even the stability of national institutions is uncertain. Until these problems are resolved, workers reasonably seek to protect themselves.

For the present, these data illuminate a recent political fact: the emergence of a "top-bottom" alliance of higher-income whites with black groups, in opposition to the felt interests of the white working class. Such coalitions led to the reelection of John Lindsay as mayor of New York in 1969 and the victory of Maynard Jackson as the first black mayor of Atlanta in 1973. On the national level, this alliance is suggested by the Democratic vote of college-educated professionals and the working class, discussed in Chapter 3.

The durability of these coalitions remains questionable. Lindsay was forced to retire in 1973, and McGovern could not forge such a national union. Lacking a direct personal interest in integration, the long-term support of the white middle class cannot be assumed, and its resistance to suburban school integration, now legitimized by the Supreme Court, provides no reason for lasting confidence. While white and black attitudes within the middle class are becoming more similar, their resemblance does not result from racial conciliation, but rather from the development of separatism among more established blacks. Not founded on the immediate interests of prosperous whites, nor even fully supported by black leadership, a stable racial union across class lines has limited prospects. Political alliances are better formed on tangible concerns. They are stronger when organized along class lines, where direct and continuing interests are involved. When—or rather if—racial conflicts abate, a class politics may shape the future.

THE RACIAL FUTURE

Peaceful resolution of the American racial drama, if it is to come, must be achieved through the electoral system. Political leaders will be hard pressed to resolve or subordinate the persisting differences between blacks and whites. The most likely means of settlement will be through the solidification of voting on the basis of economic, rather than racial, issues.

In recent elections, economic issues have not been entirely eliminated, but have been matched in importance by the newer racial issues. The relative importance of the two sets of opinions can be seen by comparing the relationship of each set to the presidential vote. In this comparison, positions on racial questions are gauged by the index of five questions on integration (presented in Table 6.5). Opinion on class issues is measured by the index discussed in Chapter 3 (p. 58), summarizing attitudes on government guarantee of jobs and provision of medical care, federal aid to education (from 1960 to 1968), and progressive taxation (in 1972).

For blacks in 1960, opinion on racial issues is somewhat more important in their vote than attitudes on economic issues, while in later years, the group's Democratic vote is so overwhelming that these factors cannot be separated statistically. Among whites, class issues have been persistently important in balloting, but a considerable increase has occurred in the significance of questions of integration. Opinion on race issues was not associated with the presidential vote of whites in 1960, but since that time there has been a continuing high association (correlations over .40) between racial views and electoral choice.[41] A new issue has thus emerged in American politics.

The relative importance of class and race issues in the voting of whites can be analyzed through multiple regression. When partisanship is disregarded, the influence of class issues is consistently greater than those of race. Since partisanship is related to class attitudes, however, the apparent correlation of vote and economic opinions may actually be a mask for the effect of party loyalty. When we include party identification in the

TABLE 6.7 / RACE, ISSUES, AND THE VOTE
(Beta Weights, Multiple Regression of White Vote for President)*

	1960	1964	1968	1972
Party Identification	.70	.55	.57	.44
Opinion on Class Issues	.12	.17	.09	.16
Opinion on Race Issues	−.00	.14	.11	.14
Region	.12	.11	.14	.10
Education	.01	−.04	.01	−.01
Class Identification	.03	.05	−.02	−.05
Total R^2	.532	.465	.392	.291
Unique R^2, Partisanship	.431	.247	.287	.185
R^2, Partisanship as First Variable	.501	.379	.337	.212
(N)	(1213)	(966)	(901)	(702)

*Positive coefficients indicate that the Democratic vote of whites is related to Democratic partisanship, liberal opinion on class issues, support of racial integration, northern residence, higher education, and working class identification. Voters without opinions are included in the intermediate categories.

analysis, as in Table 6.7, the true independent influence of each set of attitudes becomes evident.

In 1960, opinions on class attitudes have a significant effect, while attitudes toward integration have no impact on the vote. In later years, the two sets of issues are of roughly equal impact, as shown by the beta weights, and they are increasingly independent of the declining influence of partisanship. Race issues are slightly more important than class issues in 1968,[42] while class issues have a marginally greater impact in 1972. Race issues did not determine these elections, for class issues remain salient and partisanship still is the most important single factor.[43] They did, however, introduce a distinct and different dimension to voting patterns.[44]

In Table 6.7, we again see the declining effect of partisanship. The beta weight drops considerably over the twelve-year period, as does the amount of variance in the vote which can be uniquely explained by party identification, when this variable is held back to the end in the multiple regression. Even when partisanship is introduced first, the degree of explanation it provides drops continually over these four elections.

Race and class are divergent—even mutually exclusive—bases for political organization. The first is an inherited and permanent characteristic; the second, the result of life experience and somewhat subject to change. Race carries deep emotional significance and relates to a person's soul; class is of less primary importance and relates primarily to a person's wallet. Since they are different characteristics, relevant opinions concerning them are also different, and only weakly associated with each other.[45]

The vital question for the electoral future is whether race or class issues will predominate in American politics. Racial politics is inherently full of conflict. In such a politics, identifiable groups with permanent membership oppose one another. The moral and emotional issues involved are intrinsically resistant to compromise. Divergent goals are likely, expressed in utopian and chiliastic terms. Class politics, on the other hand, is more potentially manageable. The groups involved are not permanently separate, as social mobility blurs status lines. Points of dispute typically can be expressed in quantitative economic terms and therefore can be compromised; and the goals are more likely to relate to the practical conditions of life. While class politics can result in class warfare, it can also be resolved at the bargaining table. But how can there be compromise of the racial demand for equality and dignity?

The results of recent elections demonstrate the increased significance of racial questions and the development of racial polarization. Insofar as this process leads to acknowledgement and correction of the racial injustices of the past, it is to be welcomed, even at the cost of inevitable conflict. Given the intensity of feelings and the overwhelming size of the white electorate, however, it is doubtful that continued polarization will bring racial justice. Remediation of the disabilities of blacks is more likely to be accomplished as part of a reform of the overall economic and social structure of the United States.

Such reform will require voting alignments along class lines. This emphasis remains possible, and supporting evidence for it can be found if the data are carefully searched. One possible marking of this political direction is found in analyzing the 1972 vote of those persons holding opinions on all of the questions involved, about half of the electors. For this informed group, class issues are of considerably greater importance than those of race. If class issues were made more salient to the entire electorate, it is therefore possible that they would continue this predominance. Another sign may exist in regard to the particular issue of progressive taxation. Here, the racial difference is small, suggesting that programs for more equitable distribution of social burdens might win support from both blacks and whites. It may also be significant that racial differences are least among the youngest voters. If the possibility of racial agreement is low at the present time, the future prospects are more encouraging.

A new stress on class politics would relieve the gloomy prospects of America's racial future. Certainly a continued or increased emphasis on the divisive issues of race is unlikely to promote political stability. There is, however, another possible future scene in the American racial tragedy —that of revolution. Models of revolutionary change, developed in the study of foreign societies, are partially applicable to the contemporary United States as well. Whether America will eventually endure the full agony of revolution depends on the purposeful policy decisions made by its leaders and voters.

The onset of revolution, according to a leading theorist, is signaled by the loss of basic support. "When confidence has evaporated to the extent that the exercise of power is futile, when the authority of the status-holders entrusted with supervision and command rests *only* on their monopoly of force, and when there is no foreseeable prospect of a processual change in this situation, revolution is at hand."[46]

The underlying process leading to social violence is extended in time. It begins with disequilibrium between the values of a society or group and its environment. The conflict often derives from changes in the economic division of labor, stimulating new and rising expectations among large numbers of persons. Conditions of disequilibrium are evident in such personal behavior as drunkenness, venality, and violation of existing sexual norms, and in such social indicators as suicide, increasing ideological activity, rising crime rates, and augmented use of force. But unsettled conditions in themselves need not lead to political disruption. "It is in this environment of change, tension and power deflation that a system's leaders must act to bring about conservative change and to forestall revolution."[47] If they fail to take corrective action, their loss of legitimate authority and ultimate loss of coercive power will proceed.

The recent history of the United States, and the data developed here, do evidence some of the preconditions of revolution, particularly in the black community. Basic trust has been severely eroded. A large stratum of educated leaders has developed, which is politically active, but not highly supportive of existing authority. Within the mass of the black population, the values of equal and full participation in the benefits of the American life clash with the continuing facts of discrimination and inferior rewards. Separatist ideologies provide a rallying cry, while the tactics of protest provide a means of provoking necessary change. Moreover, although these marks of a revolutionary situation are most evident among blacks, instability is easily noticeable in the white community as well. Distrust of government, dissatisfaction with economic rewards, social pathology, and the resort to violence are unbounded by color.

Yet revolution is not inevitable. Indeed, revolutions "never occur as a result of forces beyond human control. Creative political action is the specific antidote to revolutionary conditions."[48] Some actions have been taken to meet the basic causes of black protest: segregation has been outlawed legally and severely curtailed in practice, deliberate programs have been instituted to equalize racial opportunities for work and schooling, and cultural norms have altered toward recognition of black identity. Retrograde actions have included coercion against some blacks and co-optation of others into the existing social structure. It is likely that these actions have prevented the outbreak of widespread black revolution.

Given the small proportion of blacks in the nation, and the immense stability of the nation's political institutions demonstrated in the presidential impeachment controversy, any revolution is unlikely to succeed. Still, men have rebelled regardless of the chances of success. The "social dynamite" of racial inequality remains combustible. Twenty years of frustration since the nation's highest court invalidated segregation have shortened the fuse, and these years have brought the flash point closer through the successive raisings and disappointments of popular expectations.

To bring the American drama to a successful conclusion, the racial issue must be solved, not suppressed. In achieving this goal, political leadership is obviously critical. Changes in popular attitudes have corresponded closely to the actions of presidents and candidates. The potential for a future response to a call for equity and justice already exists, and "the leader who thinks social conditions are suitable for leading the center even further to the left on the subject of racial integration would find strong support for his strategy."[49]

Until leadership emerges, race remains a basic defining characteristic of the nation's electoral politics, as it has shaped America for nearly four centuries. Even this hereditary factor, though, does not fully determine voters' choices. From 1960 to 1972, blacks and whites reacted in varying ways to the events of their time, to the policy questions arising from these events, and to the alternatives presented to them by parties and candidates. While color is a permanent feature of an individual, it alone does not control his attitudes. Not fixed permanently by race or age or sex or class, voters' responses are to the issues of contemporary politics.

BLACK AND WHITE ASUNDER: FINDINGS

1. In recent years, racial disparities in political participation have largely disappeared.
   1a. Blacks now vote in the South almost as frequently as whites.
2. Educated blacks have become a politically active leadership group.
3. In contrast to the past, blacks now evidence massive distrust of government.
   3a. This declining support is particularly evident among the race's young and educated.
4. Cynical attitudes toward government have developed faster among blacks than whites.
5. Blacks are more favorable than whites to protests and mass demonstrations.
   5a. This difference persists even within age and educational groups.
   5b. But acceptance of unconventional behavior is growing among both races.
6. A broad racial division has developed in regard to most political attitudes.

6a. Whites and blacks now differ in partisanship, vote, their positions on virtually all issues, and their evaluations of candidates.

7. Racial differences remain greatest on issues of integration.

   7a. White attitudes have become more favorable to integration, particularly in the South.

   7b. But black attitudes indicate a slight decline in integrationist attitudes.

8. Racial differences, in contrast to the past, are now greatest within the working class.

9. The effect of race issues on the presidential vote varies over time.

   9a. In recent elections, class and race issues have been approximately equal in their impact.

CHAPTER 7

THE CONCERNS
OF VOTERS

Despite an extensive search, we have not found a lifelike portrait of the dependent voter. While the electorate is clearly affected by its partisanship and demographic characteristics, ballot choices cannot be fully explained by these long-term factors. The voter is not only a Democrat or Republican, a member of the working or middle class, a man or woman, a youth or elder, a black or white. He is also a political being.

In the next three chapters, we examine more closely the portrait of the responsive voter. Our focus changes from the social collectivities of class, sex, age, and race to individuals. Seeing voters as active participants in the democratic process, we look directly at their concerns, their evaluations of the parties and candidates, and the particular influences of contemporary stimuli on their behavior from 1960 to 1972. The responsive voter will reach his electoral judgments on the basis of the quality of the candidates and the issues of public policy presented to him. His actions will be explicable, but not permanently predictable.

If voters are to make meaningful judgments about their government, certain conditions must be fulfilled. They must be concerned about the issues of the time and about the quality of the candidates facing them. Having evaluated these objects, they must relate them to the narrow choice facing them, typically one between the Democratic and Republican presidential candidates. If voters simply cast a ballot by party tradition or as a conditioned reflex of their social memberships, citizen participation is only a ritual. Meaningful democratic government requires that citizens act upon real and contemporary choices.

In examining the social groupings of the electorate, we have already found considerable variation in voter response, in keeping with changes in the political environment. In this chapter, where the individual voter is examined, the same pattern of change becomes evident. The problems voters stress alter with the stresses on the nation. Their evaluations of presidential nominees, of programs, and of party performance vary considerably over four elections, and are not predetermined. The factors that affect the vote, as specified statistically, are different from one contest to another. "Voters, or at least a large number of them, are moved by their perceptions and appraisals of policy performance."[1] They respond to changed needs by changing choices of Democratic or Republican ballots.

THE NATION'S PROBLEMS

A democratic citizen is expected to have a special character: an interest in the public welfare, as well as a concern for his individual needs. American voters do consider the needs of their nation. In each election·survey in 1960-72, respondents were asked, "What do you think are the major problems facing this country?" and were encouraged to designate as wide a choice of problems as they wished. Given this stimulus, the electorate did respond, naming hundreds of different problems. The public's awareness reached a peak in 1968 and 1972, when 97 percent of the sample named at least one problem. In earlier years, the concerned proportion was somewhat smaller, averaging about five out of six voters.

Although a wide variety of problems are cited in this sample, the public's concerns center on matters with direct consequences to the voters. There is a concentration on those particular parts of the body politic where the shoe pinches, thereby creating a public demand for relief of the pain. Over the course of time, as seen in Table 7.1, the location of voter distress has varied considerably. In the election of John Kennedy, for example, attention centers on problems of social welfare such as health and education, and on such foreign policy questions as the "balance of strength" with the Soviet Union. In the next two elections, two seemingly new issues take precedence. The first of these, Vietnam, is dramatic testimony to the flexible attention of the voters. As the vanguard of American advisers was entering South Vietnam in 1960 and the resumption of the Indochinese war was being prepared, not a single respondent considered the resolution of the conflict to be the most important problem facing the nation. In 1964, after passage of the Gulf of Tonkin resolution, the issue had surfaced, with a noticeable minority giving priority to the burgeoning hostilities. By 1968, with America involved in a seemingly endless jungle war, Vietnam was given prime consideration. It retained this position, although in a reduced proportion of the electorate, as U.S. withdrawal neared in the midst of the 1972 election.

TABLE 7.1 / THE MOST IMPORTANT NATIONAL PROBLEMS, 1960-72*

	1960	1964		1968	1972
Social Welfare	13.8	18.0	4.7	5.4	6.2
Poverty	1.0	6.2	0.8	6.5	3.7
Race and Civil Rights	4.4	20.0	22.5	8.9	7.7
Protest, Disorder, Civil Liberties	1.8	3.7	8.5	18.7	15.2
General Economics	8.9	8.1	4.0	6.5	20.3
Labor and Management	2.2	0.8	1.4	0.5	0.1
Agriculture and Resources	6.1	2.6	3.1	1.2	2.4
Foreign Policy	54.8	22.1	26.2	6.2	6.6
Defense Policy	6.8	5.8	1.4	1.1	1.4
Vietnam	—	9.7	15.6	43.3	32.3
General Government	0.2	3.0	11.8	1.7	4.0
(N)	(1739)	(1279)	(729)	(1509)	(1057)

*Entries are the percentages in each year designating the subject as the most important problem facing the nation. In 1964, the first column presents responses on the most important problem for government to solve; the second column, the most important problem for government to avoid. Percentages add vertically by columns to 100 percent, except for rounding errors.

Concern also came to be focused on another new issue, which is at the same time the oldest issue of American politics, that of race. In 1960, all aspects of the racial problem—poverty, civil rights, and protest—together received emphasis by only 7 percent of the electorate. In later years, attention was directed toward both the meliorative aspects of the problem, such as poverty programs, and its negative consequences, such as protest and violence. These years also saw the rise of the "social issue," anxiety over the disruptions engendered by social change. By 1968, attention to disorder and disruption was second in the minds of the voters only to Vietnam. Moreover, since protest and the war appeared to feed off one another, the two matters were not completely separable. These anxieties continued after 1968, when nearly half of the nation said "that national unrest is serious enough to lead to real breakdown."[2]

A nation, like an individual, can only pay attention to a limited number of problems. As the voters focused on Vietnam, racial problems, and disorder, other subjects were neglected. Social welfare, the condition of the economy, and foreign and defense policy aside from Vietnam received less focus in 1964 and 1968. Conversely, as the heat of the former problems appeared to diminish in 1972, there was a return to more traditional interests. After 1972, as prices and unemployment rose, an energy crisis loomed, and the Watergate investigation proceeded, new issues again came to the fore.[3] In all of these instances, we see the voters reacting to the events of the time and the actions of government. The electorate is sufficiently aware to evidence concern on current issues.

The problems interesting Americans generally are also the ones interesting smaller subgroups, to judge by the emphases in 1972. In most social aggregates, the same priorities are evident, as there is little variation in the problems stressed by persons in different regions, age groups, educational strata, or races. Thus, despite the region's historical preoccupation with race, only a small additional fraction of southerners give priority to that issue in 1972, compared to the rest of the nation. While there are some differences by age, such as greater concern with Vietnam and lesser attention to economics by young voters, overall there is a generally uniform national emphasis on common problems. Similarly, the issues stressed by loyalists of the two major parties parallel each other. About the same proportions of Republicans and Democrats are concerned with each of the major problems. To a slight extent, Republicans emphasize matters of race and public order in 1972, while Democrats are more conscious of economic and governmental questions, including official corruption. However, the differences are generally small. In the case of Vietnam, partisan stresses are identical.

The electoral impact of these national concerns comes not through emphasis on different issues, but through differing assessments of the parties. The voters do not regard the Democrats and Republicans as mirror images or as perfectly matched competitors. Rather, the two factions are seen as having different "product lines," with each handling some problems relatively better, and others more poorly. Generally, in 1972, the electorate believes the Democrats are more equipped to deal with matters of economics, welfare, and governmental corruption, while the Republicans are seen as better in handling the problems of race and Vietnam. On all of these matters, the electorate does not draw sharp distinctions between the parties. About half see no difference in their capabilities on most issues, while on the "social issue," two-thirds fail to give a nod to either group. Among those who do make these distinctions, however, a party advantage results.

Because of these different evaluations of the parties, the issues stressed in a particular election considerably influence the outcome. While the Republicans try to "sell" their "products" of peace in Vietnam and the control of public disorder, the Democrats have a better "market" for the wares of economics and social welfare. Since the issues of advantage to the GOP were of more concern to the electorate in 1972, a Republican victory was likely.

The Democrats' weakness was compounded by their campaign strategy, which played to the opposition's strength on Vietnam and other issues. While the electorate was ready to respond to a Democratic claim of greater competence on economic problems, the party neglected this asset. Among those seeing Vietnam, race, and public order as the major problems, the Democratic vote was nearly ten percentage points less than among those stressing economic and welfare matters. If attention had been focused on the latter questions, the contest would have been far closer. De-emphasis of these issues turned a likely defeat into a rout.

Stress on particular issues can even overcome the influence of party loyalty. The ballots of Democrats in 1972 are illustrative. Of all party members, three-fifths voted for McGovern. However, among those Democrats who gave priority attention to the issues of race and public disorder, an actual majority deserted their party to vote for Nixon. In the opposite direction, the small number of Republicans who emphasized the issues of government and corruption supported the moralistic appeal of the South Dakota senator.

Partisanship, however, does have effects. Whatever the problem they stress, voters tend to believe that their own party is best equipped to handle it. Therefore, Democrats find no difficulty in casting a ballot for their presumably competent party, nor Republicans in standing with the GOP. From these convenient matchings, we could rashly conclude that a process of rationalization is at work, by which partisans justify their traditional vote by declaring that their own party is best equipped to handle the urgent tasks confronting the nation.

While some of these opinions undoubtedly are rationalizations, not all can be dismissed so easily. As noted above, Republicans and Democrats do not differ on what the most important problems are. Moreover, in considering these common problems, most party loyalists do not ascribe all virtue to their own party. In a majority of cases, the voters see no difference between the parties or even concede that the opposition can handle the problem better. Evaluations also change over time, contrary to the expected behavior of blind loyalists. In most years, Republicans have been deemed better able to deal with foreign policy, but this assessment is reversed in 1964, when Goldwater's candidacy raises a threat of war. An earlier reliance on the Democrats to handle racial questions is reversed when confrontations of blacks and whites occur during the Kennedy and Johnson administrations. The voters judge the parties by performance, not simply by habit.

The vote itself is affected by both partisanship and evaluations of the parties' abilities. Commonly, these two influences point to the same conclusion, the choice of the voter's own party. Nevertheless, when voters believe the opposition is more qualified to handle the basic problems facing the nation, they are willing to abandon tradition and give their support to the alternative faction. Thus Democrats in 1952 were willing to elect Dwight Eisenhower, whom they regarded as better able to solve the major problem of Korea, as Republicans in 1960 were willing to vote for John Kennedy, whom they considered better able to maintain prosperity.[4]

Interaction of these two elements is evident in 1972 as well, as detailed in Table 7.2. The vote for Nixon is unanimous among Republicans who

TABLE 7.2 / PARTISANSHIP, PARTY COMPETENCE, AND VOTE IN 1972*

	Party Identification		
Most Capable Party	Republican	Independent	Democrat
Republican	99.0	93.5	81.1
	(105)	(62)	(37)
No Difference	92.0	70.2	49.2
	(87)	(104)	(128)
Democratic	—ᵃ	19.6	21.6
		(46)	(116)

*The percentage in each cell is that voting for Nixon. The number in parentheses is the total on which the percentage is based.
ᵃFifteen persons, of whom ten voted for Nixon.

see their party as most capable in dealing with the problem they see as "most important." He receives little support, on the other hand, from Democrats confident of their own group's competence. When these two factors conflict, the presumed ability of the parties is an important influence. American voters are concerned about the nation and bring those concerns to bear on their public choices.

PARTY IMAGES AND CANDIDATE PROFILES

To be effective, the responsive voter must express his concerns electorally. He must translate his perceptions of the nation's problems and his preferred solutions into a narrowed choice between parties and candidates. The means of translation is the "party images" that voters hold of the Republicans and Democrats. These mental pictures provide a reference point for citizens as they seek solutions to national problems.[5]

A direct approach to the sources of voting choice can be made through the elaboration of these party images and of analogous candidate profiles. Images and profiles are constructed from answers to a series of open-ended questions, which permit a respondent to give unprompted replies, rather than being confined to a possibly unthinking choice between pre-selected alternatives. At the beginning of each election survey, voters were asked whether there were any characteristics of the parties and candidates that would encourage them to vote for or against those parties and candidates. Three to five separate answers were recorded on each of the positive and negative features of the Democrats, the Republicans, the Democratic candidate, and the Republican candidate. These spontaneous statements—numbering as many as forty for a single respondent—provide a wealth of detail on the features of the political world that attract and repel the electorate.

The nature of voter reactions in 1972 is indicated in Table 7.3, which summarizes the first answers to each question. The parties are quite

TABLE 7.3 / FAVORABLE AND UNFAVORABLE CHARACTERISTICS OF PARTIES AND CANDIDATES, 1972*

	Democratic		Republican		McGovern		Nixon	
	Likes	Dislikes	Likes	Dislikes	Likes	Dislikes	Likes	Dislikes
Party Leaders	5.3	19.1	15.8	5.8	—	—	—	—
Party Organization	14.7	21.5	15.2	11.6	8.8	11.5	1.3	8.2
Managerial Qualities	1.5	6.8	7.6	7.3	0.4	0.7	3.5	4.0
Philosophy	12.1	22.1	20.7	8.4	8.4	14.1	2.3	2.6
Domestic Policies	12.3	11.4	12.5	17.2	11.4	10.5	7.8	17.6
Foreign Policies	3.5	7.5	15.8	6.5	18.7	13.3	25.6	22.5
Group Association	47.9	6.9	5.0	38.4	17.6	2.0	1.9	10.3
Candidate Experience	—	—	—	—	4.0	4.5	31.8	3.0
Candidate Leadership	—	—	—	—	2.6	19.5	3.7	4.4
Candidate Personality	—	—	—	—	24.3	20.5	15.1	21.8
Miscellaneous	2.6	4.7	7.3	4.7	3.8	3.3	6.9	5.5
(N)	(611)	(569)	(516)	(612)	(509)	(896)	(882)	(615)

*Entries are the percentages of first answers to questions on the features liked and disliked about the Democratic and Republican parties, McGovern and Nixon. Percentages add vertically by columns to 100 percent, except for rounding errors.

different in the images they present to the electorate. The strength of the Democratic party is in its domestic policies and the connections to social groups these policies have created. The party is liked because it is good for the "common man" or the "working people," because it opposes the interests of "big business," and because of its association with popular policies such as social security and economic prosperity. The positive qualities ascribed to the party clearly date to the times of the Great Depression and the New Deal. That they persist to the present, when the voters and leaders of the earlier period have largely passed from the scene, is testament to the stability of strongly felt popular attitudes. A mirror image of Democratic attractiveness is found in the features of the Republican party disliked by the voters.

The voters find somewhat different qualities attractive in the Republican party. Some persons favor the domestic policies they associate with the party, as well as the more conservative philosophy they attribute to it. It is likely that Democrats and Republicans are being judged on similar grounds, but that different terms are being applied. Democratic support of federal spending can be viewed favorably by some as action for the "common man," while it is disapproved of by others because it does not fit with "conservative philosophy." However, although different terms are employed, a clear basis for evaluative differences exists.

The Republicans' appeal in 1972 also extended beyond such domestic questions. The party was commended for its personalities, particularly Richard Nixon, for its managerial ability, and for its foreign policy. Conversely, these features were seen by others as Democratic defects. To some extent, these attributed deficiencies were only a reflection of temporary circumstances, since adverse comments about Democratic leadership referred principally to George McGovern and the incidents of his campaign, such as the nomination of Thomas Eagleton for vice-president. The deficiency of the party in regard to foreign policy, on the other hand, is a long-standing mark aginst the party.

Profiles of the candidates can also be drawn from the spontaneous comments of the voters. George McGovern drew strength from his party and from the group associations and domestic policies with which it was identified. He also gained approval from many for his Vietnam policy and was praised for such personal characteristics as sincerity. Yet, on balance, McGovern was not viewed favorably, as only half of the voters questioned could find a single positive comment to make on his behalf, while nearly nine out of ten offered a critical appraisal. Some of these critical comments represented policy disagreements, but close to half dealt with truly personal characteristics. The South Dakotan was seen as weak and indecisive, insincere, overidealistic, and incompetent in his handling of the vice-presidential nomination and withdrawal of Senator Eagleton. As we shall see below, it was these perceived deficiencies of leadership and character that were decisive in Senator McGovern's overwhelming defeat, rather than the presumed radicalism of his policies.

The image of Richard Nixon in 1972 was in sharp contrast to that of his opponent. Far more voters volunteered favorable than unfavorable comments. The Republican nominee was disadvantaged by his affiliation with a relatively unpopular party and his domestic policies and group associations. His strength lay in his foreign policies, both Vietnam and the movement toward détente with the communist powers and, even more, in his experience in office. After a quarter of a century in national politics, Nixon was seen by the electorate as having accumulated a record of political involvement that merited—at least until the Watergate revelations—"four more years."

Nixon's extended presence on the national scene provides an opportunity to examine voter responsiveness. Since the former president was a candidate in three different national elections, we have data on the features voters liked and disliked about him in varying contexts. As external circumstances altered and the candidate transformed himself, the electorate revised its appraisal. Voters' responses were not fixed by their early impressions of Nixon, but kept pace with his own remarkable variability.

Over the years, the image of this perennial candidate gained definition, as shown in Table 7.4.[6] In his first presidential race Nixon was advantaged largely by his experience in office and foreign travels, his association with President Eisenhower, presumed personal attributes including intelligence and integrity, and such characteristics as age and religion. Even his

TABLE 7.4 / PERCEPTIONS OF RICHARD NIXON IN THREE ELECTIONS*

	Voters Liked			Voters Disliked		
	1960	**1968**	**1972**	**1960**	**1968**	**1972**
Experience	21.8	16.1	18.3	8.2	4.4	1.6
Qualifications	30.3	19.4	13.3	12.8	15.4	18.6
Personal Characteristics	25.7	28.6	21.3	29.0	42.2	19.6
Party Background	9.4	5.4	1.3	24.6	9.3	3.7
Domestic Issues	3.1	5.0	9.6	13.2	8.2	24.7
Foreign Issues	4.6	2.6	12.4	4.8	1.4	5.7
Vietnam	—	8.2	17.1	—	5.0	15.9
Race and Disorder	0.8	7.4	3.4	1.7	4.8	5.6
General Ideas	4.2	7.4	3.3	5.6	9.4	4.4
(Total N)	(2406)	(1708)	(1803)	(1063)	(1344)	(1145)

*Entries are the percentages in each year liking or disliking Nixon on the basis of each of the enumerated characteristics or attitudes. Up to three comments are included for each respondent. Percentages add vertically by columns to 100 percent, except for rounding errors.

detractors concentrated on these characteristics, as well as on his Republican affiliation, and relatively little stress was placed on his positions on particular national issues.

In the later elections, individual characteristics remained important, but no longer exclusively drew Nixon's portrait for the voters. His party affiliation became insignificant, even to the critics. Experience continued to be cited in his support, and the matters of his integrity and campaign tactics remained contentious. Even before impeachment was suggested—but after many controversial political battles—a sixth of the electorate had believed Nixon to be dishonest, insincere, tricky, and lacking in principles and integrity. The most important change in voter perceptions was the greater emphasis on Nixon's policy positions. By 1972, issues and related group associations were cited as reasons for support nearly half of the time and constituted a majority of the adverse responses. Much of this issue awareness of Nixon followed his assumption of the presidency.[7] There was significant specification of his image with respect to issues, however, even in 1968, before his election to the White House.

The content of these issue emphases also changed. While Vietnam did not exist as an issue in 1960, it was a significant element in the Nixon profile in 1968, and was of major importance in 1972. In the scattered comments on the race issue in 1960, the Republican candidate was seen as favorable to civil rights as often as he was seen as opposed. By 1968, Nixon presented himself as a resolute opponent of social disorder and was viewed as unfavorable to the demands of blacks by noticeable numbers in the electorate. Similar perceptions were evident in 1972.

The greatest change in the Nixon image came on general questions of foreign policy. In 1960, a major positive attribute was his strong anticommunist stance, his ability to "stand up to the Russians," as he allegedly had done at a model kitchen display in Moscow where he debated the Soviet premier. Echoes of this debate were heard even in 1968. By 1972, the Nixon strength in foreign policy was for a reverse position, with the incumbent president praised for his trips to Peking and Moscow, and his efforts to reach peaceful accommodation with the communists he had once condemned. Nixon's political base had moved from the model kitchen exemplifying capitalist virtues to the festive banquet hall glorifying the Chinese communist leadership.

DIMENSIONS OF POLITICAL ATTITUDES

Many factors affect the vote, and the specific influences on voters and their evaluations can change greatly from one election to the next. "To assess the impact of the partisan attitudes on behavior we need to reshape the materials on perceptions of politics to measure the psychological forces acting on the individual."[8] In making such an assessment, the hundreds of comments gathered from the series of open-ended questions are grouped into a small and manageable number of categories. To aid analysis and comparison between presidential contests, nine dimensions of partisan feeling are defined:

1. The individual qualities of the Democratic candidate—his experience, qualifications for office, and personal characteristics.

2. The individual qualities of the Republican candidate—his experience, etc.

3. The policies of the candidates and parties toward issues of race, poverty, public order, and protest, as well as their attitudes toward groups associated with these issues, such as blacks, persons on welfare, young people, and feminists. This dimension will be characterized as the "social issue."

4. The policies of the candidates and parties toward all other domestic issues.

5. The policies of the candidates and parties toward the issue of Vietnam in 1968 and 1972, including the prisoner-of-war question.

6. The policies of the candidates and parties toward all other foreign policy issues.

7. The general philosophies of the parties and candidates.

8. The association of the parties and candidates with social groups other than those included in the "social issue."

9. The performance of the parties and candidates as managers of political institutions, including the party nominating conventions, the party organization itself and the national government, spending and administrative policies, and record in office.[9]

For each of these evaluative dimensions, a scale has been constructed from the open-ended responses of the total sample. The number of each individual's relevant comments favorable to the Republican candidate or party was added to the number critical of the Democratic candidate or party. This sum was then reduced by the number of responses unfavorable to the Republican candidate or party, or supportive of the Democratic party or candidate. By averaging these responses for the entire electorate, we obtain a quantitative measure of the partisan direction of the voters' feelings on these nine dimensions.

In the table below, we present the average score on each dimension for each of the elections from 1960 to 1972. A positive score indicates a pro-Republican evaluation on that dimension by the average voter; a negative score indicates an average Democratic advantage. The higher the score in either direction, the more intense is the attitude. In 1972, for example, the total electorate particularly liked the Democratic party and candidate because of their association with nonracial groups, while its strongest Republican attitude was held in reference to the party's candidate.[10]

Partisan scores on the evaluative dimensions show the particular strengths of the Democrats and Republicans, and reinforce the impressions provided by individual comments. The consistent advantage of Democrats has been in their presumed concern with the interests of social and economic groups, and this considerable electoral virtue has been reinforced by a smaller margin on matters of domestic policy. The strengths of Republicans have been evident in their party performance, in their general philosophy, and—except in the Goldwater campaign—in the greater confidence they stimulate among the voters on questions of foreign policy. In the last two elections, Vietnam has added to the GOP advantage in this area.

These voter attitudes are supplemented and supported by the self-portraits of party leaders. Democratic candidates and platforms stress

TABLE 7.5 / DIMENSIONS OF POLITICAL EVALUATION, 1960-72*

	1960	1964	1968	1972
Democratic Candidate	−.246	−.526	−.107	+.516
Republican Candidate	+.583	−.342	+.120	+.394
Domestic Issues	−.182	−.259	−.033	−.051
"Social Issue"	−.041	−.103	+.020	+.047
Party Performance	+.260	−.119	+.353	+.174
Vietnam	—	—	+.255	+.248
Foreign Policy	+.259	−.043	+.102	+.213
Group Association	−.651	−.644	−.541	−.718
General Philosophy	+.087	−.072	+.124	+.324

*A positive score indicates a net pro-Republican response; a negative score indicates a net pro-Democratic response. Entries are average evaluations of voters on a scale ranging from −12 to +12.

domestic and economic issues, and the party's representatives in Congress are particularly ready to achieve alliances between the interests of different groups. Republicans not only are viewed by voters, but present themselves, as more concerned with matters of general philosophy, more competent in governmental administration, and more skilled in the conduct of foreign policy.[11]

Neither party, however, has been clearly advantaged by the "social issue," which combines questions of race, crime, and public order. Among the voters, the problem has had little partisan impact, a surprising result given the attention paid to the subject by pundits and politicans. While candidates have hastened to raise their voices for "law and order," their frenetic activities apparently have left the electorate very unimpressed. More voters are neutral on this subject than any other, praising or condemning neither party or closely balancing their pro-Republican and pro-Democratic comments.

Several possible explanations exist for this unexpected finding. In our analysis we may have confused two separate issues—race and public order—which should actually be separated. However, even those who coined the term "social issue" concede that "race is certainly a second and key element," that "there was, and is, a clear attitudinal spillover and linkage from the crime issue to the race issue."[12] Despite the personal hope of these analysts that the issues of crime and race could be distinguished, they are united in the public mind.

The proof of that union was provided even before the social issue attracted analysis. In their book, the originators of the concept suggested that the two matters could be separated and that a black policeman taking a strong position against crime could be elected as mayor of a nonblack city, without being handicapped by his race. In 1969, Thomas Bradley, a former police captain and a black, was defeated for mayor of Los Angeles after an antiblack campaign by the incumbent mayor, Sam Yorty. Four years later, in a rematch, Bradley won election, but race was still linked to the issue of law and order.[13]

Race, in fact, is the major element in the social issue, as defined here, for most comments included in this dimension relate to color. The voters have been concerned about civil rights, the discrimination against or alleged favoritism toward blacks, and urban riots, and have linked these issues in their minds.[14] Other kinds of unrest, however, have drawn very little attention, at least in the electoral context. Despite the prominence of such matters in the mass media, the electorate has not found drugs, pornography, or the youth culture to be salient reasons for liking or disliking Republicans or Democrats. When these matters are judged on their own terms, it is very clear that most Americans are disturbed by the rapid social changes that they represent. But voters generally do not relate these concerns to their voting choices. Remarkably, of the thousands of reasons offered for evaluating the parties and candidates in 1972, only one comment was based specifically on hostility to "young people, kids, freaks, and hippies."

In terms of national political impact, the social issue has been exaggerated, and the effect is certainly not consistently in the predicted direction. Although Republicans have been seen as the beneficiaries of the social issue, the effect is actually quite balanced between the parties. To be sure, there have been some comments that the Democrats are "soft on crime," or that Nixon had the correctly disdainful attitude toward protesters. But the social issue has many components—if it is a clear issue at all. Democrats have, for instance, come in for praise on some aspects of the issue, such as their presumed support of civil rights, and Republicans have sometimes been seen as inappropriately hostile to the interests of blacks and other dissenting groups. Both parties have gained and both have lost on the matter, with the net effect on this evaluative dimension very close to a standoff.

In its general aspect, the issue has not been politicized in partisan terms. Some of the matters involved, such as sexual mores, may be too private and personal to be placed in a partisan context by voters. Even when public questions are involved, the relationship to the established parties is unclear. While race and public order have become of concern recently, as seen in Table 7.1 above, the voters tend not to see a difference between the parties on this issue, with more of them believing there is "no difference" on these matters in 1972 than on any other problem. If there is a social issue with distinct content, it is not yet a partisan controversy. To the voters, as voters, other matters are more important.

PARTISANSHIP AND POLITICAL ATTITUDES

In their evaluations of political objects, the electorate shows considerable responsiveness to the events and problems of the times. Its attitudes are not fixed in mental concrete, for there is considerable variation across the four elections. As conditions and objects change, the voters find new reasons to approve and disapprove of the parties and their candidates. The performance of the Republicans in government, for example, is usually judged positively, but the party's advantage is greatest when it is actually out of office and does not bear the responsibility for an ongoing administration. Similarly, the Democratic appeal to group associations is greater when it constitutes the opposition party and does not have the power to alienate some groups by its actions.

The greatest variation in voter response comes in attitudes toward the candidates, the political objects that change most frequently. Richard Nixon, for example, saw his reception vary considerably over the course of the twelve years, and had fallen into widespread public disfavor by the time of his resignation.[15] Even more change is evident in regard to the other candidates. While the electorate has tended to look favorably on whatever presidential nominees are chosen, there have been two conspicuous exceptions. Barry Goldwater was distinctly unpopular and added to the general disadvantage Republicans bore in 1964. George McGovern was regarded even more critically, and his candidacy represents the most pro-Republican element affecting electoral choice in the last presidential contest. Aside from their individual inadequacies in the voters' mind, both of these candidates held policy views considerably different from those of a large proportion of their own party members, as well as from the views of the general electorate.

While voter evaluations do change over the years, they still might be dismissed as simply the rationalizations of partisans. Evaluations of the candidates provide a direct test of this negative view. If rationalization is to be found on any dimension, it is most likely in judgments of the personal characteristics of the nominees. Historical memories and personal experiences might affect voters' responses on issue dimensions, but they are little help in appraising the party leaders, whose partisan label is their most obvious characteristic.

Lacking reliable data on the nominees' integrity, intelligence, and related qualities, voters might well attribute favorable features to the candidate of their own party and find fault with the opposition choice. Since the nominee is legitimized as a potential president by the party, judging him on partisan terms is a convenient and timesaving means to save the costs of acquiring more detailed information. Moreover, such a partisan decision would relieve the voter of potential psychological conflict. In an effort to achieve "cognitive consistency,"[16] he could rationalize that virtue resides in his party's leader, vice in the contender.

Partisanship indeed does provide a distorting lens through which electors appraise the candidates. Although they are considering the same persons, opposing partisans are quite distinct in their evaluations of the candidates' individual qualities—even if we set aside comments about policy positions or remarks tying the nominees to other figures in the Democratic or Republican parties. In the four elections we are considering, favorable personal comments about the Democratic candidates were always more frequent among Democrats than critical statements, while the balance was in the opposite direction when the Democrats spoke of the GOP candidates. Republicans reacted in exactly the opposite way.

The evidence thus far does indicate considerable rationalization by voters to make their perceptions of the candidates fit their party loyalty. However, the evidence does not show consistent rationalization. Some of the voters' statements are probably related to policy considerations. A belief that Barry Goldwater is "impulsive," for example, may relate to his alleged adventurism in foreign policy, just as disbelief in George

McGovern's "integrity" can derive from his inconsistencies on tax reform. A significant number of voters do find virtues in the opposition nominee and faults in their own leader, moreover, and the distribution of responses is not fixed from one election to the next. Static partisanship alone cannot explain these variations in evaluations of the candidates. Rather, responsiveness is evident.

Change and balance is evident even among the most ardent partisans, those strongly identified as Democrats and Republicans. While ardent Democrats more frequently find favorable characteristics in their own party's choice and unappealing ones in the alternative candidate, Republicans show the same responses with respect to their party choice. It is not really surprising, of course, that strong partisans favor their own party's candidate. Yet, even among these loyalists, we see considerable variability over the four elections. In 1964, a fifth of the strong Republicans were attracted to Johnson as an individual and repelled by Goldwater. Among Democrats, the same proportion was attracted to Nixon in his early years, and later was unimpressed by their own party candidate, McGovern, in 1972. Thus, flexible perception is evident even among those voters who might be presumed to be particularly subject to the tunnel vision created by partisan blinders. The less strongly partisan voters and the Independents show even greater variability.[17]

On the other evaluative dimensions, partisan rationalization is less evident. Generally, voters are able to see virtues and defects in both the Republicans and Democrats. In fact, about two-thirds of the respondents in the past two decades have expressed comments opposite to their vote—admiring Democratic domestic policy even when voting for Nixon or speaking well of Eisenhower even while preferring Stevenson. Clearly, as has been pointed out by others, this "is not what people do when giving good 'reasons' for a decision made on other grounds, or, to make the point in another way, it is not the sort of behavior to which the term, 'rationalization,' is usually applied."[18] Reasonable judgment, rather than rationalization, is evident in such responses.

The degree of partisan bias in political evaluations varies with the object being evaluated. There is a considerable effect when voters consider those issues that have been traditionally identified with the parties, such as questions of economic and welfare policy, but there is less impact on newer issues. Assessment of a party's performance in managing governmental institutions is less affected by partisanship than by the events of the time. The party in power is the particular object of judgments on performance, since its record is the basis of the electoral decision. Evaluations on this dimension "graphically reflect the electorate in its great, and perhaps principal, role as an appraiser of past events, past performance, and past actions."[19]

The varying effects of partisanship are illustrated when the nine evaluative dimensions are examined for 1972. On five of the nine scales, evaluations are strongly conditioned by party loyalty: judgments on each of two candidates, and views on domestic policy, group associations, and general philosophy. While these views are alike in their susceptibility to partisan influences, the direction of the effects is quite different. Democrats are more favorable to McGovern and more hostile to Nixon than are Republicans, but they are close to the neutral point on these scales. Conversely, the net effect of views on domestic issues and perceived party associations with social groups is heavily favorable to the Democrats. Even strong Republicans barely support their own party on these dimensions.

Partisan influence is little evident on the dimensions of foreign policy and the social issue. The general, but limited, Republican advantage on these issues exists at comparable levels throughout the electorate, across the spectrum from Democrats to Republicans. Attitudes on Vietnam and party performance occupy moderate positions. While evaluations do become increasingly favorable to the Republicans as we view them across the range of partisanship, the effect is not as strong as in the evaluations of candidates or social associations.

A representative number of these scales is illustrated in Figure 7.1. Their total import is to relieve the voter of the charge that his evaluations are fully dependent on his partisan loyalties. Democrats do not show much enthusiasm for McGovern, and Republicans do not see their party as friendly to important group interests. On newer issues—such as foreign policy, race, and public order—partisanship has little effect on political evaluations. The voters' choice has been a choice of parties, but not a choice determined by party.[20]

THE EFFECTS OF POLITICAL ATTITUDES

Voter evaluations are important for their effects both on the electoral outcome and on the general shape of American politics. When citizens like or dislike the candidates, or find praise and blame in the parties' policies, they manifest these attitudes in their ballots. We can now examine the specific impact of these dimensions of political attitudes on presidential contests.

In any particular election, the vital data are the percentages of the vote gained or lost because of a particular set of attitudes. For example, the question of interest might be how much McGovern lost for the Democrats, or how much opinions on the social issue benefited the Republicans. The direct effect of an attitude is comprised of two elements. First, an attitude can influence the vote if popular reactions tend to favor one candidate and party over the other. The measurement of this party advantage is the average attitude of all voters on this dimension. The more the average evaluation diverges from a neutral point, the more potential there is for

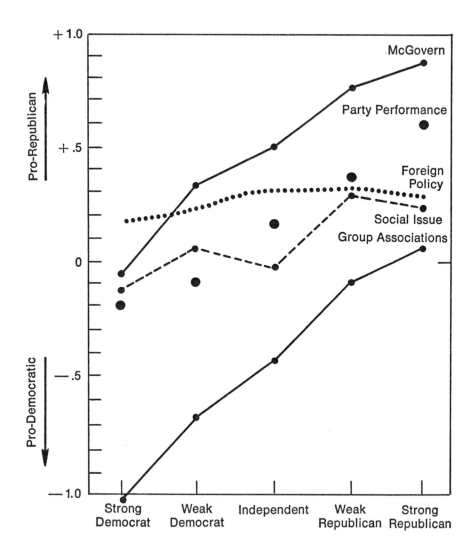

FIGURE 7.1 / PARTISANSHIP AND POLITICAL EVALUATIONS, 1972

this dimension to affect the vote. Second, there must be an actual relationship to the vote. Even if attitudes on a given dimension favor the Democrats or Republicans, that dimension may not be salient to the voters in the particular election. The total effect of a given dimension is therefore a combination of the party advantage in underlying attitudes and its actual impact. The latter factor is measured by the regression coefficient.

To illustrate the concept, we can use the metaphor of a rock thrown into a lake. The resulting ripples in the water will vary according to the weight of the rock and the force of the throw. In this analysis, the vote constitutes the ripples, whose magnitude depends on the weight of the attitudes and their force. Mathematically, the impact of attitudes on the vote is derived by multiplying the partisan deviation of evaluations from a neutral point (as specified in Table 7.5), by the regression coefficient of the dimension, as derived from a multiple regression with the presidential vote.[21]

The electoral effects from 1960 to 1972 of the evaluative dimensions are portrayed in Figure 7.2, which provides explanations for the divergent outcomes of these contests. In 1960, represented by the top bar in each category, the national choice was most clearly one between two traditional parties and two individually appealing candidates. Both Kennedy and Nixon were generally praised as intelligent and capable persons, and contributed to their parties' causes. The Democrats also gained votes on their established strengths, domestic issues, and their association with social groups. Nixon stressed his own record and the performance of the Eisenhower administration in ending the Korean war and preventing corruption. These differing emphases were both invoked by the candidates and responded to by the voters.[22] Having reasons to support both parties, the electorate split down the middle, giving Kennedy only the narrowest victory.

The choice was considerably different in 1964. Lyndon Johnson was now president, having successfully managed the national trauma of President Kennedy's assassination. After securing the passage of long-delayed domestic and civil rights legislation, he campaigned on a program of "fair shares."[23] The Republicans countered with Barry Goldwater, who campaigned on the philosophic premise of "a choice, not an echo." To many voters, however, Goldwater appeared to threaten the economic benefits of Democratic policy and to imperil world peace. "Between a party of prosperity and peace, as against a party of depression and war, there is little room for hesitation."[24] Assuming a pro-Democratic stance on virtually every attitudinal dimension, the electorate gave the Democrats their largest victory in history.

By 1968, the voters again had a new political world to consider. Evaluations of the two major-party candidates made little impact, as neither Hubert Humphrey nor the resuscitated Richard Nixon brought noticeable personal strengths to the contest. Traditional Democratic advantages were overcome by adverse judgments on the party's performance in its raucous nominating convention and on the conduct of the Johnson administration. Further votes were lost from the electorate's anti-Democratic reaction to the Vietnam war. A substantial majority of the electorate voted for the opposition candidates, Nixon and George Wallace, with the Republicans narrowly winning the presidency in the three-party contest.[25]

FIGURE 7.2 / EFFECTS OF POLITICAL ATTITUDES ON THE VOTE, 1960-72*

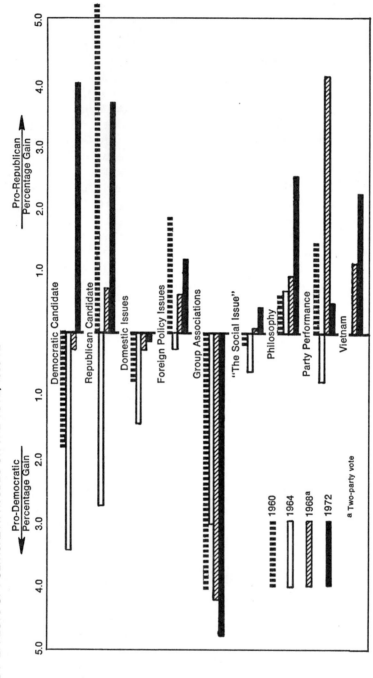

*Bar length measures the percentage of the national vote that was gained from each dimension. Elements aiding the Democratic party display bars to the left of the neutral point; dimensions aiding the Republican party extend to the right. No bar is seen for a dimension that had no effect favorable to either party.

The electoral cycle closed in 1972. Richard Nixon was again the Republican candidate, again emphasizing his experience in office, and again winning support on the basis of his individual attributes and the party record in office. Established appeals on the basis of foreign policy were buttressed by a claimed success in bringing "peace with honor" in Vietnam and by the attractions of a conservative philosophy grounded in the maintenance of public order. Democratic strengths were limited to the traditional domestic issues and group associations. These few Democratic advantages could not overcome the considerable weakness of the party candidate and the approval of the Nixon record. The electorate combined these diverse Republican appeals into a Nixon landslide.

Voter reactions over the years evidence both stability and change, but generally reveal responsiveness to the varying stimuli of the times. The consistent Democratic advantage is in the group loyalties it has inspired. However, the impact of the domestic policies associated with the party has diminished over time. Continuing a trend that can be traced back at least to 1952, these dimensions now tend to add only about one percent to a Democratic plurality.[26]

In recent years, foreign policy has come to have a greater impact upon the electorate. Attitudes on foreign policy have been favorable to the Republican party in all but one election since 1952, and their influence has been supplemented by the electorate's pro-Republican reaction to the Vietnam war in 1968 and 1972. The GOP performance in government also has been generally praised. Nevertheless, in 1964 these evaluations were reversed by the Goldwater candidacy. While voters' images of the party continue over time, they are also subject to reconsideration.

The most surprising finding of this entire analysis is the limited impact of the social issue. Considering the attention devoted to the subject in the popular press and by politicians in their campaigns, the net effect on the vote itself has been small and inconsistent. Rather than acting as a continuing threat to the Democratic party, the issue actually contributed to Kennedy's and Johnson's victories. Its adverse effect in 1968 is very limited, and this conclusion is unchanged even if we include the Wallace vote with Nixon's. Little impact is evident in 1972 either. To be sure, voters are concerned about the components of the social issue, such as race, crime, disorder, and the decline of traditional ways of life. But even as the concern is real, the political effect may be ambiguous. The social issue has both pro-Democratic and pro-Republican components, as well as many elements that do not have a national partisan reference. To be electorally significant, a concern must be made an issue between the parties. To the present time, only the purely racial elements of this concern have been translated into the language of partisan debate. The other aspects remain nonpartisan in their impact.

In the future, the social issue may be resolved into two distinct questions. To the extent that it is involved with race, candidates and parties may take differing positions, such as favoring or opposing laws to promote civil rights. A partisan effect on the vote could then become evident. However, even this impact may be exaggerated. An analysis of southern whites has found that the importance of race actually declined in their evaluations after 1964,[27] while a general analysis of both national and state voting in 1968 finds civil rights and law-and-order issues to be of only moderate significance.[28]

A partisan effect of the second element in the social issue—disorder and change—is even less likely. Matters such as this are likely to be "valence issues,"[29] such as motherhood, which have only one side a candidate can logically support. Neither Democrats nor Republicans are likely to endorse crime, advocate disorder, or oppose motherhood. We may find more aspirants wearing miniature American flags in their lapels or hear more denunciations of sin. The very prevalence of flags and ubiquity of piety, however, will make it impossible for voters to choose among candidates on this basis. Political rhetoric may reflect a concern for the social issue, but not a political choice.

In the four elections from 1960 to 1972, the voters have made their decisions on the basis of a range of evaluations that have changed with the times. Their choices have resulted from a combination of party initiatives, thrusting of new issues into political consciousness, and eventual considered judgment of the electorate. Parties and candidates initiate programs, and seek to focus public attention on their favorite topics. Indeed, much of campaign strategy consists of trying to define the issues advantageously. If the domestic issues and group associations that favor the Democrats can be brought to center stage, that party is likely to win the contest. If, on the other hand, a concern for foreign policy and party management is accorded priority, the normal Republican dominance.in these dimensions makes a GOP victory likely.

The final judgment is that of the voters. From the conflicting stimuli offered by the parties, they select those worthy of their consideration. They decide both how to evaluate aspirants on various dimensions and how important each of these dimensions is in their vote. From 1960 to 1972, voters evaluated their choices on reasonable criteria, changed these evaluations with changes in external stimuli, and varied the importance of different dimensions in line with different circumstances, different partisan initiatives, and their own judgments. Their behavior is a reasonable likeness to the portrait of the responsive voter.

In the future, these voter evaluations are likely to have continuing effects on the political system. Assessments of policies and candidates are becoming ever more prominent. By contrast, past analyses of voting behavior have relied on party identification as a basic and originating factor. However, party loyalty itself may be understood not simply as the cause, but in part as the effect of political evaluations. Citizens often become Democrats or Republicans because they like particular policies and candidates, rather than letting their past partisanship determine their present preferences. The relationship is particularly evident when examining changes in party loyalties. While stability in partisanship is most common, persons who develop unfavorable images of a traditional party do tend to change parties. "In fact, the more one's party image favors the party one did not identify with in the past, the more likely is one to convert to that party in the present." There is, then, an independent effect of political evaluations.[30]

In the vote itself, these evaluations are important, as we have seen, and their significance is increasingly independent of partisanship. The relative effect of voters' attitudes and of partisan loyalty can be gauged by the familiar technique of multiple regression, employing party identification and all of the evaluative dimensions as independent variables. As expected, party identification is closely related to the vote. But, as discussed in previous chapters, its importance appears to be declining relative to the evaluations. In 1960, party alone accounted for three-fourths of the explained variance in the presidential vote, when entered first in the regression. In 1964 and 1968, partisanship remained the most important explanatory variable, but now accounted for two-thirds of the explanation. By 1972, even though the first variable in the procedure, party alone could explain only half of the total variance.[31]

As partisanship alone becomes less determinative of the vote, other factors are likely to be more influential. One possibility is that the vote will be more candidate-oriented. Individual characteristics such as honesty and intelligence are certainly appropriate characteristics for judging political candidates, particularly for such a unique office as the presidency and particularly after the exposure of "the White House horrors" of the Nixon administration. There is a danger, however, that greater candidate orientation in the vote may encourage focus on politically irrelevant characteristics such as personality or religion.

The evaluative dimensions developed in this chapter provide some data on this point. When we undertake a multiple regression of these dimensions to show their influence (exclusive of partisanship) on the vote, we consistently find that presidential choice is most highly correlated with the candidate dimensions. This high relationship is to be expected, since asking whether the voter personally likes a candidate and whether he will vote for that person is virtually asking the same question in different form.[32]

Over time, however, there is increasing independence between the vote and candidate evaluations. In 1960, electoral choice could be largely explained in terms of these reactions to the party nominees, with more than four-fifths of the explained variance attributable to reactions to

Nixon and Kennedy as individuals. In the later elections, reactions to candidates explain far less of the variance—about half in 1964 and three-fifths in 1968 and 1972.

Aside from being influenced by these personal features of the candidates, the voters have come to cast their vote more on impersonal grounds, such as the record of the parties and the policies the voters identify with the candidates and their factions. The point is partially illustrated by the 1964 voter who, when asked what he liked about Goldwater, replied, "He's got guts." To the next question on what he disliked about the Republican candidate, however, he made an implicit judgment on issues, replying, "More guts than brains."

For the voter to express his policy preferences effectively, a link to the political system is necessary. Candidates provide a possible link, but since candidates change frequently, such change may make it difficult for voters to focus their issue concerns. A more stable connection is needed, and parties provide the most obvious possibilities. Through these permanent organizations, the electorate may be able to transmit its concerns to its government.

The responsiveness of the voters makes it possible for an election to be more than a registration of traditional fealty. The voters are sufficiently concerned and flexible enough to render a judgment on candidates and parties. Other conditions must be fulfilled for this judgment to be effective. A forceful electoral choice requires potent electoral organization. The voters must be able to see a difference between the parties and to discern the direction of party difference. In the next chapter, we will consider these qualifications of the electorate.

THE CONCERNS OF VOTERS: FINDINGS

1. The national problems cited by voters vary with the electoral context.

    1a. The problems cited vary little among social and partisan groups.

2. The parties are perceived as different in their abilities to deal with particular issues.

    2a. Democrats are seen as better able to deal with economic issues, and less equipped to deal with racial and foreign policy.

    2b. However, there is little perceived difference on the "social issue."

3. Voting choices are affected by perceptions of party competence as much as by party loyalty.

4. The "party images" of the Democrats and Republicans differ considerably.

    4a. The profile of Richard Nixon gained policy definition over three presidential elections.

5. Of nine dimensions of political attitudes, a consistent Democratic advantage is evident in economic policy and the party's identification with social groups.
6. On these same dimensions, a consistent Republican advantage is evident in political philosophy, party performance and, except in 1964, in foreign policies.
7. Neither party is advantaged by the "social issue."
8. Partisan loyalty does not determine voter response on these political attitudes.
   8a. In contrast to past findings of constant distortion, the effect of partisanship varies among the dimensions of political attitudes.
9. The effect of particular attitudes varies considerably from one election to another.
   9a. The Republican victory in 1972 results from favorable voter evaluation of Nixon and his foreign policies, and an unfavorable evaluation of George McGovern.
   9b. "The social issue," contrary to popular belief, has had little net effect on the vote.
10. The effect of political attitudes on the vote is increasingly independent of partisanship.

CHAPTER 8

FROM CONFUSION
TO CLARITY

Observers of politics, from Plato to Herbert Marcuse, have frequently sneered at the inability of the "masses" to discern political reality. As Plato believes they are misled by the shadows on the wall of a mythical cave, so Marcuse argues they are deceived by the shadows of the television tube. To both, citizens are fundamentally unequipped politically. Allegedly, they lack the capacity to control governmental leaders and to direct public policy rationally.

These premises lead to the portrait of the dependent voter, a representation that has been unverified by the analysis to this point. The electorate is not controlled by its traditional loyalties or sociological characteristics. Its ballot choices are significantly associated with its policy preferences, its concerns, and its evaluations of candidates and their tickets. The responsive voter lives.

To be effective, however, voters must express their choices in an organized way. Political parties have developed over the centuries as the most potent means of converting mass preferences into public action. A party is not necessarily organized for this purpose, and Edmund Burke was surely too generous in defining a political faction as "a body of men united for promoting by their joint endeavors the national interest upon some particular principle."[1] More realistically, parties develop to promote the profit and position of individual activists and social interests. But in their search for power, parties in a democracy must seek popular favor. This search is likely to require some measure of satisfaction of the masses' policy demands.[2]

Parties are a potential link between the issue preferences of the voters and the actions of government. This link has not always been forged in American politics. Republicans and Democrats often have won the presidency on other grounds, such as personal popularity or the emotional memories evoked by "waving the bloody shirt" of the Civil War. To establish the link, the parties must be somewhat distinctive: Democratic or Republican loyalty must mean something relevant to the issues of the day. Furthermore, the parties must be perceived as different, so that voters will know how to express their policy preferences at the ballot box.

Compared to the recent past, the evidence presented below shows a considerable increase in voter consciousness. Twenty years ago, there was little association between issue preferences and the party loyalties of the electorate. Amid the turmoil of the 1960s the two sets of attitudes came into closer alignment. Similarly, when Dwight Eisenhower was president, the electorate found difficulty in distinguishing the parties on policy grounds. In the present, voters do see the parties as different with respect to policy and do know where the parties stand. American voters have become more aware of party differentiation, more coherent in their own thinking, and more responsive to policy questions in their vote. As a result, American politics has become more ideological, and potentially more meaningful.

PARTIES AND POLICIES

These relationships can be analyzed first by tracing the association over time of party loyalty and policy views. For this purpose, six precise policy questions are available that have been asked consistently of national samples in each quadrennial study from 1956 to 1968. In 1972, there is a considerable change in the format of the questionnaire, and these responses require additional analysis.

The six policy questions concern federal aid to education (or, in 1972, progressive taxation), government provision of medical care, government guarantee of full employment, federal enforcement of fair employment and fair housing, federal enforcement of school integration, and foreign aid. Although the questions are not worded identically in the different surveys, wording is sufficiently close to be highly comparable. Moreover, we are not concerned with the trend of opinion itself, but rather with comparisons of the structure of opinion in each of the election years, so that identical wording is not critical.[3]

In Table 8.1, positions on these issues are presented along the five-point scale of party identification; the statistic reported is the percentage taking the "liberal" position (i.e., in favor of federal government action).[4] For 1956, the data clearly support the contention of *The American Voter* that issue preferences are essentially unrelated to party identification.[5] A linear relationship between the two variables exists only on the issue of medical care. The situation changes substantially, however, over the next twelve years. By 1968, a linear relationship exists essentially on all issues but foreign aid. This change is not gradual, but becomes suddenly apparent in the election of 1964. When John Kennedy was elected president, the relationship of opinion and party identification was hardly different from that of the Eisenhower period. By 1964, though, linear relationships are evident on four of the six issues, and they begin to appear on the other two as well.

The same pattern is evident in the increasing spread between the extremes. Strong Democrats and strong Republicans are already distinct on the issue of medical care in 1956, but the difference almost doubles in 1964 and remains considerably widened in 1968. The same pattern is evident on the other issues as well. Party differences become quite high by 1964 and then decrease slightly (on job guarantees, fair employment, and foreign aid) or increase slighly (on aid to education and school integration) four years later.

The increased policy distinctiveness of partisans is summarized by the increases in the ordinal correlation included in the last row of Table 8.1. Policy and party preferences become far more congruent in 1964, and the correlation is very similar in 1968. The only major exception is the issue of school integration. For the first three elections in this period, no meaningful correlation exists between party identification and support of federal action in the issue (gammas = .04, −.01, .08). But by 1968, there is a considerable relationship, and the gamma statistic (.43) is higher than in any other instance. On five of the six issues—all but foreign aid—party identification means something by 1968 other than a traditional reaffirmation: it is now related to the policy preferences of the voter.

It is difficult to compare the views of the voters in 1972 to those in earlier years, because the questionnaire changed considerably. Some

TABLE 8.1 / PARTY IDENTIFICATION AND POLICY POSITION, 1956-72*

Party Identification	Education, Taxation					Medical Care					Job Guarantee				
	1956	1960	1964	1968	1972	1956	1960	1964	1968	1972	1956	1960	1964	1968	1972
Strong Democrat	80.0	66.8	51.0	53.6	52.6	74.2	74.5	78.2	81.3	67.4	75.6	71.2	52.6	53.1	62.6
Weak Democrat	78.1	59.0	44.1	38.3	66.5	67.3	60.2	65.2	72.1	53.1	64.0	62.4	38.4	39.7	44.4
Independent	71.0	53.2	39.3	32.9	55.2	55.8	56.7	57.2	55.3	56.7	55.0	56.6	31.0	27.0	39.5
Weak Republican	68.7	39.1	21.5	22.5	59.3	51.4	47.5	43.5	39.3	36.2	59.5	43.9	25.9	24.9	24.0
Strong Republican	67.7	44.5	15.5	12.0	39.8	45.9	54.2	23.6	42.7	40.9	51.5	52.7	16.1	25.4	20.5
Gamma	.15	.20	.34	.36	.11	.24	.18	.45	.41	.22	.19	.16	.31	.25	.36

Party Identification	Fair Employment					School Integration					Foreign Aid				
	1956	1960	1964	1968	1972	1956	1960	1964	1968	1972	1956	1960	1964	1968	1972
Strong Democrat	73.3	63.0	56.3	61.9	64.9	38.7	39.8	53.7	58.9	55.3	49.5	51.4	64.7	51.3	38.9
Weak Democrat	71.3	63.1	42.9	43.5	53.0	44.4	37.5	43.2	44.6	43.1	55.4	48.8	59.2	45.8	44.7
Independent	66.6	65.4	50.3	37.7	55.2	48.8	47.1	49.0	37.3	45.6	49.9	53.2	57.5	42.7	47.4
Weak Republican	70.8	62.7	36.3	37.8	51.0	49.3	43.0	50.5	37.4	45.4	48.2	54.0	56.6	47.0	44.0
Strong Republican	66.8	65.9	20.6	31.3	39.4	38.8	41.5	34.8	31.5	34.8	51.4	61.5	49.7	41.8	47.8
Gamma	.04	−.02	.22	.24	.15	.04	−.01	.08	.43	.11	.01	−.03	.08	.04	−.06

*The percentage in each cell is that supporting the "liberal" position.

questions asked in the past, such as that on federal aid to education, were not repeated. The substitute item on progressive taxation clearly is not identical, even though both generally concern the redistribution of income. On other matters, particularly medical care and job guarantees, the newer form of the question tends to diminish differences between groups. Rather than being asked to choose between two alternative policies, as in the past, the respondent locates his preferred position on a seven-point scale. While this procedure is more methodologically interesting, it prevents direct comparison with past replies.[6] Only the last three questions—on fair employment, school integration, and foreign aid—are comparable to previous queries. Even in these cases there has been some change in wording, and subsequent questions on perceptions of the parties have been omitted.

Leaving these difficulties aside, the 1972 data show continuing, but reduced, policy differentiation among party loyalists. On the basic issue of job guarantees, however, the statistical difference actually increases in the last election and reaches a level close to the highest on any issue over the entire period. Since, of the three economic questions, this issue was most salient in 1972, these responses indicate one persistent partisan differentiation. With regard to other economic questions, the parties show less distinctiveness.

On racial matters, there has been an apparent diminution in factional divisions in 1972. Nevertheless, at the extremes, Republicans and Democrats remain quite split, with the reduction in polarization coming principally from the more liberal attitudes of the intermediate groupings. This reduction can also be attributed to the lessened salience of this particular question. By 1972, there was little argument over formal school integration and equal employment. The argument had shifted to other grounds, particularly that of positive government action to promote racial equality. When queried on direct government aid "to improve the social and economic position of blacks and other minority groups" and on school busing, sharp differences again emerge between Republicans and Democrats. As in the past, there is a monotonic relationship on both of these relevant questions. While 56 percent of strong Democrats favor aid to minorities, only 30 percent of strong Republicans take the same view (G = .20). Busing is not popular with any partisan group, but 22 percent of the most loyal Democrats approve, compared to a microscopic 4 percent of committed Republicans. On the real issues of the day, position on racial issues and party loyalty retain their link.

Withal, voters in 1972 were less clearly differentiated by party lines than in the 1960s. Issue and partisan alignments were becoming closely aligned through the 1968 election. The introduction of new issues and the fading of older controversies slowed, or even reversed, this development. Party and policy became disconnected. The potential for clear party differentiation remains, however, as evidenced by opinions on guaranteed employment and the emerging questions of busing and aid to minorities. This potential is further seen in the electorate's characterizations of the Republicans and Democrats.

PERCEPTIONS OF THE PARTIES

A further binding is needed for the parties to serve as links between voter preferences and public policies. A reasoned choice between policies requires an observable choice between parties. Their programs must be perceived as somewhat distinct and reasonably clear. In recent times these connections have been drawn far more frequently.

Since 1956, voters have become more aware of party differences on the policy questions under examination. Earlier, the Survey Research Center found little awareness of differences. It subjected its respondents to a series of questions on each policy question, eliminating those who had no interest in, or opinion on, an issue, as well as those who, holding an opinion on the issue, could not decide if "the government is going too far, doing less than it should, or what?" This latter question typically eliminated more respondents than the query on the issue itself. Those who were left after the multiple screening were then asked whether there was a difference between the parties. This remaining sample was presumably a relatively knowledgeable group, but in 1956 even they found rather little distinction between the parties on most issues.[7] In later surveys, the question on the government's program was eliminated. Therefore, the remaining sample asked to differentiate the parties was larger and presumably less informed. Nevertheless they perceived more of a difference between the parties.

This changing awareness is seen in Table 8.2. Because of question changes in 1972, the data for that year are not strictly comparable and will be discussed separately. In the direct comparisons from 1956 to 1968, a growth in voter consciousness is clear.

In particular, the parties have come to be seen over time as more different on questions of federal government power. Again, the issue of foreign aid is exceptional. The critical effect of the 1964 election is evident once more, as the proportions seeing party differences changed most dramatically in the Goldwater-Johnson contest. In 1968, there was a regression downward toward lessened perceptions of party differences, although it was not a full regression. Only on the distinct issue of foreign aid was the perception of party differences in 1968 at or below the level of the Eisenhower period. For the other issues, during the decade of the 1960s, the data indicate that a significant and apparently enduring political lesson was learned about the existence of party differences. The lesson was particularly well learned by strong partisans. On virtually all issues

TABLE 8.2 / PERCEPTIONS OF PARTIES ON POLICY ISSUES, BY PARTY IDENTIFICATION*

| | Existence of Party Differences | | | | | | | | | | | | | | |
| | Education, Taxation | | | | | Medical Care | | | | | Job Guarantee | | | | |
Group	1956	1960	1964	1968	1972	1956	1960	1964	1968	1972	1956	1960	1964	1968	1972
Strong Democrat	58.1	62.8	73.8	75.7	83.5	63.2	68.6	86.4	85.8	80.2	73.0	74.5	80.3	78.1	86.9
Weak Democrat	44.2	53.2	60.9	53.0	74.6	48.9	59.0	77.2	71.2	64.7	54.2	66.3	69.3	65.4	82.0
Independent	43.4	52.3	53.5	48.0	70.9	41.2	45.3	77.4	62.3	52.6	36.4	57.6	55.2	54.2	60.2
Weak Republican	48.0	41.8	58.9	53.3	73.0	50.0	68.6	75.3	65.8	74.2	50.3	50.5	61.3	64.1	76.8
Strong Republican	59.0	63.0	78.4	73.3	77.4	64.9	66.7	87.7	75.9	69.5	63.7	42.5	76.7	79.1	89.5

| | Fair Employment, Minority Aid | | | | | School Integration, Busing | | | | | Foreign Aid, Defense Spending | | | | |
Group	1956	1960	1964	1968	1972	1956	1960	1964	1968	1972	1956	1960	1964	1968	1972
Strong Democrat	50.0	52.5	77.5	78.5	71.2	55.6	50.6	70.0	75.9	72.7	46.5	44.7	61.5	64.7	57.6
Weak Democrat	46.9	38.7	70.1	64.9	62.7	55.6	34.9	63.7	62.5	64.1	40.4	37.5	52.7	43.8	53.1
Independent	38.5	38.7	58.8	55.0	55.7	42.3	30.8	59.0	51.1	61.3	33.6	32.7	50.8	39.3	42.4
Weak Republican	46.0	44.3	53.2	47.7	68.6	50.0	36.4	52.1	53.1	72.0	50.0	32.0	50.3	42.8	47.0
Strong Republican	52.3	50.0	75.0	60.5	58.4	57.5	39.2	66.2	60.5	74.0	63.9	47.4	61.8	48.0	53.0

*Cell entries are percentages of voters with opinions perceiving party differences.

and in all elections, strong partisans were more likely to see party differences than were weak partisans, who in turn were more likely to see differences than Independents. These results clearly accord with the concept and significance of party identification.

A more important finding is involved in a change relating to the ideological identity of the parties. In 1956, even among the sample remaining after various filterings, there was relatively little consensus on the ideological position of the parties with respect to the six issues we are considering. The greatest ideological consensus existed on another question, one dealing with ownership of electric power and housing. On this item, three-fourths of those who saw party differences also agreed that the Republicans were more favorable to private ownership of these industries.[8] The identification of the parties' ideological positions was lower on the six issues. (The item on power and housing was not used in later surveys, so it cannot be analyzed here).

By 1968, as seen in Table 8.3, each of the two parties seemed to have a much clearer identity. The proportion seeing the Democrats as the more liberal or activist party had risen on every question, even on foreign aid. It is particularly significant that in almost all cases the perceptions of the parties showed a consensus greater than that which existed on the exceptional issue of ownership of industry in the Eisenhower period. In other words, by 1968, to judge by six important items, the majority of the electorate had become more aware of party differences and had come to agree that the Democratic party was the liberal party.[9]

This change in perceptions of the parties' positions is not affected by controls for party identification. In all partisan groups surveyed, the Democrats were increasingly recognized as the liberal party on each of the

TABLE 8.3 / CONSENSUS ON POSITIONS OF PARTIES ON POLICY ISSUES, BY PARTY IDENTIFICATION*

| | Consensus on Party Positions | | | | | | | | | | | | | | |
| | Education, Taxation | | | | | Medical Care | | | | | Job Guarantee | | | | |
Group	1956	1960	1964	1968	1972	1956	1960	1964	1968	1972	1956	1960	1964	1968	1972
Strong Democrat	90.5	95.2	96.5	94.1	64.6	93.9	95.8	98.2	98.8	84.0	85.5	98.8	98.8	97.0	83.1
Weak Democrat	86.5	90.5	93.6	82.6	71.4	84.6	90.4	95.8	88.7	80.6	71.8	93.3	93.9	88.5	80.1
Independent	66.3	74.6	83.8	64.3	76.1	76.4	87.7	93.5	82.7	90.5	61.9	82.3	89.3	71.4	83.0
Weak Republican	37.2	60.9	55.8	58.7	77.7	64.3	52.2	77.6	85.0	88.5	60.0	67.3	72.5	69.4	91.4
Strong Republican	31.6	47.9	55.0	41.2	83.1	57.8	51.3	79.8	63.6	89.7	47.0	32.3	63.8	53.9	83.0

| | Fair Employment, Minority Aid | | | | | School Integration, Busing | | | | | Foreign Aid, Defense Spending | | | | |
Group	1956	1960	1964	1968	1972	1956	1960	1964	1968	1972	1956	1960	1964	1968	1972
Strong Democrat	64.6	83.5	96.9	97.3	78.5	39.1	34.7	96.2	95.3	65.6	57.1	80.9	98.1	93.0	76.4
Weak Democrat	63.6	65.5	93.9	88.3	81.3	51.5	42.5	90.3	87.1	64.6	53.0	60.2	94.2	89.2	84.6
Independent	49.4	53.4	89.5	75.6	72.4	45.8	46.4	91.8	83.4	68.0	54.5	46.8	88.1	83.1	84.4
Weak Republican	23.6	18.3	81.0	70.2	79.6	45.1	49.3	83.9	75.4	86.0	46.2	13.0	67.8	81.5	86.1
Strong Republican	6.0	17.2	67.6	56.4	88.5	59.4	48.5	71.3	69.5	94.0	29.3	21.4	70.8	61.6	81.0

*Cell entries are percentages of voters that select Democrats as liberal among those voters who perceive party differences.

six issues. Democrats were most likely to make this judgment, but by 1964 a majority even of strong Republicans recognized the liberal credentials of the opposition. In 1956, by contrast, the strong Republicans conceded this "honor" to the Democrats on only two issues.

The acceptance of the liberalism of the Democrats is most evident in the 1964 survey, conducted during the contest between Goldwater and Johnson. It is not solely related to that election, however, for important changes in perceptions of party position on the economic issues of aid to education, medical care, and job guarantees can be located as early as the 1960 campaign. The identification of the Democratic party as the liberal faction largely persists through the 1968 election as well, although there is some lessening of perceived party positions, most notably on the issue of federal aid to education.

The most striking change in perceptions of parties is evident on racial issues. In 1956, there is no consensus on the parties' stands on the issues of school integration and fair employment. Differences between the parties are less likely to be seen, and Republicans are as likely as Democrats to be perceived as favoring federal action on civil rights. A startling reversal has occurred by 1964: all partisan groups recognize the existence of a difference on this issue, and all are convinced that the Democrats stand more for government programs on behalf of blacks. Even strong Republicans concede the point they argued in the Eisenhower years. The identification of the Democrats with civil rights is slightly attenuated in 1968, but it still is a clearer perception than exists on any other issue.

In 1972, the survey instrument used was considerably different from previous elections. For that year, opinions are analyzed here on aid to minorities rather than fair employment, on school busing rather than school integration, and on defense spending rather than foreign aid. Obviously, these are different questions from those asked in the past. Even for those items that deal with the same policy area, perceptions of the parties' stands are not measured in the same way. The voter is not asked directly to compare the two parties, but to locate each separately on a scale. These distinct placements are then compared statistically.[10]

Despite changes in questions and methods, the voters continue to perceive differences between the Democrats and Republicans. On the newer economic issue of progressive taxation, as well as the established issues of medical care and job guarantees, there is a high degree of consensus on the more liberal position of the Democrats, with even the most ardent Republicans agreeing to this characterization. On the bread-and-butter issues, voters of all tastes know which side has their favorite spread.[11]

Most voters also see the parties as distinct on racial matters. While there is virtual unanimity that the Democrats are more favorable to economic aid to minorities, there is less agreement on busing. Republicans are particularly ready to attribute this unpopular policy to the Democrats. On the one foreign policy issue, defense spending, there is the least awareness of party differences.[12] Dealing with the level of defense spending, this question is quite different from the earlier item on foreign aid. While liberalism on this item is defined as reduced expenditure, the earlier question considered increased spending as the more liberal attitude. The general consensus on the Democrats' liberalism on this issue in 1972 therefore does not concern the parties' alleged foreign policy, but their domestic spending priorities.

The two developments we have discussed show that the American party system now provides a possible means for the responsive voter to transmit his policy preferences: at least from 1956 to 1968, party loyalties became more congruent with issue stands; still more persistent, continuing through 1972, is the electorate's perception of greater differences between the parties, and its agreement on the positional placement of those competing for power. The causes of these shifts remain to be explored.

SOURCES OF CHANGE

The shifts that have just been detailed are closely related. Particularly vital are the stable, new perceptions of the parties as holding relatively distinctive and identifiable positions on particular issues. Generational change is one possible explanation of these new perceptions. Younger, more ideologically attuned voters may have replaced older and less sensitive electors. To test this possibility, age is controlled in Table 8.4. Respondents in the age groupings used in the 1956 surveys are compared to cohorts four, eight, twelve, and sixteen years older in 1960 to 1972, respectively. If generational replacement is the main reason for the changed perceptions, the greatest differences would be seen between the upper-right and lower-left segments of each set of percentages. If political aging is not an explanation, changes would be most evident among cohort groups.[13]

The data show that both conclusions are valid to some extent, but that generational turnover is not an adequate explanation in itself. In virtually all comparisons, the new generation (below aged 23 in 1964, or aged 31 in 1972) is more aware of party differences and more perceptive of Democratic liberalism than those it replaces (those 65 or older in 1956, or 69 or older in 1960, who were too depleted by 1964 to be included). These differences are not as large, however, as are the changes of matched cohorts. Some political learning has occurred in all age groups. In 1956 and 1960, for example, most age groups did not see a party difference on racial issues, and all of them tended to identify the Republicans as more liberal. Particularly since 1964, all age groups have come to perceive a party difference on racial issues and to agree on the Democratic party's greater support of fair employment and school integration.

The data give some indication of greater growth in awareness among older, rather than younger, voters. The cohort aged 25-34 in 1956 (41-50 in 1972) appears to have become particularly aware of Democratic liberalism in 1964 and to have held to its new perceptions in 1968 and 1972. Speculating on the source of this change, we could note that this group came of age politically just after the realignment of the New Deal. Hence this group may not have been immediately affected by the political events of that period, but may have been particularly susceptible to the effect of similar issues in 1964.

Degree of educational achievement might be an alternative explanation for the new perceptions of party differences. The average level of schooling has increased considerably in the United States in this sixteen-year period. Greater perceptions might result from the intellectual upgrading of the population, with less informed grade school or high school graduates being replaced by informed college alumni. Controlling for education would reveal this effect by indicating relatively little change by educational level. This control is presented in Table 8.5, which clearly shows that educational upgrading does not explain the shift in perceptions. Awareness has increased at all educational levels.

In fact, the disparities in perceptions among persons of varying schooling have tended to lessen, particularly in regard to identifying the Democrats as the liberal party. This effect was most marked in the 1964 campaign; in that year, on every issue, respondents with only a grade school education were clearer in their perceptions of the parties than college graduates were in 1956. The educational gap widened again in

TABLE 8.4 / PERCEPTIONS OF PARTIES ON POLICY ISSUES, BY AGE*

Existence of Party Differences

Age in 1956	Age in 1972	Education, Taxation					Medical Care				
		1956	1960	1964	1968	1972	1956	1960	1964	1968	1972
—	Under 31	—	—	60.6	52.2	72.2	—	—	84.7	64.6	69.2
Under 25	31-40	49.1	67.2	58.4	56.7	76.8	57.8	74.0	83.9	68.7	67.2
25-34	41-50	49.1	45.7	65.3	59.8	78.9	49.0	51.4	82.5	77.8	64.9
35-44	51-60	45.2	53.1	72.7	62.9	77.3	50.2	66.1	81.0	68.6	76.2
45-54	61-70	53.3	58.0	65.9	59.6	69.2	54.0	52.0	76.6	71.4	66.7
55-64	Over 70	52.2	58.8	55.2	56.5	78.5	59.0	58.0	78.1	74.9	61.7
65 and Over	—	54.0	59.3	—	—	—	53.5	52.6	—	—	—

Age in 1956	Age in 1972	Job Guarantee					Fair Employment, Minority Aid				
		1956	1960	1964	1968	1972	1956	1960	1964	1968	1972
—	Under 31	—	—	65.8	65.8	76.6	—	—	78.1	60.5	64.8
Under 25	31-40	46.6	68.7	66.0	61.5	83.2	50.7	57.3	69.9	64.3	64.3
25-34	41-50	55.3	66.3	73.0	70.8	77.0	51.5	37.8	68.1	63.3	61.9
35-44	51-60	49.5	66.0	68.2	74.6	82.0	44.1	39.0	66.3	65.0	65.5
45-54	61-70	58.0	62.3	71.8	62.2	74.7	50.2	48.5	66.8	54.0	64.3
55-64	Over 70	63.9	59.0	66.2	70.3	73.3	39.1	42.6	65.6	58.2	66.7
65 and Over	—	58.8	54.5	—	—	—	52.7	46.7	—	—	—

Age in 1956	Age in 1972	School Integration, Busing					Foreign Aid, Defense Spending				
		1956	1960	1964	1968	1972	1956	1960	1964	1968	1972
—	Under 31	—	—	75.6	56.2	66.8	—	—	54.5	42.2	63.4
Under 25	31-40	58.2	41.1	67.1	59.6	67.5	42.5	42.3	55.1	39.2	52.9
25-34	41-50	52.7	38.4	61.6	65.4	68.1	48.8	38.9	60.6	49.3	51.3
35-44	51-60	50.2	46.6	64.9	57.7	62.4	40.4	37.4	55.0	47.5	45.6
45-54	61-70	49.3	40.6	61.9	61.3	73.7	44.5	37.8	55.6	47.2	44.9
55-64	Over 70	53.1	28.5	54.7	56.9	72.4	44.9	33.0	54.8	50.6	46.9
65 and Over	—	50.0	34.4	—	—	—	47.2	46.6	—	—	—

Consensus on Party Positions

Age in 1956	Age in 1972	Education, Taxation					Medical Care				
		1956	1960	1964	1968	1972	1956	1960	1964	1968	1972
—	Under 31	—	—	89.9	65.6	70.6	—	—	96.7	86.0	88.6
Under 25	31-40	51.8	77.9	86.2	72.3	79.5	73.8	82.4	92.2	88.6	85.0
25-34	41-50	66.0	73.5	84.8	79.4	74.1	78.9	89.4	94.1	91.5	85.9
35-44	51-60	75.8	74.6	77.4	67.0	71.7	81.6	80.0	87.5	87.6	78.8
45-54	61-70	69.7	90.2	86.5	73.1	79.6	80.2	82.7	95.5	83.3	91.7
55-64	Over 70	67.1	72.6	74.0	73.1	75.3	72.0	71.3	90.6	80.8	99.7
65 and Over	—	51.8	60.8	—	—	—	64.5	75.9	—	—	—

Age in 1956	Age in 1972	Job Guarantee					Fair Employment, Minority Aid				
		1956	1960	1964	1968	1972	1956	1960	1964	1968	1972
—	Under 31	—	—	92.0	79.0	85.3	—	—	93.6	83.7	83.5
Under 25	31-40	76.0	82.6	92.7	78.3	82.1	54.7	55.4	93.0	83.0	81.6
25-34	41-50	65.0	82.4	88.5	85.9	83.6	43.6	52.5	88.3	83.5	85.9
35-44	51-60	72.2	81.6	85.4	66.7	82.5	42.7	45.3	85.8	84.7	83.5
45-54	61-70	65.8	85.2	89.0	83.9	87.0	53.0	63.1	91.5	82.0	78.2
55-64	Over 70	62.5	72.1	90.8	74.5	82.3	48.0	42.0	89.3	75.6	78.8
65 and Over	—	71.4	64.9	—	—	—	47.7	56.2	—	—	—

Age in 1956	Age in 1972	School Integration, Busing					Foreign Aid, Defense Spending				
		1956	1960	1964	1968	1972	1956	1960	1964	1968	1972
—	Under 31	—	—	91.2	85.5	70.7	—	—	87.5	85.2	88.5
Under 25	31-40	50.0	34.9	92.6	84.5	72.2	34.8	50.0	90.6	85.8	89.2
25-34	41-50	42.6	44.6	92.0	90.0	82.0	60.1	44.0	88.1	87.7	77.7
35-44	51-60	46.8	40.0	85.8	85.3	68.6	40.6	46.0	86.5	85.9	78.0
45-54	61-70	51.0	50.0	90.0	84.6	83.7	48.1	60.1	88.0	83.2	73.1
55-64	Over 70	57.2	35.2	86.9	79.6	78.0	47.3	50.0	83.7	80.5	86.8
65 and Over	—	49.0	52.3	—	—	—	38.6	46.0	—	—	—

*Entries in the first half of the table are percentages of voters with opinions in each group that perceive party differences, as in Table 8.2. Entries in the second half of the table are percentages of voters in each group that select Democrats as liberal among the voters who perceive party differences, as in Table 8.3.

TABLE 8.5 / PERCEPTIONS OF PARTIES ON POLICY ISSUES, BY EDUCATION*

| | Existence of Party Differences | | | | | | | | | | | | | | |
| | Education, Taxation | | | | | Medical Care | | | | | Job Guarantee | | | | |
Group	1956	1960	1964	1968	1972	1956	1960	1964	1968	1972	1956	1960	1964	1968	1972
Elementary School	45.7	51.8	61.6	56.1	76.9	49.2	53.4	76.0	70.7	66.3	59.9	65.3	68.8	63.7	75.1
High School	52.2	55.4	51.6	53.0	71.2	50.0	60.0	80.6	68.0	63.7	52.3	71.2	65.5	61.4	76.9
Some College	49.0	58.2	66.9	61.7	78.0	57.0	63.8	84.3	68.9	70.9	48.1	56.4	71.2	68.1	84.9
College Graduate	65.2	60.2	73.2	67.4	80.6	61.7	63.9	87.8	84.1	77.7	55.2	56.5	71.9	74.9	85.8

| | Fair Employment, Minority Aid | | | | | School Integration, Busing | | | | | Foreign Aid, Defense Spending | | | | |
Group	1956	1960	1964	1968	1972	1956	1960	1964	1968	1972	1956	1960	1964	1968	1972
Elementary School	47.2	45.9	68.2	62.5	63.5	50.0	35.2	63.3	61.9	67.9	40.2	39.0	51.0	46.3	46.3
High School	49.1	36.3	67.7	61.2	62.2	54.1	37.3	61.3	57.1	64.6	43.1	35.5	54.8	47.5	51.8
Some College	46.5	48.3	67.5	63.1	65.4	51.7	34.4	66.7	60.2	71.8	47.1	42.3	55.7	42.4	64.0
College Graduate	44.3	44.4	65.8	57.6	70.4	51.8	41.2	58.9	61.7	78.1	62.0	36.5	68.3	51.6	53.1

| | Consensus on Party Positions | | | | | | | | | | | | | | |
| | Education, Taxation | | | | | Medical Care | | | | | Job Guarantee | | | | |
Group	1956	1960	1964	1968	1972	1956	1960	1964	1968	1972	1956	1960	1964	1968	1972
Elementary School	65.7	71.8	86.4	75.0	63.4	70.9	75.3	92.7	84.0	75.3	68.8	78.0	90.1	82.0	75.7
High School	62.3	73.9	77.6	70.3	69.1	75.5	85.0	90.3	87.0	84.2	69.9	83.6	87.2	76.2	82.3
Some College	67.5	78.9	77.4	71.6	82.0	82.9	81.1	89.4	86.4	89.1	65.0	80.0	85.6	79.2	88.4
College Graduate	75.8	88.7	86.9	75.8	85.6	89.0	93.9	95.4	92.0	94.1	72.2	82.9	90.0	84.4	90.6

| | Fair Employment, Minority Aid | | | | | School Integration, Busing | | | | | Foreign Aid, Defense Spending | | | | |
Group	1956	1960	1964	1968	1972	1956	1960	1964	1968	1972	1956	1960	1964	1968	1972
Elementary School	49.7	53.7	91.6	79.7	71.3	45.5	51.5	87.2	84.8	69.4	46.5	47.8	88.4	84.8	75.0
High School	53.0	63.8	88.5	81.3	78.2	44.5	41.7	91.2	83.3	68.2	40.6	58.2	86.0	83.5	81.6
Some College	39.2	44.0	85.3	83.6	88.2	51.0	36.7	87.0	87.7	77.6	51.0	40.5	83.6	84.3	87.0
College Graduate	46.5	39.5	91.3	88.9	95.6	56.0	35.8	96.6	87.0	88.7	56.0	54.8	97.2	86.4	91.9

*Entries in the first half of the table are percentages of voters with opinions in each group that perceive party differences, as in Table 8.2. Entries in the second half of the table are percentages of voters in each group that select Democrats as liberal among the voters who perceive party differences, as in Table 8.3.

1972, but the level of awareness remained substantially higher in all educational strata. In one sense, therefore, the political events of this period provided a tax-free learning substitute for the political education that might otherwise have occurred in high school and college classrooms.

A final control may be made for region and race, since the changed perceptions noted above may have been concentrated in particular segments of the population. Such differences do exist, although the changes are also apparent in both the North and South, and among whites as well as blacks. The change in southern whites stands out particularly. Their perceptions vary widely over the course of the four elections, but the net result has been a notable rise in their awareness of party differences and their ideological identification of the parties. The change is greatest in their identification of the Democrats as the more liberal party on issues of civil rights. These changing perceptions may well be related to the growth of Republican voting in the white South.[14]

Blacks' opinions also vary widely, but the net result has been a substantially increased awareness of party differences and a clear identification of the Democrats as the liberal party. This change is most dramatic on civil rights issues and among southern blacks, but it is not confined to these issues or to the South. Both northern and southern blacks have become more cognizant of differences between the parties and of Democratic liberalism on economic issues. Given their perceptions of increasing differences between the parties, it is not surprising that blacks now overwhelmingly identify with and vote for the Democrats.[15]

There is no obvious demographic cause for the changed awareness of party differences by the electorate. Neither the passing of generations, nor improved education, nor regional and racial variations provides a simple explanation. The fact remains that, during these sixteen years, all segments of the population displayed considerable political learning (or misperception, depending on one's view of the "real" character of the parties). The alternative to a demographic explanation is a directly political one: the events and campaigns of the 1960s and 1970s made politics more relevant and more dramatic to the mass electorate. In the process, party differences were developed and perceived. Democrats divided from Republicans; Democrats became more liberal; and voters became more aware.

There are many correspondences between the events of the political world and the voters' perceptions of the parties. In the 1960 campaign, John Kennedy and Richard Nixon, and the Democratic and Republican platforms, differed on federal aid to education.[16] The voters consequently became more likely to regard the Democrats' position on the issue as the more liberal. Medicare became a major partisan issue during the Kennedy administration, resulting in a series of partisan congressional roll calls on the issue and a platform conflict during the 1964 campaign. Perceiving the disagreement, the voters were much more likely in 1964 to see a difference between the parties on the issue of medical care and to identify the Democrats as more favorable to governmental action on the issue. When a Republican administration acted vigorously to promote school integration, as in Little Rock, the voters tended to believe that the GOP was more favorable to this policy. This opinion was particularly common in 1956 and 1960 among southerners and blacks. When a Democratic administration came to support new civil rights legislation, when it sent marshals and National Guardsmen to desegregate the University of Alabama and the University of Mississippi, when it reacted sympathetically to the protests of Martin Luther King in Birmingham and Salem, the voters drew the conclusion that there was a difference between the parties and identified the Democrats as more favorable to the cause of the blacks. When the Republican party adopted a "southern strategy" in 1968 and its candidate largely ignored the issue of civil rights, the voters continued to hold this position and clearly to distinguish the parties.[17] When new issues of economic security, busing, and defense spending were raised in 1972, the electorate recognized the parties' programs.

The most important electoral event of this period appears to be the 1964 presidential campaign. Senator Barry Goldwater consciously sought to clarify and widen the ideological differences between the parties. The evidence presented here indicates that he accomplished his goal, although this did not benefit the Republican party. Voters, previously unable to see differences between the parties, learned the lesson of "a choice, not an echo." They accepted the senator's characterization of the Republicans as conservative and the Democrats as liberal, and, on the specific issues involved, they preferred the liberal alternative.[18] This process of political education was not confined to the insightful young, to the formally trained college population, or to committed white segregationists and black integrationists. It was general and apparently persistent.

The party characteristics that had been so clearly marked in 1964 remained relatively evident to the voters four and eight years later. The lessons remained learned even though differences between the candidates had narrowed considerably on some matters and although some of the previous issues, such as aid to education and medical care, had been partially resolved. Differences were not perceived as clearly in 1968 and 1972 as in 1964, but they were far more apparent to the voters than in the Eisenhower years. When newer matters such as busing came to the political forefront, these past lessons provided a framework for perception of the parties. Having previously characterized the Democrats as relatively liberal on economic matters such as aid to education or on racial matters such as school integration, the electorate would perceive it as more liberal on issues such as progressive taxation or busing. Clarity was further promoted when the Republicans loudly proclaimed their opposition to these new policies. Thus, a new potential basis for American voting has been established. Its full development, however, depends on the parties more than on the voters.

THE DEVELOPMENT OF IDEOLOGY

Along with a clearer view of the political parties, voters over the past decade have also clarified their own political ideas. Their "political consciousness" has been raised, so that they are now better able to place issues into a general and coherent framework, to see parties in that framework, and to respond electorally on the basis of particular issues, as well as more general and ideological stances.

The conventional wisdom about American voters has been that they lack a coherent ideological viewpoint. While radicals have been upset at the lack of ideological consciousness on the part of the electorate, defenders of American political tradition have seen the absence of an ideological public as one of the major sources of the political stability in the United States.[19]

The assumed nonideological character of the electorate empirically is based on research primarily conducted in the 1950s, when the benign administration of Dwight Eisenhower seemed to quiet divisions within the electorate. The cold war eased with the achievement of a truce in the Korean war, but Americans still faced an obvious and formidable foreign threat. Republican acceptance of the progressive legislation of the New Deal moderated domestic political conflict, and the absence of new policy initiatives restricted disagreement. A pervasive national consensus on social and personal goals was unassailed by countercultures or radical critiques.

In this environment, voters had little reason to think seriously about politics. Consequently, few persons introduced general or philosophic ideas to their discussions of politics. When asked their likes and dislikes of the parties and candidates, voters gave shallow answers. In a careful review of each interview, Converse was able to classify less than 3 percent of the electorate as clearly ideological. Relaxing his standards, he was able to add another 9 percent of the citizenry, or 12 percent of the actual voters, as "near-ideologues." Even this classification was quite generous to the respondents. Virtually anyone using such terms as "liberal" or "conservative" was included, except for obviously unknowledgeable persons as the college graduate who, "when asked what she meant in styling herself as 'liberalist,' replied that she liked *both* of the parties."[20]

The bulk of the electorate did not fit in this category. Rather, most persons viewed the political world in terms of "group benefits" and the "nature of the times," with the parties and candidates praised because they favored the interests of workers or farmers, or condemned for bringing war and depression. These voter reactions were largely reflections of short-term factors and were rarely placed in a broader ideological perspective.[21]

The ideological consciousness of the voters can also be gauged more directly, by assessing their responses to particular issues. Using data from the same era, Converse later tested the degree to which responses on issues evidenced "constraint." If their responses constituted a constrained, coherent belief system, voters would show similar positions on similar issues. A person who favored federal aid to housing would be expected also to favor federal programs of full employment.

Applying this test to the actual beliefs of the citizenry from 1956 to 1960, Converse found very low levels of constraint.[22] Persons who favored one program of government activity were hardly more likely than others to favor another such program. Moreover, opinions changed during short periods of time—two to four years—and in no systematic fashion. Indeed, for one set of opinions, the changes observed could be explained best as being purely random, rather than following any clear pattern.

The findings of the low level of ideological awareness of the electorate became widely accepted in the early 1960s and were seen by some as a threat to the very continuance of democracy.[23] Whether or not one is personally happy with these conclusions, they were largely validated by the data and methods available at the time. But the times did change, even as one textbook after another was published, each proclaiming that no more than 15 percent of the electorate could be regarded as ideological.

After the 1950s, events made politics more salient, and an increased voter consciousness became more likely. The most profound questions of individual liberty and equality were raised by the civil rights movement; basic constitutional issues were brought to the fore by the Vietnam conflict; moral problems became politically significant with the advent of a new generation and its disquieting life-styles. The very language of American politics changed in the 1960s, as "alienation" replaced "consensus," "Negroes" was supplanted by "blacks," and "go along" gave way to "turn on."

As politics has become more pressing and more relevant, Americans have developed a more coherent, constrained belief system. Of particular interest in this regard is the work of Nie and Andersen, who have precisely replicated the methods of Converse, while employing data from the 1960s and 1970s. The general level of ideological constraint has risen considerably during this period, as seen in a substantial increase in the correlations between positions on different issues. In regard to issues of substantially different content, from foreign policy to racial integration, the average coefficient has increased from a bare .14 in 1946 to .38 in 1972. Using only domestic issues, the average correlation between issues has doubled, to .49.[24]

The voters now do make the logical connections between attitudes on war and welfare, or on school integration and aid to education; and this new coherence of mass beliefs is evident even on such disparate questions as civil liberties and crime. Furthermore, and paralleling the findings above, this change cannot be explained by increased levels of education, for the increased consistency in mass attitudes actually has tended to be greater among persons of lower education.[25]

These changes must be seen as a remarkable development of popular political consciousness. Its dramatic quality is seen in Table 8.6, Nie and Andersen's comparison of recent mass attitudes with those of congressional candidates in 1958, a highly informed and articulate group. Greater issue constraint is found in the general public after 1964 than among the presumedly sophisticated activists of an earlier period. This growth of public political awareness must be attributed to the new environment of American life. "The political events of the last decade, and the crisis atmosphere which has attended them, have caused citizens to perceive politics as increasingly central to their lives."[26]

TABLE 8.6 / COMPARISON OF LEVELS OF ATTITUDE CONSISTENCY BETWEEN ELITES AND MASS PUBLIC*

	Index of Attitude Consistency Within Domestic Issues	Index of Consistency Between Domestic and Foreign Issues	Overall Index of Attitude Consistency
Congressional Candidates, 1958	.38	.25	.31
Mass Public, 1956	.24	−.01	.14
Mass Public, 1958	.23	−.07	.17
Mass Public, 1960	.24	−.04	.13
Mass Public, 1964	.49	.29	.41
Mass Public, 1968	.51	.23	.40
Mass Public, 1971	.51	.24	.38
Mass Public, 1972	.49	.27	.38

Source: Norman Nie, with Kristi Andersen, "Mass Belief Systems Revisited: Political Change and Attitude Structure," Journal of Politics, XXXVI (August, 1974), 566.
*Entries are the average gamma correlations among designated issues for the groups listed. High correlations show high levels of constraint.

The voters now have a clearer ideological framework in their own minds and are more able to apply such constructs to the political parties. Previously, such terms as "liberal" and "conservative" had little meaning to the voters. More recently, however, these descriptions have been applied by voters to the parties. Paralleling the increased consensus on the parties' attitudes toward specific issues, there has been an increased consensus on the parties' general placement on an ideological scale.

In three of the last four elections, the voters have been asked about the relative conservatism of the Democrats and Republicans. In 1960, when political conflict was still limited, the voters were uncertain. As seen in Table 8.7, partisanship significantly affected their replies. Almost half of the Democrats claimed the conservative mantle for their own party, or saw no difference between the parties, while about three-fourths of Republicans insisted on the greater moderation of the GOP.

TABLE 8.7 / PARTISANSHIP AND PARTIES' PERCEIVED IDEOLOGICAL POSITIONS*

	1960					1968					1972				
	SD	WD	I	WR	SR	SD	WD	I	WR	SR	SD	WD	I	WR	SR
Democrats More Conservative	19.9	15.2	7.8	6.2	0.7	13.9	9.9	8.6	4.0	4.5	16.5	12.5	8.4	5.7	6.3
No Difference Between Parties	27.3	33.3	24.9	23.6	21.5	22.1	36.4	27.9	28.1	14.9	5.9	17.8	21.1	9.1	8.8
Republicans More Conservative	29.5	31.2	46.2	49.2	37.5	27.0	32.9	42.8	51.3	36.5	32.0	40.2	39.5	38.7	37.7
Republicans Much More Conservative	23.2	20.4	21.1	21.1	40.3	37.1	20.9	20.6	16.6	44.0	45.7	29.5	31.0	46.4	47.2
(N)	(366)	(442)	(398)	(242)	(288)	(267)	(335)	(383)	(199)	(134)	(188)	(343)	(478)	(209)	(159)
			G = .23					G = .07					G = .09		

*Percentages add vertically by columns to 100 percent, except for rounding errors.
SD = Strong Democrat; WD = Weak Democrat; I = independent; WR = Weak Republican; SR = Strong Republican

By the end of the period, however, the character of the parties was more clearly defined. The proportion of Democrats claiming conservatism for their party or seeing no difference was halved by 1972. There was a general consensus that the Republicans were less liberal, and indeed that there was a considerable partisan difference. As shown by the almost insignificant gamma correlations, there is now virtually no association between partisanship and ideological characterizations of the parties.[27]

These clear views of the parties are relatively unclouded by the voter's own ideology. Less than a fifth of conservative Democrats delude themselves in 1972 that their party is more conservative than the Republicans, and only an eighth of the spartan band of liberal Republicans believe that their own party is their rightful ideological home. For the most part, voters of all ideological persuasions know where they belong.

Furthermore, most voters not only know their place, but are in the right place. More than four times as many liberals are in the Democratic party as are Republicans, while there are half again as many conservatives in the GOP as in the opposition. The matching of ideology and partisanship is even greater among the strong partisans and, as discussed in Chapter 5, among the young. Because similar questions were not asked in earlier surveys, we cannot determine if these matchings have increased recently. The other data of this chapter, however, surely suggest that the electorate increasingly sees the parties as means of expressing both its specific and general attitudes toward political questions.

THE FUTURE OF PARTY POLITICS

The American electorate today shows an increasing sophistication and a potential for clear political choice. Mass belief systems are internally coherent and constrained. The voters do see differences between the parties, both on general ideology and on particular issues. At appropriate times, they align their party loyalty to their issue preferences. A link has been forged that can promote a "responsible party" system, in which the parties put forth programs, receive popular approval of these programs, and then carry out the popular mandate.[28]

Despite the major changes that have taken place in the electorate, however, the linkage is not fully tempered. While there has been an enormous increase in issue consciousness, and in the effect of issues on the vote, the connection to the political parties is still weak. Indeed, there is an apparent disjunction between voter choices in the voting booth and their reactions to the parties between which they choose.

In the vote itself, issues are becoming more important. Two indications of the change may be cited among the many data that are available. In 1972, the Democratic candidate received 72 percent of the vote from persons who favored government medical insurance, but only 30 percent from those who opposed the program. By contrast, there was only a difference of 25 percent among 1956 Democratic and Republican voters relative to this issue.[29] More generally, the correlation between issue positions and the ballot has risen substantially. In 1956, the average correlation with the vote over all policy areas was only .16. Rising precipitously to .58 in 1964, it remained high, at .53, in 1972.[30]

At the same time, however, the party connection to political decisions has weakened. The citizenry seems to be unconcerned with party organizations. Not only are there more Independents, but the substantive "images" of parties, as developed in Chapter 7, are less defined and increasingly neutral. Voters are not ignorant about the Democratic and Republican appeals, but disdainful. While they show more awareness of issues, and even of party stands on issues, they do not consistently adjust their loyalties accordingly. Particularly in 1972, as we have seen, there is decreased correspondence between party loyalty and such established issues as medical care and school integration.

Accordingly, the electoral impact of parties has dropped. This decline is not only evident in the falling impact of party identification on the vote, but even in the lessened effect of party images that are freer of a purely traditional component. As one of the established institutions of the nation, the party system has been included in the general alienation from traditional politics. Voters make a direct connection between their policy preference and their ballots, but omit any connecting link to the parties.[31]

An independent analysis of the evaluative dimensions used in Chapter 7 confirms this conclusion. In this study, the electoral effect of party loyalties and of perceived party positions on issues is found to have decreased from 1952 to 1972, while the relative importance of attitudes toward the candidates has increased. The greater importance of candidate orientations is not simply a reflection of a candidate's personality, but also of attributes more directly related to his likely performance in office—his administrative ability and experience—and his attitudes on the questions of foreign and domestic policy. Thus, "the impact of issues on the vote has increased during the 1960's and early 1970's—yet these issues are linked and responsive to candidate images."[32]

The American electorate today seems clear about where it stands and where the parties stand, and apparently separates these perceptions increasingly when it votes. It understands the parties more, but finds them less salient to its concerns. Seen as not relevant, parties are bypassed, with the voters making their choices on the basis of their own issue preferences and those of the candidates. An essential link for continuing democratic control of the government is being eroded.

The development of a complete system of political accountability requires that the parties be restored to a central place. Only through the permanent organizations of parties can the voters exercise a continuing control, rather than sporadically intervening to favor one candidate over another, or voicing a preference for a particular and transient set of issues. Electoral accountability demands that Democrats, rather than Lyndon Johnson, be held accountable for Vietnam, and that Republicans, rather than Richard Nixon, be brought to political judgment for Watergate.

Reconstruction of the parties is chiefly the task of the parties and their leaders. They can promote the necessary congruence between the issues voters emphasize and their perceptions of the parties. They can emphasize those issues on which the electorate is now aligned along partisan lines, such as guaranteed employment. Alternatively, they can change their emphases to speak to emergent questions and to structure the citizenry's growing issue consciousness. Or they can fully atrophy.

For their part, voters have shown themselves ready to respond, to realign their loyalties, to comprehend abstract belief systems, and to fit their votes to their ideology. Their response depends on the stimuli they receive from the political environment. If these stimuli are issueless and static, as they largely were in the 1950s, the citizenry is likely to react in like manner. If these stimuli are seen as irrelevant, the link drawn to the parties will be weak, as in 1972. If the stimuli are more ideological and dynamic, on the other hand, we are likely to see different perceptions and behavior, such as that evidenced in the 1964 and 1968 elections. Confused voters reflect confused parties; clarity among the voters follows from clearheaded parties.

FROM CONFUSION TO CLARITY: FINDINGS

1. In contrast to the past, party loyalty and policy views are significantly related.

    1a. These differences are most evident on economic and racial issues.

2. Over time, the parties have come to be seen as different from one another.

    2a. The perception of party differences first becomes evident in the 1964 election and continues through 1972.

3. In contrast to the past, there is consensus in the electorate on the relatively more "liberal" position of the Democratic party on specific issues.

    3a. These perceptions remain even when partisanship is controlled.

    3b. These perceptions continue through the 1972 election.

4. Changed perceptions of the parties cannot be explained by generational differences.

5. Increased education in the United States cannot explain the changed perceptions of the parties.

5a. The growth in awareness of party differences has been greatest among persons of limited formal education.

6. Both blacks and whites, regardless of region, have become more aware of party differences.

7. Political events are the most likely explanation of changed perceptions.

8. In contrast to the past, voters show considerable ideological coherence in their attitudes.

9. The electorate now has a clearer perception of the general ideological character of the major parties.

   9a. This perception is unaffected by the voter's own partisanship or personal ideology.

   9b. Partisanship and ideological position are now largely congruent.

10. The effect of issues on the vote has risen considerably, while the effect of partisanship has decreased.

CHAPTER 9

VARIABILITY IN ELECTORAL BEHAVIOR*

Our search for "the" American voter has been fruitless. There is no single voter, nor any simple explanation of electoral behavior. While affected by their partisanship and their social characteristics, Americans are not permanently controlled by these factors. Instead, there is a substantial responsiveness in their actions. Ballot choices are significantly influenced by the voters' concerns, their evaluations of the parties, and their own policy preferences.

Variability is the most constant feature of electoral behavior, as it is a persistent characteristic of social life. The nation reacts to its political environment. The voters of 1956 respond to a static politics, in which the "great issues" are given an official funeral; public questions do not touch individual lives; and party divisions are obscure. The voters of more recent times also respond—but now to a time in which war, race, freedom, and conscience are evocative symbols; issues spur action; and parties differ.

Given these new stimuli, the citizenry has exhibited greater capacity. Previous findings of low mass interest and knowledge were interpreted as evidence of the public's "inherent limitations."[1] In later years, however, the public has shown considerable understanding of issues and awareness of party positions, and an increased susceptibility to voting on the basis of these issue positions.[2]

Because the context of elections varies considerably, it is dangerous to

---

*Mark Schulman has provided most of the data analysis and interpretation in this chapter.

reach general conclusions about voter behavior from a single event. Reliance on "synchronic" data, that derived from one election, presents two related problems. The first and most general problem is that such analyses tend to provide a view of society "suspended at a given moment, giving the illusion of a static structure that may be quite at variance with both theory and reality."[3] Different behavior existing in different circumstances cannot be discovered in these analyses. Thus, time itself is disregarded as a variable of possible explanatory power.

This problem is illustrated by contrasting findings of cross-sectional surveys of a single election with the findings of time-series investigations, which use official results from a series of elections. The latter studies have indicated a high degree of voter dynamism and responsiveness, with perhaps half of American presidential elections considered as "deviating" from stable patterns.[4] Yet analyses of single elections have cast aspersions on the ability of the electorate to think coherently and understand issues, to discern party differences on issues, and to free itself from traditional party loyalty.

These contrasting conclusions point to the second problem resulting from reliance on synchronic data, that of overgeneralization from time-bound results. The tendency to draw long-term inferences from such data is evident in the major work in the field, whose authors conclude that "the relationships in our data reflect primarily the role of enduring partisan commitments in shaping attitudes toward politics."[5] Yet, as one of these authors later mused, such conclusions may have been a chance product of selecting static campaigns for investigation.[6] The original finding, while accurate for 1952 and 1956, may well have been a time-bound description rather than a continuing reality. Static description inadvertently can become mixed with general explanation.

With the extensive accumulation of survey data, these problems can be met. Surveys can serve, to some extent, as a continuing data source to test general hypotheses in varying empirical situations. Theory can then be focused on the analysis of stability and change in the relationships between different variables over time. The unit of analysis becomes the particular election, rather than the individual voter.

In this chapter, the emphasis will be on comparative analysis of similar questions in different electoral contexts. These comparisons, however, must avoid a third problem, the tendency for methodological innovation to be joined with the use of synchronic data. The first findings on the limited and dependent character of the electorate were founded on data developed through use of valid but limited techniques. Spurred both by the political context and their own normative concerns, later analysts became concerned that a demeaning portrait of the voter would result in scornful leadership. V. O. Key warned of politicians' possible response: "If they see voters as most certainly responsive to nonsense, they will give them nonsense. If they see voters as susceptible to delusion, they will delude them."[7]

With new research, the later analysts have come to endorse the essential rationality of the electorate. However, their findings are often based on new methods that limit clear comparisons to earlier conclusions reached through other techniques. Thus, one author argues that preworded, preselected issue questions used in previous studies may have depressed issue-voting relationships existing in the data.[8] Multidimensional scaling of attitudes has been employed to detect the coherence of voter attitudes on a series of questions,[9] while computer simulation has been used to test their basic rationality.[10] Upon using a different technique, one which deals with the comparative similarity in the issues positions of candidates and voters, electoral rationality is found to be considerably higher than in previous studies.[11]

Such innovative findings may reflect only innovative procedures. In themselves, new techniques would not invalidate previous conclusions, or necessitate a focus on changed temporal circumstances. A meaningful comparison requires that similar data be investigated by similar methods, in this way isolating the effect of differences in the political environment.[12] Since sets of election data are never precise duplicates of one another, variables must be carefully selected. Methods change frequently, therefore methodological strategies must be carefully chosen to enhance comparability.

Two kinds of comparisons are made in this chapter. First, the single issue of Vietnam is isolated in 1968 and 1972, and its effect on the vote observed. Second, all of the variables previously analyzed in this book are combined, using the complex technique of causal path analysis, in an effort to trace their relative importance. In both of these comparisons, we will see the critical effect of the electoral context and of the clarity of choice presented by Republican and Democratic candidates.

VIETNAM AND THE VOTE

American involvement in Vietnam was the major campaign issue in both 1968 and 1972, and can therefore provide a critical test of the influence of issues on electoral behavior and of the effect of different electoral circumstances. In this analysis, we will examine the relationship of a voter's own position to his ballot choice. Other variables, however, can facilitate or interfere with this relationship. Perceptions of the candidates and their policy positions may be clear or confused. Partisanship may cause distorted vision. Sex affects issues involving the use of force, as suggested in Chapter 4. All of these factors must be taken into account.

For opinions on Vietnam to have an actual influence on the vote, two links must be established. The voters must see the candidates as representing identifiable positions on the war, and then they must actually vote for that candidate whom they perceive to represent their opinions. Although these links were indeed forged by the voters in both elections, clear perceptions were far less common in the earlier one. As a result, the relationship of opinion and the vote is weaker in 1968 than in 1972.

Unclear perceptions of the candidates in 1968, the first Vietnam-oriented election, resulted from the candidates' deliberate similarity. Both Hubert Humphrey and Richard Nixon were consistent in their positions—but consistently alike—with neither tending to favor either of the clear options of withdrawal or escalation. "Taken as a whole, the Vietnam positions of both candidates amounted to advocacy of war as usual, with a rather gradual de-escalation of American effort if and when certain conditions were met."[13]

The campaign situation was quite different in 1972, when the major nominees emphasized distinct positions on Vietnam. George McGovern called for immediate withdrawal from Southeast Asia, while Richard Nixon defended his policy of extended negotiations and continued military intervention. The party platforms endorsed these conflicting positions, offering the electorate two definite options. The Democrats pledged "an immediate and complete withdrawal of all U.S. forces in Indochina. All U.S. military action in Southeast Asia will cease." The Republicans were less pacific: "we stand unequivocally at the side of the President in his effort to negotiate honorable terms, and in his refusal to accept terms which would dishonor this country." Continued military involvement was forecast, until a final treaty.[14]

These differing stimuli brought corresponding differences in popular reaction. In 1968, the voters found it difficult to distinguish the two major candidates. Respondents were asked to place the nominees on the seven-point Vietnam Action Scale (Table 4.5), with alternatives ranging from withdrawal to additional force. Table 9.1 presents the average score attributed to each candidate by the voters. In 1968, these scores are very similar.

TABLE 9.1 / PERCEIVED POSITIONS OF CANDIDATES ON VIETNAM, 1968 AND 1972*

	Men			Women		
	1968 Less Interested	1968 More Interested	1972	1968 Less Interested	1968 More Interested	1972
Humphrey-McGovern	4.30	3.95	2.15	4.22	4.09	2.53
Nixon	4.48	4.41	4.53	4.24	4.46	4.43
Wallace	5.59	5.86		5.24	5.68	
Voters' Position	4.60	4.64	3.83	3.91	3.95	3.50
(N)	(309)	(243)	(465)	(386)	(304)	(597)

*Entries are the average score given to candidates on the seven-point Vietnam Action Scale.

With their vision blurred, voters tended also to project their own policy preferences onto the presidential aspirants. Whatever their own position, voters in 1968 rationalized that the major candidates agreed with that position. For example, among men who placed themselves on positions 1-3 on the Vietnam scale, 40 percent also saw Hubert Humphrey at that end of the scale, and only 29 percent saw him as a hawk (positions 5-7). The figures are exactly reversed among men who regarded themselves as hawks, with 40 percent considering Humphrey relatively forceful and 29 percent placing him at the softer position. Women tended toward even greater cognitive consistency between their own position and their perception of Humphrey, while both sexes tended to interpret Richard Nixon's position in similarly congruent fashion. There is less bias in the voters' perceptions of Wallace, particularly among women.[15]

We find greater clarity among these voters when we distinguish between those giving greater or lesser emphasis to the Vietnam issue. Those who were more concerned with Vietnam could discern at least some distance between Humphrey and Nixon, and clearly regarded Wallace as extreme. At least among these voters, the basis for a policy-relevant vote did exist. However, even they showed only limited differences in their characterizations of the candidates, as well as distorted and rationalized perceptions.

In 1972, by contrast, voters of all persuasions and of both sexes were agreed on the positions of the candidates. In Table 9.1, there is considerable difference between the average ratings of McGovern and Nixon on the Vietnam scale. While these perceptions of the candidates were somewhat affected by the voters' own preferences, the biases are not extreme, particularly among women. Of female doves, 69 percent believed McGovern held a similar position, while only 5 percent saw him as a hawk. Of the sparse female hawks, only 5 percent believed that McGovern agreed with them, while 76 percent characterized him as tending to favor withdrawal. Views of Nixon were subject to more distortion, particularly among men, but all groups placed the former president toward the more aggressive end of the scale.

Between the two contests, the electorate achieved a clear choice. In 1968, in a direct comparison of Humphrey and Nixon, relatively few could separate the candidates, and even those "who saw a big difference were quite unable to agree which candidate was more of a hawk, and which more of a dove."[16] When the same measure was applied to 1972 responses, as in Table 9.2, the voters did distinguish the candidates, and the vast majority placed McGovern at the relatively more dovish position.[17]

Sex made no difference in these perceptions of the candidates in 1972. Less than 6 percent of the men and 9 percent of the women believed McGovern was more of a hawk than Nixon, while 73 percent of the men

TABLE 9.2 / PERCEIVED DIFFERENCES BETWEEN CANDIDATES ON VIETNAM, 1968 AND 1972*

		1968	Scale Difference	1972		
Humphrey More Hawkish	17%	1%	6	2%	9%	McGovern More Hawkish
		0	5	1		
		1	4	2		
		6	3	2		
		9	2	2		
Difference Slight or Nonexistent	57%	11	1	3	19%	Difference Slight or Nonexistent
		29	0	10		
		18	−1	6		
Nixon More Hawkish	26%	14	−2	12	72%	McGovern More Hawkish
		9	−3	22		
		2	−4	18		
		0	−5	10		
		1	−6	10		

*Entries are the percentages of respondents seeing a given amount of difference between the two candidates on the Vietnam Action Scale. Percentages add vertically by columns to 100 percent.

and 61 percent of the women believed him to be more of a dove. Among those who actually voted, nearly 90 percent of men and over 80 percent of women saw McGovern as more dovish.

Clarity is necessary for a policy-oriented vote. The choice in 1968 between Nixon and Humphrey lacked such clarity and was completely uncorrelated to policy preference on Vietnam.[18] If ballots for Wallace are included, as in Table 4.6 above, an association between issue and the vote does become evident, but only among those who are more interested. In 1972, however, there is a clear relationship between issue choice and candidate choice (G = .62).

Policy voting seems evident in 1972 on the Vietnam issue. It is theoretically possible, however, that these correlations are due to rather different processes. One possibility is rationalization, by which voters misperceive a candidate's position as agreeing with their own. Such distortions were quite evident in 1968, but the 1972 data exclude this explanation. Another possible process is persuasion, by which voters change their opinion on an issue to conform with that of the candidate they prefer for other reasons. This possibility cannot be excluded on the basis of these data. On an issue like Vietnam, however, such massive alteration of views during the 1972 campaign seems unlikely. The question was of long standing by this time, it had been fiercely argued, and it was of primary importance to the voters. It would be difficult to change popular opinion rapidly in these circumstances.[19]

To this point, we have considered only the direct relationship of position on Vietnam and the vote. However, there is another way to evaluate this relationship, by including perceptions of the relative positions of the candidates. In the real world, voters must consider not only their own positions, but also must relate their stands to those of the party nominees. The individual cannot just vote for withdrawal or escalation in Vietnam. Rather, he must seek to find the candidate whose position most closely matches his own. To examine this process, "proximity" measures have been created. Of particular interest is the measure of "relative proximity: how close is a voter to a particular candidate or party on a given dimension, relative to how close he sees himself as being to the other candidates or parties on the same dimension."[20]

When this measure is employed, the war issue shows major impact on the vote, even in 1968. "Surprisingly, upon refining relative proximities to account for the relative distances that citizens perceived between candidates, Vietnam policy turns out to be a major correlate of candidate choice." Using multiple regression, this factor explains about a fourth of the variance in the presidential vote.[21] In 1972, again employing the measure of relative proximity, the same strong relationship exists, with almost 30 percent of the vote accounted for by the perceived closeness of voters to candidates on the question of Vietnam.

Relying on the relative proximity of the issues, however, may not contribute to an effective vote. Since the candidate's positions were unclear, a dove on Vietnam might have voted with equal reason for either Nixon or Humphrey. Conversely, the two candidates may have received the support of voters of all persuasions. Rationalization was likely, and there was no clear message transmitted to public officials. In this confused situation, policy voting "has significance only at the level of individual choice. Variable perceptions of candidates subvert the popular control of public policy."[22] Vietnam certainly affected the vote in 1968, but this vote could not mandate the nation's future policy.

Four years later, with the candidates presenting clear differences, the effect of Vietnam is apparent even when the simplest techniques are used for analysis. The correlation between policy position and vote is almost as explanatory as that between relative proximity on the issue and the vote.[23] The necessity for rationalization, and its probability, are sharply limited when candidates offer a comprehensible choice. In 1972, both men and women voted according to their policy views on Vietnam, with the previous sexual difference on war minimized by political clarity.

The varying impact of Vietnam can be seen further if we introduce the factor of party identification. Partisanship, rather than policy position alone, could be the real explanation for these statistical associations. In other words, Democrats might be both doves and Humphrey or McGovern voters, while Republicans might be both hawks and Nixonites. To see the influence of policy position alone, we need to control for Republican and Democratic loyalties.

In Table 9.3, we see the effect of both policy position and partisanship. Their relative importance is quite different in the two elections. In 1968, there is very little effect, within partisan groupings, of opinion on Vietnam. Humphrey received only slightly greater support from the doves in his party than the hawks, while Republicans of all orientations endorsed Nixon's candidacy.

In 1972, there is less partisan influence and more direct impact of policy views. Republicans were still primarily affected by their party ties; but there was a noticeable effect of the war issue on the choices of Independents, and Democrats showed particular sensitivity. The critical effect of Vietnam in 1972 was to sharpen policy polarization in the majority party, strengthening the McGovern vote among the party's doves and stimulat-

TABLE 9.3 / PARTISANSHIP, OPINION ON VIETNAM, AND THE VOTE*

	1968 Policy Position		
	Withdrawal	**Neutral**	**Force**
Partisanship			
Democratic	79.8	72.6	63.5
	(124)	(143)	(162)
Independent	40.3	30.5	15.0
	(67)	(72)	(113)
Republican	11.3	5.2	4.8
	(79)	(77)	(104)
Total	50.2	44.4	32.9
	(270)	(292)	(379)

	1972 Policy Position		
	Withdrawal	**Neutral**	**Force**
Partisanship			
Democratic	75.8	46.5	30.2
	(311)	(144)	(142)
Independent	54.1	23.5	13.3
	(207)	(102)	(150)
Republican	14.7	5.6	1.1
	(122)	(125)	(180)
Total	56.9	26.3	13.6
	(640)	(371)	(472)

*Cell entries are percentages voting for the Democratic candidate, Humphrey in 1968 or McGovern in 1972. Numbers in parentheses are the totals on which the percentages are based.

ing defection among its hawks. A multiple regression on the vote leads to the same conclusion. While the correlation of vote and partisanship declined in this period, the impact of Vietnam opinion increased substantially.[24] A distinct alternative allowed voters in 1972 to make a definite decision affected by policy views, while earlier ambiguity required them to rely more on their traditional loyalties in reaching ballot choice.

By comparing the impact of Vietnam in 1968 and 1972, we have again seen the critical importance of the political context. Deaths were as frequent in Southeast Asia during one campaign as the next, and the voters gave primary attention to the issue in both elections. Their national leaders, however, frustrated a direct expression of citizen views in 1968, while they facilitated such expression in 1972. Given the opportunity, the electorate made its choice as responsive voters.

THE CAUSES OF THE VOTE

The second kind of comparison in this chapter is more complex, involving the technique of causal path analysis. Statistically, this method is an extension of simple correlation and multiple regression, as used previously in this book. In these previous methods, however, we dealt with only one dependent variable at a time, seeking explanations for such factors as party identification or presidential vote. In causal analysis, we test hypotheses and models that involve a sequence of variables, which may be related to one another in a variety of ways. For example, we try to analyze together the combined effects of social class on partisanship, class on the vote, and partisanship on the vote. Before proceeding with the causal path analysis, however, we need to explain the method, the variables, and the data used.[25]

Strictly speaking, causal analysis does not explain relationships. More exactly, it permits a test of hypothesized relationships among variables, as summarized in a statistical model. A model is an abstraction, a selection of a limited number of influences from the many causal agents that exist in the real world. Through exercising this selectivity, we can concentrate on the most critical factors, rather than seeking to explain everything. "By using such abstract models, the scientist can then make certain predictions about what should occur under given conditions. He then returns to the world of reality and attempts to assess how well his predictions work."[26] After this, the model can be retained or modified.

Once the model is tentatively validated, the next step is to assess the relative strength of the different variables in the model. We will seek to discover not only whether class and partisanship affect the vote, but the proportionate impact of each variable, or the combined direct and indirect effect of class. In a more exact sense than employed metaphorically in

Chapter 3, we can evaluate the importance of each of the "base paths" in the "baseball diamond" of voting. The technique of causal path analysis offers a number of advantages. It provides a convenient summary of complex relationships among a number of variables. For each election, analyzed separately, the technique has the further quality of summarizing relationships among variables in one time period. Furthermore, by comparing elections, causal path analysis permits us to designate variables as relatively stable or relatively changeable in their effects over time.

We must also recognize, however, that there are some critical and even questionable assumptions involved in this technique. The most important is that causation is assumed to be one-way. To employ this technique we must make a reasoned judgment on the direction of causality. Presidential vote, for example, is the dependent variable in this analysis, and we therefore assume that issues and partisanship influence the vote, but are not reciprocally influenced by the ballot choice. In the real world, it is possible that people change their issue positions and even their party loyalty to conform with their vote. Because our basic purpose is to explain the vote, we will proceed to ignore the latter possibility, but we must acknowledge the existence of alternative interpretations.[27]

The usefulness of our model is increased by a deliberate replication of previous research. In this analysis, we will use a model that has been modified from an earlier work on national elections.[28] Since the variables employed encompass all of the various topics we have investigated, this analysis serves as a summary of the preceding chapters. We have considered the effects of parental tradition and inherited partisanship; of demographic factors such as class, sex, age, region, and race; and of political factors, such as party identification, evaluation of candidates, and position on the issues. All of these influences will be included in the causal analysis. The last variable in the hypothesized chain is the basic electoral behavior, the vote for president.

Specifically, seven variables are included in the analysis:[29]

1. Family Socioeconomic Partisan Predispositions. This factor is a measure of the likely partisanship of a respondent's father or mother, whoever was more interested in politics. It is based on the parent's race, religion, region, place of residence, and social class identification. The prototype of a Republican partisan would be a parent who was a white Protestant living in a northern small town and self-identified as middle class.

2. Family Party Identification. The remembered party loyalty—Republican, Independent, or Democratic—of the parent more interested in politics.

3. Respondent's Socioeconomic Partisan Predispositions. As in the first variable, this measure gauges the likely partisanship of the voter himself, based on the five demographic characteristics.

4. Respondent's Party Identification. The present partisanship—Republican, Independent, or Democratic.

5. Partisan Issues Index. This variable gauges the likelihood of an individual's vote on the basis of his positions on the five issues most frequently mentioned by the national sample as affecting its choices in a given election. For example, persons who took a dovish position on Vietnam, and who were in accord with Democratic voters on the other issues emphasized in 1972, would be expected to have voted for McGovern.

6. Candidate Evaluation. The open-ended responses considered in Chapter 7 are employed here, specifically the responses to questions concerning voters' "likes" and "dislikes" of the party nominees. The measure summarizes these feelings as relatively favorable to one or the other candidate. It is calculated as a simple arithmetic sum of pro-Republican and anti-Democratic candidate evaluations, *minus* the total of pro-Democratic and anti-Republican candidate evaluations.[30] References to issues and parties are excluded.

7. Respondent's Vote. Republican or Democratic.[31]

The issue variable presents the greatest problem in this analysis. A measure is needed which includes issues that are salient to each election, which is comparable among elections, and which is little subject to voter rationalization. Open-ended inquiries on the salient issues are not available in all of the surveys. Similarly, scales measuring the "proximity" of respondents and the candidates are another recent innovation, and are subject to considerable rationalization as well. Limiting ourselves to those few questions asked in all surveys could result in the inclusion of past issues that have faded from the "zone of relevance"[32] and the exclusion of such vital, but latter-day, questions as Vietnam. To include all questions asked would be excessive, while excluding issues not included in the interview schedule.

The approach adopted here establishes an issue-selection criterion based upon the five issues mentioned most frequently in the series of open-ended questions, common to all surveys, about what the respondent likes and dislikes about candidates and parties. The Partisan Issues Index then is constructed from the respondent's position on the closed-ended equivalents of those issues. The selection criterion achieves comparability over time, therefore, with the issues selected being clearly salient to each election.[33] Furthermore, by use of the respondent's actual issue position, the index specifically excludes rationalization, whereby the voter projects his own issue stand upon the candidate he favors. An artificial inflating of the correspondence between issue position and the vote is avoided.[34]

The variables are ordered as follows: (1) Family Socioeconomic Partisan Predispositions; (2) Family Party Identification; (3) Respondent's Socioeconomic Partisan Predispositions; (4) Respondent's Party Identification;

(5) Partisan Issues Index; (6) Candidate Evaluation; (7) Respondent's Vote. While the correct ordering of variables cannot be determined by statistical derivation, the variable ordering follows established practice and theory. Party identification temporally precedes the issues and candidates of a particular election, as has been shown in past electoral research and socialization studies.[35] Issues, in turn, tend to be more long-standing than the particular candidates running in a given election.[36] In our particular cases, moreover, some of the issues are present in more than one election, while there is no overlap of candidates.

The order of variables is important because of the assumption that causation runs in only one direction.[37] Therefore, variables that are placed earlier in the sequence are assumed to be unaffected by variables that are later in the sequence. By placing the parent's partisanship before the respondent's, we assume that children may be influenced by their father's or mother's party loyalty, but that parents will not be affected by their children's partisanship. In this particular instance, the assumption seems reasonable, but the conclusion is not so clear in other cases. While party identification certainly contributes to issue positions, the reverse relationship could also hold. The ordering of the variables, however, is that which is most logical and most widely accepted. Substantive conclusions would not be changed by reasonable alternative models.

After ordering the variables, the impact of each one is assessed through a series of multiple regressions. The quantitative measure of this impact is the "path coefficient." Statistically, these coefficients are equivalent to the beta weights we have employed earlier. Pictorially, they are placed on the "paths" which trace the causal influences on the vote, as can be seen in Figures 9.1 to 9.3. The path coefficients are derived through a two-step procedure. First, each possible connection between variables is assessed, and those connections that fail to reach statistical significance are eliminated.[38] Then, each variable in the path model is treated as the dependent variable in a multiple regression, with beta weights, or path coefficients, calculated for the variables for which there is a single direct path to that dependent variable. The complication here is that we are dealing not with one dependent variable, but a series. Thus, the respondent's party identification is dependent on social characteristics and parental partisanship. In turn, his partisanship becomes an influence on the later dependent variables—issue position, candidate evaluation, and the vote.

The data for this analysis are drawn from three recent presidential elections. The first is the 1956 contest between Eisenhower and Stevenson. This election has been a basic source for leading works of electoral analysis.[39] From its data flow findings on the low salience of issues to the mass public, the central role of partisanship in shaping perceptions and the vote, and the importance of inherited party loyalty and the impact of social characteristics on partisanship. As the benchmark of voting studies, it must be included in a comparative analysis.

The 1964 election, on the other hand, provides the original data base for many of the newer studies emphasizing the importance of issues to the vote and the increasing political consciousness of the electorate. Coherence in mass ideology and clarity in identifying the parties' positions first becomes evident in the race between Johnson and Goldwater. In fact, the features of the 1964 election have led some observers to the conclusion that it was a "critical election," initiating a new political era in the United States.[40] Characteristic of such elections is increased voter consciousness of policy questions and the establishment of a new and enduring cleavage in the electorate. Such realignments occur rarely, but they are the decisive moments in American political history.[41] Given the partial evidence of realignment in 1964, the election merits detailed examination.

The 1972 results provide the most recent time point available. They are not only of intrinsic interest, but also allow a comparison to both the relative quiet of 1956 and the relative turmoil of 1964. By examining the Nixon-McGovern race, we may attempt a tentative guess as to the future character of American voting. Throughout this work, we have found much evidence of continuing change in the electorate's behavior. Including the 1973 presidential election may inform us about the persistence of these developments. In the process, by analyzing three elections which have widely different outcomes and which span sixteen years of intensive scholarly research, we hopefully avoid concentration on the unique characteristics of isolated events.

VOTING PATHS FROM 1956 TO 1972

The causal flow of the 1956 vote is drawn in Figure 9.1. There are eleven individual paths that are statistically significant and therefore are part of the explanation of the outcome. This explanation can be divided into two parts, which correspond in the diagram to the upper quadrilateral and the lower diamond.

In the first part of the diagram, the respondent's party identification is the "pivotal encapsulator" of prior political socialization, with no direct links existing between background demographic characteristics and the respondent's vote. A voter's partisanship is affected by his own social characteristics and his inherited party tradition. However, there is no direct link between social characteristics and the vote, nor any direct link between childhood sociological characteristics and adult party identification. The omission of the causal links between these variables and voting behavior "certainly justify the qualms of the authors of *The American Voter* about the sociological explanations of voting behavior."[42] The effects of

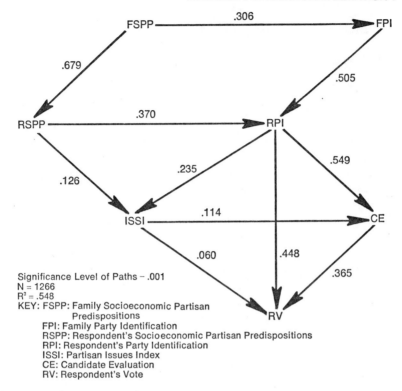

FIGURE 9.1 / CAUSAL MODEL OF THE 1956 PRESIDENTIAL ELECTION (Beta Weights)

demographic variables are only indirect, through their influence on partisanship. Voting is not a dependent act.

In the second part of the diagram, we see the more immediate influences on the vote. Previous research on the 1956 election found a "dual mediation" of respondent's vote by party identification and an index of political attitudes. However, this earlier index combined both candidate evaluations and positions on issues. In light of our interest in issue voting, the effects of these two variables are calculated separately in this chapter. The result indicates that the preponderant factor in 1956 political attitudes consists of candidate evaluations rather than policy preferences. The relative importance of the paths is shown by the coefficients associated with them. The direct path from issues to the vote has a very low coefficient, and the more complicated route, from issues to candidate to vote, also has a low value. There is a much greater impact of candidate evaluations on the vote.[43] In short, the 1956 results had more to do with Eisenhower's personality than his policies.

Party identification has an important effect on ballot choice. Reviewing the link between party identification and the vote, both RPI's direct path and its indirect path through candidate evaluations are strong. At the same time, the path between respondent's party identification and the issue index, while significant, is relatively weaker. This attenuated relationship supports these researchers who have emphasized the often "nonrational" nature of party identification in this period.

In summary, the 1956 vote may be viewed as being dominated by a dual mediation process, in which the two factors immediately affecting the election are party identification and candidate evaluation, with issues only weakly linked to the vote. The model seemingly comports well with previous conclusions emphasizing the powerful and enduring strength of partisanship in shaping attitudes, candidate evaluations, and policy preferences.

The 1964 model, in Figure 9.2—using the same variables, methods, and pattern as in the 1956 analysis—reveals relationships quite different from those in 1956. For the most part, moreover, these differences continue to be evident in the 1972 model (Figure 9.3), indicating that the contest between Johnson and Goldwater was not a completely unique event. Three implications are suggested by these new patterns, each consistent with the conclusions of previous chapters.

First, we see an evident breakdown in the New Deal's socioeconomic

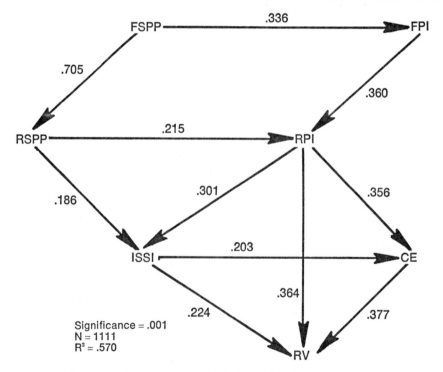

FIGURE 9.2 / CAUSAL MODEL OF THE 1964 PRESIDENTIAL ELECTION

party coalitions. The parental generation shows a rather stable effect of demographic characteristics on party identification, measured as the path from FSPP to FPI. However, this relationship is fast diminishing among current voters, as seen in the path from RSPP to RPI. The relationship between socioeconomic variables and partisanship weakens from one election to the next, falling to a very low weight in 1972. Our earlier finding of a decreased effect of class in the younger generations supports this conclusion.

A shift in the nature of the partisan coalitions is also shown by the falling into insignificance in 1972 of the path between FSPP and RSPP. The demographic factors associated previously with partisanship no longer are predictive of Democratic and Republican loyalty. Further analysis reveals the same conclusions, showing that most of the transmission of partisanship between the generations now occurs through FPI, by tradition itself, rather than by the replication of the relationship of demographic variables to the current electorate's loyalty.[44] In Chapter 2, also, partisan transmission was seen to be increasingly dependent on unsupported tradition.

Second, the importance of issues to the vote has been enhanced consid-

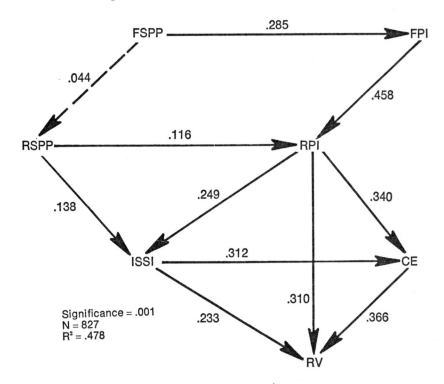

FIGURE 9.3 / CAUSAL MODEL OF THE 1972 PRESIDENTIAL ELECTION

erably, consistent with the evidence emphasized in the last two chapters. This development is evident in the 1964 diagram both in terms of the direct impact of issues and their indirect influence through candidate evaluation. In 1972, the impact of issues is still greater, both marginally on the direct path, and more emphatically on the indirect path, as issues affect the evaluation of candidates and the resultant vote. Johnson and Nixon are not simply chosen because of their individual qualities, but because voters approve their actions and promises.

Third, there has been a decline in the impact of partisanship on the vote, a repeated finding of our previous analysis. This decline is evident in the coefficient of the direct path from respondent's party identification to the vote, where there is a continuing drop in weight from 1956 to 1964 and, again, from 1964 to 1972. The decline is evident as well in the indirect effects of RPI. Candidate evaluations have become far more independent of party loyalty, while the direct influence of these evaluations themselves on the vote has remained largely unchanged. The importance of party identification remains, but it is seemingly more than a simple reflection of traditional loyalty. An increasing proportion of its impact is through the relationship with issue preferences. Voters are going well beyond traditional partisanship in casting their ballots.

The relative importance of the political variables can be gauged by an analysis of the complex paths, involving more than two variables, between respondent's party identification and the vote. This type of analysis, a further refinement of the causal method, is an attempt to gauge both the direct and indirect effect of a variable. Party identification, for example, may be the immediate cause of the vote. It can also affect the election by influencing the way persons judge candidates or by bending their views on issues. To measure these indirect influences, a "compound path coefficient" can be calculated, equal to the product of the coefficients of the included single paths.[45]

This technique is applied in Table 9.4 to the various paths between respondent's party identification and the vote. While the direct path between the two variables (RPI/RV) remains primary, the contribution of the indirect paths through the issue index has risen considerably. Excluded from the model by the assumption of one-way causality are those issue preferences that influence party identification itself. Therefore, the total impact of issues on the vote in these years is underestimated.[46] At the least, there has been a fourfold increase in the ability of issue preferences to explain the presidential vote.

The most obvious difference among these elections is the apparently greater importance of issue preferences in 1964 and 1972. The vote has become less dependent on sociological characteristics and traditional loyalties and is related more to the electorate's position on public policy and its corresponding evaluation of the candidates. Such influences bring

TABLE 9.4 / COMPOUND PATH COEFFICIENTS TO RESPONDENT VOTE

Path	1956		1964		1972	
	Coeff.	Relative Importance*	Coeff.	Relative Importance*	Coeff.	Relative Importance*
Direct:						
RPI/RV	.448	66.6	.364	61.8	.310	59.5
Through Candidate:						
RPI/CE/RV	.200	29.8	.134	22.8	.125	23.9
Through Issues:						
RPI/ISSI/RV	.014	2.1	.067	11.4	.058	11.1
Through Issues and Candidate:						
RPI/ISSI/CE/RV	.010	1.5	.023	3.9	.028	5.4
Total	.672	100.0	.588	99.9	.521	99.9

*Figures in these columns are the percentages of the total relationship between RPI and RV that are explained by the given paths.

results as disparate as the Democratic landslide of 1964 and the overwhelming Nixon triumph eight years later.

To explain these changes in the level of issue voting since 1956, one might hypothesize that a new, issue-oriented younger generation in 1964 and 1972 replaced older, less issue-oriented cohorts. To examine generational shift, the magnitudes of the direct issue-voting paths for 1956 age groups are compared, in Table 9.5, to those of their generational cohorts in 1964 (age in 1956 + 8 years) and in 1972 (age in 1956 + 16 years). The method is similar to that used in Chapters 5 and 8.

If common generational learning experiences were responsible for low levels of issue voting in 1956, similarly low levels should be evident within the same cohorts across the three elections. Little variation would appear, then, in the rows of Table 9.5. If a new issue-oriented generation is changing overall voting behavior, the highest coefficients would be evident in the first entry in each column.

Data in Table 9.5 soundly disconfirm the hypothesis of a generation distinct in its concern for issues. While new voters in 1964 and 1972 demonstrated greater policy responsiveness than the older 1956 cohorts they presumably replaced, a substantial increase in issue voting is evident across time in all generational cohorts (i.e., the rows of the table). In fact, viewing each election separately, it is not necessarily the new voters who demonstrate the greatest influence of issues on their votes. Although the aged might be considered inflexible by some, they show more responsiveness to issues, particularly in 1972, than do many younger cohorts.

The data also permit us to draw some inferences about life-cycle or maturational effects on voting behavior. If position in the life cycle is a predominant influence, relatively little variation should be present along

TABLE 9.5 / DIRECT PATHS FROM ISSUE INDEX TO VOTE, BY AGE*

Generational Cohort	Age in 1956	Age in 1972	1956	1964	1972
		18-25			.244
		26-33		.220	.162
1.	18-25	34-41	.121	.277	.323
2.	26-33	42-49	.116	.279	.217
3.	34-41	50-57	.074	.169	.168
4.	42-49	58-65	.039	.258	.206
5.	50-57	66 and Older	.016	.253	.268
	58-65		−.008	.123	
	66 and Older		.035		

*Entries are the path coefficients, for the designated cohort and election, for the direct path from ISSI to RV.

the diagonal lines of Table 9.5, which indicate the same maturational groupings. Persons of a particular chronological age, whether in 1956 or 1972, would behave similarly. Furthermore, if aging reduces susceptibility to issue influences, as is sometimes implied, the coefficients across the horizontal rows should diminish. Precisely the opposite conclusions must be drawn from the data. There is wide variation along the diagonals and a general increase along the horizontal rows. Maturity does not mean rigidity.[47] The time period men and women live in, rather than the length of their lives, is more important.

The real change from 1956 to 1964 and 1972—and the most likely explanation for upward shifts in issue voting—was not the passing of generations, but the changing of the generations' political environment. The point can be statistically demonstrated by the technique of analysis of variance, which can apportion the variance in issue voting into one part due to generational differences and another part due to the elections themselves.[48] Of the total variance, three-fourths can be accounted for by the differences in the elections, only a quarter by differences in the generations. The technique also shows that the two contests of 1964 and 1972 are quite similar to one another, but that each is different from the 1956 election. These results are another indication that we have entered a new and persistent electoral era.[49]

A second possible explanation for upward shifts in issue voting might be increasing educational achievement among the electorate from 1956 to

1972. Table 9.6 presents the results of controlling for level of education on direct paths from issue index to vote. Substantial increases in issue voting are apparent at every educational level in 1964 compared to 1956, and this development generally continues in 1972. Interestingly, issue voting is more pronounced in 1964 and 1972 among respondents in the lowest educational categories than among college-educated voters in 1956. Thus, the electorate in the latter two elections was responding quite differently from the way it did in 1956, and the transformation is evident throughout the national sample. Consistent with the findings in Chapter 8, we must reject the hypothesis that educational upgrading explains these upward shifts.

Given the inability of demographic variables to account for heightened issue voting, the third and most obvious explanation must be offered, namely politics itself—the contrasting circumstances and styles of the three elections and their impacts on the electorate. In 1956, both Eisenhower and Stevenson described their policy positions in terms so general that "their statements lacked any clear relation to issues on which voters had to decide."[50]

Both were for peace, social welfare, full justice for farmers, honest government, a strong national defense, the expansion of civil liberties, full employment, the development of individual talents, a vigorous economy, a flourishing world trade, and a large number of other objectives of similarly general appeal. . . . At no time did either candidate declare himself to be opposed to any statement of fundamental belief that his opponent had advanced.[51]

Any major differences that may have existed did not transform themselves into effective and cognitive links with the voters.

By contrast, the 1964 and 1972 campaigns surely marked a departure from "Tweedledum-Tweedledee" politics. The Johnson-Goldwater contest presented the electorate with two clearly different sets of domestic and foreign blueprints, Goldwater representing a challenge to the New Deal legacy of "positive government." Sharp differences between the candidates were also evident in 1972 and were perceived as such by the voters. Regardless of their own positions on the issues, as previously discussed, the electorate saw McGovern as more dovish and welfare-minded, and Nixon as more aggressive on Vietnam and economically conservative. With a choice available, the voters chose.

TABLE 9.6 / DIRECT PATHS FROM ISSUE INDEX TO VOTE, BY EDUCATION*

Education Level	1956	1964	1972
Grades 0 through 8	.008	.158	.213
Grades 9 through 12	.094	.189	.217
College	.109	.295	.258

*Entries are the path coefficients, for the designated educational stratum and election, for the direct path from ISSI to RV.

THE VARIETIES OF POLITICAL EXPERIENCE

Using comparable variables and techniques, we have sought to gain a summarizing, longitudinal perspective on two divergent hypotheses on voting behavior. The first hypothesis yields the portrait of the dependent voter. In this portrait, continuity and stability are stressed, and the electorate is viewed as the captive of its social backgrounds or its "inherent limitations" in conceptualization. The second hypothesis, presenting "the perverse and unorthodox argument . . . that voters are not fools,"[52] yields the portrait of the responsive voter.

On the issue of Vietnam, the behavior of the electorate differs considerably in 1968 and 1972. In both years, the electorate was concerned with the issue, and its choices showed a strong association between its perceptions of the candidates' positions and its own policy preferences. In 1968, however, the obscurity of the candidates and the parties made a direct policy mandate difficult to establish. Voters tended to project their own positions onto the presidential nominees, and partisanship distorted the results. Four years later, a clearer choice was presented. Responding to the clarified options, the electorate showed little distortion, a reduced susceptibility to partisan bias, and a high degree of association between its own positions and its selection of a president.

More generally, we have constructed causal models of the vote that encompass all of the influences we have analyzed separately in the previous chapters. Three elections, spanning sixteen years, and each featuring an incumbent president, have been matched by using analogous data and comparable methods. The differing impact of the factors studied in 1956, 1964, and 1972 demonstrate the extensive variability in electoral behavior.

The 1956 election comports well with the emphasis on continuity in the portrait of the dependent voter. Three conclusions are justified: (1) party identification was the "pivotal encapsulator" of prior political socialization, with a strong linkage between parents' partisan attachments and those of present voters; (2) links between party identification and issue positions were not strong, raising questions about the ability of political parties in 1956 to aggregate issues meaningfully for purposes of electoral competition; (3) the voting decision was mediated primarily by party identification and candidate evaluations. Issues were only weakly associated with the voting decision, indicating the electorate's inability to discern issue positions.

The 1964 and 1972 elections, by contrast, lead to conclusions more supportive of the portrait of the responsive voter. These findings indicate that: (1) the linkages between (a) demographic factors and partisan tradition to (b) voter partisanship diminished considerably; (2) while party identification was still a significant indicator of the vote, it retained this significance partially because of the greater weight of the causal paths from partisanship through issues; (3) issues played a meaningful role in voting decisions in the two elections.

Significantly, the changed voting behavior evident in 1964 continues into 1972. Many observers at the time dismissed the Johnson-Goldwater contest as an aberrant event, but the distinct causal relationships established then persisted in the quieter time of the Nixon-McGovern race.[53] The effects of social background and parental partisanship diminished still further in the later election; the direct impact of issues on the vote remained at its new level; and the influence of partisanship still flowed in the new and indirect channels. Along with the shifts in party identification that occurred in 1964, these changed relationships suggest that a new period of American politics originated in the turmoil of the 1960s and is being sustained in this decade by the new attitudes and new awareness of the voters.

Comparative causal analysis shows that the voters are capable of a wide range of behaviors and are not inevitably dense. These behavioral changes cannot be explained by generational or educational alterations in the electorate, nor can they be dismissed as the artifact of new methodological and conceptual tools used to measure the impact of issues on voting. The relationship of issues to the vote was not constant during these sixteen years, nor disguised by flawed techniques. Rather, actual changes in the level of policy voting may now be inferred from 1956 through 1964 and 1972. In the appropriate political circumstances, such as in the later, clearer contests, the electorate will respond to issue differences between the candidates.

That response, however, depends critically on the options provided by political parties and candidates. As is evident on the Vietnam issue in 1968 and 1972, even an aware electorate in contentious times can be confused by uncertain leadership. "The leading statesmen in a free country have great momentary power. They settle the conversation of mankind. . . . It is by that program, by a comparison of the programs of different statesmen that the world forms its judgment."[54]

The greatest American politicians have acknowledged this power and responsibility. They have sought to focus public attention on the major issues facing the nation, not to obscure policy questions through a false consensus. As George Washington in the Constitutional Convention called upon the delegates to "raise a standard to which the wise and honest may repair," so Franklin Roosevelt recognized that the presidency is "pre-eminently a place of moral leadership." The need for direction is no less in the contemporary United States, uncertain of its future, doubtful of its world mission, and beset with problems of racial conflict and economic instability.

The American electorate is able to understand and respond to political leadership. Our analyses show that general conclusions about voter incapacity derived from time-bound data are necessarily incomplete and static. When voters are studied comparatively, in a variety of empirical and temporal contexts, they evidence responsiveness to these differing environments. We must conclude, with V. O. Key, that "in the large the electorate behaves about as rationally and responsibly as we should expect, given the clarity of the alternatives presented to it and the character of the information available to it."[55]

VARIABILITY IN ELECTORAL BEHAVIOR: FINDINGS

1. Voters perceived candidate positions on Vietnam quite differently in 1968 and 1972.
   1a. In 1968, the voters see the major candidates as similar to their own positions and alike to each other.
   1b. In 1972, whatever their own views, the voters see a distinct difference between the major candidates.
2. The effect of Vietnam policy preferences on the vote is quite different in 1968 and 1972.
   2a. Position on Vietnam was unrelated to the vote in 1968.
   2b. There is a close relationship in 1972 between position on Vietnam and vote.
3. In both years, the vote is significantly affected by the relative proximity between the voters' and candidates' views on Vietnam.
   3a. But policy views have a more direct effect on the vote in 1972.
4. The effect of Vietnam policy views on the vote remains greater in 1972 when partisanship is controlled.
5. Causal path analysis shows the vital importance of party identification in the 1956 election.
   5a. Social characteristics and family tradition affect the vote through party identification.
   5b. Party identification itself has a large direct influence on the vote.
   5c. The most important immediate influences on the 1956 vote are candidate evaluations, not issues.
6. Causal path analysis shows considerable change in the factors affecting the 1964 and 1972 elections.
   6a. The socioeconomic character of the parties breaks down in these elections.
   6b. The importance of issues to the vote has been enhanced considerably.
   6c. The importance of partisanship to the vote has declined substantially, in both its direct and indirect effects.

7. Increased issue voting cannot be explained by generational differences.

   7a. Nor does issue voting diminish with aging.

8. Increased issue voting is evident even with education controlled.

9. The chief source of variation in electoral behavior is the electoral context.

CHAPTER 10

THE NEW AMERICAN POLITICS

If it were not necessary to make such an assertion, it would be trite to declare that American politics has undergone basic change in the past two decades. The statement is obvious when we review the mental newsreel in our memories that has recorded the assassinations of leaders, the protest marches, the agony of Vietnam, the transformation of racial and sexual status, and the rise and fall of Richard Nixon. Yet the assertion is necessary because many Americans want to believe that the past can be recaptured. The mass culture of the 1970s is drawn tropistically toward that of the 1950s. Similarly, a political analogy is made between the two periods, with President Gerald Ford compared to President Dwight Eisenhower, and the aftermath of Vietnam likened to the aftermath of the Korean war.[1]

The events, the reactions, and the remembrances of these years cannot be forgotten. Still, American institutions may well endure in their accustomed form. Their stability has been tested for nearly two hundred years, most recently in the resignations of both a vice-president and president. In other nations, military intervention or insurrection in the streets might have followed such events. In the United States, even with these traumatic shocks, the national institutions persisted with hardly a trace, on the surface, of permanent damage.[2]

Below the surface, however, change is more evident. In speculating in this chapter on the future of American politics, we should avoid the easy course of "persistence forecasting," of simply asserting that what happened in the past will continue to happen in the future. The evidence of recent political history is that the American electorate has significantly changed in character. The dependent voter has been supplanted by the responsive voter. With a different electorate, a new American politics becomes likely.

The character of the new politics will be defined by the resolution of two divergent factors. On the one hand, the nation gives evidence of political modernization. The public is participating more broadly in public life; traditional restraints have been loosened; national integration has proceeded; and politics has become more ideological. On the other hand, the political institutions of the nation have not developed sufficiently to stabilize and integrate these new forces. Required now are governmental agencies that are both capable and democratically responsible. The survival of America as a democracy depends upon the construction of such institutions.

THE MODERN AMERICAN VOTER

The signs of political modernization have been evident in the analyses of previous chapters. Broadened participation in public life can be seen in the most obvious measure, voting turnout. Blacks, formerly disenfranchised by semilegal and illegal measures, now cast ballots almost as frequently as whites. Previous psychological and socioeconomic limitations of blacks have been reduced, with advocates of "black power" and college graduates at the forefront of racial activity.[3]

Women show a similar increase in ballot turnout, with the only remaining sex differences with respect to turnout confined to traditional elements in the South. Even there, women with advanced education or who have been raised outside of the region vote no less frequently than men. Still more female participation can be expected in the future, as education becomes more widespread; egalitarian sex role definitions are diffused; and migration continues. Moreover, women are no longer political carbon copies of men. Their differing partisanship and policy views portend change, not simply expansion, of the American political universe.

Increased participation in politics is evident in other groups as well. Politics has become an important leisure activity of the middle class. The involvement of the young has been augmented by the constitutional enfranchisement of 18-year-olds, who will continue to swell the voting lists for another decade. Among partisan Independents, who already outnumber Republicans and approach the proportion of Democrats, a different quality of participation is appearing. No longer unknowledgeable or apathetic toward public affairs, this growing group evidences a commitment to politics generally, even while it remains less interested in the narrower activities of elections.

Greater political involvement is evident beyond the voting booth. Indeed, turnout itself has actually declined from its high point in 1960 to a scarce 55 percent in the 1972 presidential election. Greater concern, however, is evident in peaceful activities such as letter writing and in more disruptive activities such as protest marches and civil disobedience.[4] Even as they detour away from the ballot box, Americans turn toward other forms of political action.

These movements are indicative of another element in the modernizing process, the decline of traditional authority. Protest activity is not only more widespread, it is more accepted—and by both whites and blacks. Such nonconventional behavior cannot be dismissed as the anomic actions of the "riffraff." To the contrary, protest has become an accepted form of political activity by persons of all social strata, used as "a means of gaining access to councils of power by groups which have been denied legitimacy."[5]

The decline of traditional authority is evident also in attitudes toward the political system. Individuals feel less competent politically; government is less trusted; and favoritism is suspected more often. These adverse judgments are particularly evident among college-educated persons and blacks, two vital segments of the population, but they are not confined even to these critical groups. Dissatisfaction and cynicism toward established authority is evident and growing nationally.[6]

In voting itself, we have found other indications of the lessened effect of tradition. While Americans still express a duty to vote, even this ritualistic action is performed less frequently. Turnout has increased recently only in social groups that have been restricted from the ballot in the past, such as blacks and women. Among the general population, particularly youth, the felt duty to participate has been displaced by skepticism and alienation.

When ballots are cast, additional signs become evident of breaks from existing conventions. Partisanship is less frequently inherited from one generation to the next. Voters are freer of both social and political ties. The importance of categorical social memberships to party loyalty and to the vote has virtually disappeared by 1972. While partisanship itself is still important in voting choices, its weight has decreased continually. Its remaining impact occurs not as purely traditional loyalty, but in association with the issue preferences and candidate evaluations of the electors. The conservatizing influence of party tradition, whether for good or ill, has diminished.

Another modernizing development is national integration. On the societal level, the trend is apparent in residential mobility, the spread of the mass media, the decline of regional cultures and speech, and the consolidation of the corporate economy. Politically, two-party competition exists in every state. Within government, the federalist division of power between the nation and the states remains vital, but the states' activities are closely tied to standards established in Washington and revenues provided through national taxation.[7] Despite the traditional American reverence for grass roots government, important functions of defense, health care, law enforcement, welfare, and transportation have been assumed or financed by the national government. The economic and social integration of the country assures the continuation of these trends.

National unification is also evident on the individual level. The concerns of Americans are relatively uniform, with no significant variation in the issues emphasized by the different classes, sexes, generations, races, or regions. Perceptions, such as an awareness of social class, similarly vary little among demographic categories. Even with respect to the most important political factor, party identification, many group contrasts have diminished. There are fewer religious, class, educational, and regional differences between Democrats and Republicans now than in the past.

The political map of America increasingly is the same for all Americans. They agree on the policy directions and ideological positions of the parties, and they react to the same issues. Vietnam was the critical concern throughout the nation in 1968 and 1972, and the entire country has been affected by common domestic issues as well. In the past, southern politics centered on questions of race and subordinated issues of economics, while northern politics exhibited the opposite characteristics. Migration, political change, and cultural diffusion have closed the geographical fissures. Class politics is as evident in Arkansas as in Michigan, while racial conflict is as prominent in Boston as in Birmingham. America has become one nation, divisible on the same lines of conflict throughout the society.

Finally, political development in the United States is evident in the growth of an ideological politics. Consciousness of group identity has become more prevalent. Most conspicuously, blacks have come to endorse the concepts of "black power,"[8] and a defined leadership stratum and political structure has developed among them. Greater self-awareness is also evident among women, and youth has developed a distinct configuration of political attitudes and life-styles. American politics is no longer a clash of atomized, separate persons, as imagined in doctrines of liberal individualism. Neither is American politics accurately described as a meeting place for interest groups organized for transient and particular purposes.[9] Contemporary groups are more aware, more encompassing, and potentially more conflictful.

A more ideological politics is also seen among individual voters. Citizens have clearer perceptions of differences between the parties on a series of policy questions and are more agreed on the particular directions of the Democrats and Republicans. Given these clearer perceptions, their ballot choices show a greater effect of issue preferences. As the importance of traditional partisanship, candidate personality, and sociological influences has declined, the impact of issue preferences on the vote has increased. Changes in the issues presented to the voters every four years have brought changing responses—and wide variation in the election results.

The development of ideology is more than a responsiveness to specific and changing issues. The character of salient issues has been transformed, with an emerging new emphasis on such basic matters as war and race. These questions are not ones that can be bargained out and eventually compromised. They involve fundamental normative questions, ultimately about the very quality and purpose of human life. Political deals can be struck on the allocation of the pork barrel; they cannot be made on the morality of force.

Issue preferences have also become more coherent. Voters grasp the connections between different policy questions, rather than reacting to each matter separately.[10] Their outlook on politics is more integrated, as they can more readily place preferences on individual issues into a general ideological framework and also can see the parties in the same framework. Given the use of such frameworks, the impact of issues on the vote is likely to be persistent. As new issues arise, they will be interpreted in consistent terms.

American politics is likely to become even more ideological. The increasing numbers and influence of the young and the educated point in this direction. The fundamental divisions in the electorate are no longer largely sociological or traditionally partisan, but ever more conceptual. The generations differ because of their ideas, not because of their inherited party loyalty or their biological maturity. Ballots are cast differently because persons have different beliefs, not because they were raised in different homes. Greater emphasis on ideology, along with the other elements of political modernization, has created the basis for a new American politics.

THE DECAY OF INSTITUTIONS

In a period of political modernization, effective government is a basic requirement, for "without strong political institutions, society lacks the means to define and to realize its common interests. The capacity to create political institutions is the capacity to create public interests."[11] Absent such institutions, there is a distinct likelihood not only of instability, but of authoritarian government, whether in the form of mass movements with demagogic leadership or in the form of elite manipulation of the public. In such a society the mass is atomized and unstructured, characterized by "strong feelings of alienation and anxiety, and therefore the disposition to engage in extreme behavior to escape from these tensions. In a mass society there is a heightened readiness to form hyper-attachments to symbols and leaders. . . . Total loyalty is the psychological basis for total domination."[12]

The United States has had a fortunate history in which it could avoid the need for strong governmental institutions. Stability was possible because of the restricted role of government. No severe foreign threats existed. The dominant values left economic expansion to individual capitalists and to the capricious movements of the invisible hand of free enterprise. With the activity of government limited, formal popular participation in politics could be expanded safely. Since the power of government was not likely to be employed by an aroused electorate, the problems of political modernization could be avoided.

These favorable conditions no longer exist. International involvement cannot be avoided in the age of intercontinental missiles, and a mature economy requires government direction. In response to these changed conditions, popular intervention has increased, and the scope of governmental institutions has grown. The two developments, however, have not been joined in the evolution of institutions that are both capable of meeting modern problems and responsible democratically to a modern electorate. The capable institutions are not responsible, while the responsible institutions are not capable.

The power of the presidency has grown to meet the policy problems of the country, but in the process the office has become increasingly distant from popular controls. Its swollen capability is well known, demonstrated by the chief executive's command of Jovian powers of world destruction, his supervision of a budget of incomprehensible size, and his veneration by trusting school children and fearful adults. Increased presidential power has resulted from real national needs for leadership coordination and dispatch in meeting modern problems, not from devious conspiracies in the White House.

Accompanying these largely inevitable developments has been the separation of the office from the political process that provides democratic accountability. This separation is evident in the election results, for example, where there is little relationship remaining between presidential and congressional ballots. In the last presidential election, Democratic loyalists far outnumbered Republicans. On election day, however, a Republican landslide for Nixon was accompanied by solid Democratic majorities in both the House and the Senate. This outcome was not unique, but rather was the culmination of a trend building for nearly thirty years. Furthermore, a historic high was reached in 1972, when split results developed in 45 percent of the individual districts, producing presidential and congressional winners of different parties.[13]

The disjunction in the 1972 results is part of a larger fission in which the presidency has been effectively separated from partisan politics. Nixon could win reelection as president while his party continued to decline in Congress and party loyalties because voters no longer consider the office in partisan terms. This perception goes beyond the act of splitting the ticket. Rather, in the voter's mind, there is no ticket. He sees one ballot for president and another ballot for everything else—as is literally true in some states. Party is relevant only to the latter choice, while the presidency is becoming a plebiscitary office. Parties serve mechanically to nominate candidates, but they have little organic connection with the White House.

The political isolation of the presidency results partially from deliberate actions by chief executives and partially from a modern fact, the predominance of foreign affairs in the conduct of the office. Foreign policy decisions are obviously more critical to the nation than domestic issues, but they are also more attractive to a president and beckon his attention. The ritual of foreign visits or the thrill of disposing of megatons is more attractive than dispensing sewer grants. And it is easier, in the sense that the president can make his decisions with less opposition from competing politicians and less need to win democratic consent from Congress or the mass public.

A focus on foreign policy limits partisan debate—a comfort to the president, but also a curtailment of electoral control. Until recently, these issues have not been organized along party lines, and the tradition of bipartisanship has been reinstituted with the end of the Vietnam war. Even when such questions do become partisan, they cannot be easily argued and subjected to the constant tests of domestic issues. The inability of Congress effectively to control the Vietnam involvement underscores the difficulty.

Ultimately, foreign policy questions can become, for the electorate, questions only of personal competence. Which man can be trusted with the nuclear trigger? Which candidate can negotiate better or stand up to the Russians? The nature of the issues thereby furthers the movement toward making presidential elections a choice of individuals, not a choice of parties. In the process, we approach an end to political control over the conduct of the presidency.

Changes in the character of the executive office have been supplemented by deliberate presidential attempts to divorce the presidency from partisan politics. Even national executives with extensive party experience have treated their factional fellows with contempt.[14] Disdain and neglect crested in 1972, when the last Nixon campaign was conducted through a fully independent Committee for the Re-Election of the President, which consciously ignored other Republican candidates. Although the committee collected over fifty million dollars, very little was shared with House and Senate candidates of the president's party. In fact, the Watergate investigation revealed that the funds were instead administered to help those Democrats who had supported Nixon on Vietnam or who were endorsed by organized labor, his temporary ally.[15] These actions surely reflected the ultimate "aggrandizement of the president's personal power at the direct expense of the continuing electoral viability of his own party."[16]

Separation of the president from his party has been accompanied by attenuation of other constraints. Increasingly, occupants of the office have taken on the appearance of majesty, leaving them free not only of criticism but of freely expressed advice. "These circumstances surround a man with an atmosphere of adulation, composed of both sycophancy and genuine respect for the office, which can find parallels only in divine-right monarchies."[17] Indeed, "by the twentieth century, the presidency had taken on all the regalia of monarchy except ermine robes, a scepter, and a crown."[18] The failure of all advisers to challenge Richard Nixon in the Watergate cover-up is dramatic testimony to this presidential isolation and adoration.

The press, another possible constraint, has also been limited in its effects. The growth of presidential power has brought deference from reporters, a debilitating increase in the White House press corps, and consequent difficulties in achieving intimate knowledge and free criticism. Press conferences illustrate the change. Free exchanges during the administration of Franklin Roosevelt, they have become stage-managed affairs, held infrequently, briefly, and in forums of the president's choice, with almost no opportunity for probing, but with unspoken sanctions available against the overly inquisitive reporter.[19]

The presidency has become both restricted in its political depth and extended in its governmental reach. The events of the Nixon administration, while uniquely outrageous, also represented the consolidation and culmination of long-standing developments. Previous executives also emphasized foreign affairs, scorned their party organizations, surrendered to false flattery, and disregarded public criticism. Earlier presidents, too, tried to extend their power, and not always in pretty fashion.

What makes the Nixon experience distinctive is the combination of activities that took place. Political constraints were almost completely dissolved, and executive authority was stretched almost to the breaking point of the Constitution. The various exercises of presidential power that had been scattered historically through the lifetime of the nation were now gathered together. The attempt was made to combine in one time and place the precedents of Polk's use of executive privilege, Lincoln's temporary suspension of civil liberties, Theodore Roosevelt's expansive view of American world power, Wilson's personal diplomacy, Franklin Roosevelt's use of emergency power, Eisenhower's frustration with the bureaucracy, Kennedy's approval of wiretapping, and Johnson's control of the military services.

The attempted fusion can be charitably regarded as an improper attempt to create the strong national institutions needed as the United States confronts the problems of modernization. By placing loyalists in key bureaucratic positions, rational centralized authority could be achieved. By centering power in the White House, the clumsiness of separated institutions could be overcome. By placing election funds in the right hands, the crisis of broadened popular intervention could be managed. The attempt, of course, was not only improper, but pernicious. Yet it can be seen historically as an effort to meet the real problem of modernization.[20]

An analogy can be drawn to the period of constitutional development in Great Britain in the eighteenth century. In that era, the Tudor balance of power between king and Parliament had vanished; the Stuart attempt at monarchical supremacy had been defeated; but parliamentary sovereignty had not been achieved. With the release of the economic power of capitalism and the development of political consciousness in the middle class, strong governmental institutions were needed. The necessity was met by a system frankly called "influence" and "corruption," which "comprised, in effect, a private, informal constitution."[21] A court faction was created to control politics in the name and in behalf of the crown. Formal parliamentary power was acknowledged, but elections were controlled by the executive through payments to electors; the manipulation of constituencies and "rotten boroughs"; and the proffering of office, titles, and bribes to important politicians. A capable system was achieved, but one well insulated from control by even the small electorate of the time.

Presidential sovereignty is the analogous American attempt to deal with modern problems. It, too, has employed corruption and the control of elections. It, too, lacks accountability to the voters. Its control, also, may come through the means achieved in British development, the creation of strong and legitimate opposition. Faced with the power and influence of the crown, British Whigs argued for a coherent party system, for "duty demands and requires that what is right should not only be made known, but made prevalent; that what is evil should not only be detected, but defeated."[22]

The same necessity exists in the United States today. Political parties are the best instrument available for democratic control, for "freedom of opposition seems almost meaningless . . . in the absence of effective oppositional structures in the form of one or more political parties."[23] Unfortunately, the very institution that could promote responsibility shows very limited capability to do so. The recent course of the parties is toward dissolution, not development.

Parties evidence decreasing ties with, and control over, public officials. As discussed above in relation to the president, this change is partially due to the deliberate decisions of politicians and partially due to changes in campaign techniques. In periods of indirect communication between nominees and the voter, party loyalty was the major basis of ballot choice; individual canvassing was the major campaign method; and parties were the principal mobilizing organization. They registered voters, persuaded or bribed them, and brought them to the polls. It was therefore in a president's self-interest to lead and strengthen his party, in the process necessarily subjecting himself to a measure of control.

In the contemporary period, a presidential candidate does not need much more than a party label as a means of securing access to the ballot (and George Wallace even did without that). He can appeal directly to the voters through the mass media, prerecorded telephone messages, and computerized mailings. Individual canvassers cannot reach 140 million voters sprawled across a continent. Instead, the candidate himself presents his personality, style, qualifications, and issue positions to an electorate increasingly independent of party loyalty. It is no longer in the self-interest of the president to identify himself with other persons sharing his Republican or Democratic label.

Organizational developments strengthen this trend. Little party patronage is left to the president, as civil service has been extended to virtually all positions. Revenue sharing decreases the discretionary spending power of the national executive, even as it increases the opportunities for local boodle. Of course, there is still much discretion left in the granting of such favors as defense contracts or airline routes. As shown in the Watergate revelations however, these powers promote direct contributions to a president's individual campaign, not to his party.

Parties have been greatly weakened as campaign organizations. In presidential campaigns, the load is largely carried by volunteers who are enthusiasts for particular candidates or advocates of specific issues, but who have little interest in long-term commitments. While some volunteers do become devoted to their parties, they also tend to be persons with particular ideological viewpoints they wish to promote, rather than steadfast loyalists. Their ability to persist in party activity, and thereby to control public officials elected under their name, is still unproven.[24]

The most important control parties have over politicians is that of nominations, but this weapon is weakening. Culminating a trend of the twentieth century, every state now chooses its candidates by direct primaries, and the party organizations are less able to intervene successfully in these selections. At the national level, presidential primaries are now held in almost half of the states, and there are recurrent proposals to bypass the party nominating conventions entirely by selecting presidential candidates in a single national primary.

In the Democratic party, the reforms of recent years constituted another step in this direction. The guidelines for the 1972 convention promoted direct choice of the candidate not by the entire party, but by its most enthusiastic and organized factions, and specifically prohibited ex-officio representation by public officials elected under the party label. Here is the pure plebiscitary ideal—the direct choice of a presidential candidate by self-styled party members and the exclusion of the putative "machine." But, after the nomination and the possible election, what organization then remains to provide democratic control over the new president?

We have come to a time of institutional decay. The constitutional system of checks and balances, when it works, will be insufficient to handle the forces of political development. The presidency has grown in power, but has decayed as an office that is democratically controlled. Alternative power structures, such as the bureaucracy or national corporations, hardly promise any greater accountability to the public.[25] The Congress, a potentially democratic institution, still lacks capabilities. The most potent instrument for voter control, the parties, are in an accelerating state of decay. It is a time for political reconstruction.

TOWARD A RESPONSIVE POLITICS

In prescribing for the future, the simplest course is to resort to traditional remedies. Particularly in the aftermath of the impeachment proceedings against Richard Nixon, it is inspiring to hear, and comforting to believe, that "Our Constitution works; our great republic is a government of laws and not of men. Here the people rule."[26] Indeed, given the uncertain attitudes of the public, it may be necessary at first "to try to calm a troubled nation with uncritical reassertions of the legitimacy of our traditions, symbols and institutions."[27]

Tradition alone, however, will not meet the needs of an untraditional politics. The prudent and decent investigation that led the House Judiciary Committee to vote for impeachment of the president was a testament to the resilience of American institutions and a historic defence of law and individual liberty. Three times, by overwhelming and bipartisan votes, the committee declared that "Richard M. Nixon has acted in a manner contrary to his trust as President and subversive of constitutional government, to the great prejudice of the cause of law and justice, and to the manifest injury of the people of the United States."[28] Within a week, it was evident that presidential resignation was the only means to prevent formal impeachment by the House of Representatives, conviction by the Senate, and removal from office.

These actions resurrected impeachment as a safeguard against presidential obstruction of justice, violation of the rights of citizens, and invasion of congressional powers. However, they did not deal with specific policy issues or with basic institutional problems. In fact, the committee generally refused to consider impeachment on the basis of policy matters and decided against impeachment on the one specific matter that came to a vote, the U.S. bombing of Cambodia. The institutional consequence of impeachment has been therefore to revive the traditional checks and balances, by increasing the power of Congress. Rather than development toward a modern state with articulated and strong political institutions, the effect has been to recreate the character of the United States as a "Tudor polity," with fractured power and divided authority.

The necessity for institutional change remains, as the causes behind the growth of presidential prerogative persist. Centralization through executive corruption has been checked, but surely will revive unless alternative structures are built. As when the Constitution was adopted, it remains true that, "In framing a government, . . . the great difficulty lies in this: you must first enable the government to control the governed; and in the next place oblige it to control itself."[29] In the contemporary concern to control the government and to deter abuse, the need for effective political direction must not be forgotten.

The rebuilding of American institutions first requires a strengthening of Congress. The national legislature, weakened in recent decades in comparison to the executive, also lacks sufficient mechanisms for democratic control. Its potential for competency and responsibility remain. The historical conditions seem right for the development of fuller democratic policies and procedures, with Congress as the fulcrum of these efforts.[30] In the wake of the Nixon presidency and threat of impeachment, substantial changes have already been made toward the revival of congressional powers. If combined with party reform, they may point the way to further invigoration.

In the early 1970s, a series of statutes and court decisions have limited the powers and potential corruptibility of the presidency. Presidential secrecy has been curbed by the Supreme Court in two cases. In the first, the court permitted publication of "The Pentagon Papers," detailing the history of American involvement in Vietnam, despite White House claims of military security.[31] In the second, the Court established an authoritative definition of "executive privilege," declaring that presidential claims to papers and tape recordings pertinent to the Watergate investigation were subordinate to the judicial need for complete evidence in criminal cases.[32] Public access to the operations of the executive has been increased as well by the Freedom of Information Act and its liberalizing amendments, passed over a presidential veto in 1974.

Congress has also moved to increase its controls over the executive branch. Presidential appointees are being evaluated more carefully than in the past. When vice-presidents were nominated by Presidents Nixon and Ford, under the new provisions of the 25th Amendment, they were given detailed consideration by both chambers. Appointees have been pledged to follow specific policies, such as the condition imposed on recent attorneys-general, that they respect the independence of a special prosecutor in the Watergate case. Officials free of legislative control in the past are now subject to Senate confirmation. Particularly important in this regard are the Director of the FBI and the chief budget officer of the

United States, the Director of the Office of Management and Budget. A precedent for further legislative involvement may also have been established by the voluntary appearance of President Ford before the House Judiciary Committee to explain his pardon of Richard Nixon.

Attempts are also being made to avoid recurrence of the abuses of power revealed in the Watergate and other investigations. Beginning in 1976, presidential nominations, conventions, and elections will be financed from public funds and individual contributions from the wealthy will be limited. Presidential use of troops in military situations abroad is to be restricted to ninety days without congressional approval. Secret funds available to the White House, particularly for covert operations, are being curtailed or more oversight will be implemented. Presidential emergency powers in existence for four decades have been repealed. Lavish government spending on presidential residences will no longer be permitted. In these many ways, the national government has responded to the most obvious sources of popular discontent in recent years.

Beyond this increased control of the executive, the ability of Congress to formulate national policy has been improved. The most important potential step in this direction has been the Budget Act of 1974. Unlike its practice of the last fifty years, Congress will now seek to examine the fiscal and economic policy of the nation on a comprehensive annual basis. Special committees in each chamber will set spending, appropriations, and debt limits, and divide the total spending of government among its various functions. Furthermore, Congress will be able to control and overrule presidential impoundments of appropriated funds.[33] In another step, the expert advice needed on scientific matters is now being furnished by another new agency, the Office of Technical Information.

More is needed. The presidency should be checked, but not enfeebled. The Congress should become an active participant in the formulation of policy, not a stronger opponent to the president. Institutions should not be made incapable of doing anything, in order to insure that they are incapable of doing evil. They must be made capable of doing good, for much needs to be done, while they are made more democratically responsible.

Congressional reforms have not fully developed in this direction. The primary thrust of recent changes is toward control over the president. The seniority system has been modified formally, by requiring party or committee approval of chairmen; but only the first steps have been taken to reduce the emphasis given to longevity of service, and to increase the emphasis on individual ability or loyalty to a party program. Committees retain most of their autonomy, and an attempt to rationalize committee jurisdictions and curtail independent power has been severely compromised.[34] Although contributions and total spending in legislative elections have been limited, Congress deliberately exempted itself from the law providing public financing of elections.

The vigor of the party system must be restored in order to provide effective and responsible institutions. Parties are not only the most effective democratic institutions available, they also perform the critical modernizing function: "to organize participation, to aggregate interests, to serve as the link between social forces and the government."[35] Their revival is necessary to the successful political development of the United States.

Party revival can be promoted by institutional changes. Within Congress, the power of leaders chosen on the basis of seniority must be subordinated to that of leaders who are party representatives. Committee assignments, including chairmanships, should be made by secret ballots in party caucuses. Party programs should be developed by the respective policy committees in each chamber, and by joint party committees of both House and Senate. It is unrealistic to expect to enforce party loyalty by caucus votes, but representatives and senators who repeatedly oppose the party can be disfavored in the distribution of committee assignments, congressional patronage, and party funds.

In the current Congress, the House Democratic party has moved in these directions. Spurred by the demands of 75 freshmen representatives, the Democrats have given the power of committee assignment to a representative steering committee, the Speaker has been given the power to appoint the majority members of the Rules Committee, and the party caucus has established legislative priorities and has endorsed an economic program. Most significantly, four chairmen were challenged for reelection, one resigned, and three were actually removed because of their opposition to the programs of the congressional party. If these new powers are vigorously used in the future, and extended to the Senate and the Republican party, the basis for party responsibility will exist.[36]

The greatest potential for party coherence lies in the electoral system. If elections become universally financed from public funds, the party organization may revive as the central object of candidates' loyalty. Recent practices have encouraged nominees to be individual entrepreneurs, raising their own funds and selling their own wares, with no regard for a common party program. If election finance were centralized in the party organization, there would be a strong incentive for candidates to achieve a united platform. It is important, therefore, that any public funds for elections not be distributed to individual candidates, but to parties.

The new federal law meets these prescriptions only in part. Its main purpose is to limit contributions, spending, and potential corruption, not to strengthen the parties. Public funds will go to candidates, including participants in presidential primaries, with the parties receiving support only for the national conventions. The only means provided for financial intervention by the parties is a provision which allows the national organizations to contribute up to $10,000 to a House candidate and up to $20,000 to a Senatorial nominee. To increase the democratic accountability of the party system, however, it would be preferable to funnel most funds through the Democratic and Republic organizations. Such action has been taken in Montana, Rhode Island, and Utah, and deserves imitation.[37] A similar step would be to provide equal and free time in the mass media for the parties, rather than for the individual candidates. This change would promote both meaningful competition and party coherence. Direct subsidies to the parties, a common practice abroad, would also be helpful.

The party organizations themselves need to be strengthened as political bodies. The Democrats have held the nation's first mid-term party convention, establishing standards for state party procedures and declaring authoritative party policy on economic matters. This precedent should be followed and expanded. The parties should move toward financial independence of large contributors and toward reliance on the support of a dues-paying membership, ideally with encouragement of tax deductibility. The integrity of the parties should be safeguarded by legislation that restricts the raiding of state party primaries by members of the opposition.

More coherence and stability is needed in political campaigns. The decentralized character of American institutions has been unnecessarily exaggerated by the parties, which rarely have attempted to coordinate their electoral efforts. Greater reliance on mass financing, as in recent national telethons, will enable the parties to conduct unified campaigns on agreed programs, thereby reflecting the facts of national integration and increased voter interest in issues. A permanent enlargement of the national committee staffs and the recruitment of inhouse experts will also make for more effective efforts.[38]

Party leaders also must be restored to a central role in the nominating process. While presidential primaries need not be abolished, they certainly should not be extended, but would better be restricted to a manageable number of representative contents to provide tests of popular sentiment and candidate abilities. A single national primary, or restrictions on the participation of elected party officials, is clearly adverse to the establishment of meaningful party competition. Rather, what is needed is more frequent meetings of nationally representative bodies, whether as party conventions or reconstituted national committees.

These reforms constitute a partial program for the renewal of American democratic institutions. The alternatives are grim, including demagogic movements, continued drift, and social division. A generation ago, a choice was presented to students of politics between a strengthening of the political parties or incoherence in public policies, a dangerous enlargement of presidential power, public cynicism, and the growth of extremist movements.[39] By neglect or design, the choice was made to permit the further decline of the parties. Not coincidentally, the baleful alternatives have developed. It is now time for another effort at party revival.

Institutional changes, however, can only provide the parties and their leaders with the opportunity to win popular support. The responsibility remains theirs to develop programs that are relevant to the concerns of the electorate and offer significant choice. More coherent parties that debate only the personal charms of their candidates, or their relative commitment to law and order, will not resolve the doubts or meet the aspirations of the American people.

Party revival will certainly be difficult. The "onward march of party decomposition"[40] continues, spurred by new campaign techniques and the proliferation of autonomous voters. Basic disagreements within the parties, particularly among the Democrats, make difficult the achievement of any unified programs.[41] The growing dependence of the parties on ideological volunteers restricts their ability to develop coherent and hierarchical structures.[42]

With all these difficulties, the possibility for party renewal exists. The internal coherence of the parties, a necessary precondition, has increased considerably. The Republican party has become a more consistently conservative party, as dissidents such as John Lindsay and Donald Riegle have changed loyalties. In the opposite direction, the once-numerous faction of conservative southerners has been reduced to an aging corporal's guard in Congress. As "Dixiecrats" such as Strom Thurmond and John Connally join the Republicans, they are being replaced by a new generation of moderate and liberal southerners. Among the voters, partisanship and policy preferences have become considerably more congruent in the past two decades. The vote itself is cast more on the basis of these preferences. The spread of two-party competition throughout the nation facilitates these realignments.

Coherent parties and meaningful ballot choices are even more likely if the vital issues of campaign debate match the salient concerns of the electorate. An economic crisis is bringing to the fore basic problems of economic development and income disparities. The crisis is evident in the nation's shortage of energy, an uncertain balance of trade, the simultaneous growth of inflation and unemployment, resistance to the level and incidence of taxation, the paucity of public services, and an unchanging, inequitable distribution of wealth. Critical decisions must be made by the nation's leaders and faced by the national electorate.

For any new economic policies to work, they must be based on popular approval. Strong parties will be needed to win this approval, but they must be parties that pose the real questions, and are based on relevant class and economic alignments. In our analyses, we have seen many signs that there is a readiness among the American public for such politics, such as the growth of class voting in the South and the interracial agreement on taxation policy. A class politics not only is salient today, but it also has the potential to overcome other divisions in the nation. As the citizenry's focus turns to these issues, then, there is "much reason to believe that in the shorter run the headlong march toward decomposition that marked the late 1960s will be checked and even reversed, the New Deal party system will be reinvigorated, and most of those who ceased identifying with one or the other major party in the recent turmoil will reidentify."[43]

The capacity of the parties, as of American institutions generally, remains to be tested; their democratic accountability remains to be proven. For their part, when called upon, the voters in recent years have demonstrated their abilities and responsiveness. In a period of upheaval and torment, the electorate has made varied, meaningful, and reasoning choices. As the nation celebrates its bicentennial, its desire for life, liberty, and equality continues; leadership remains necessary to secure these rights; and the truth is still self-evident that governments derive their just powers from the consent of the governed.

NOTES

CHAPTER 1 / THE OBSCURE AMERICAN VOTER

[1] Max Farrand, ed., *The Records of the Federal Convention of 1787* (New Haven: Yale University Press, 1911), I, 364.

[2] *Ibid.*, II, 31.

[3] James Madison, *The Federalist*, Nos. 51, 10.

[4] Farrand, I, 288.

[5] See Samuel Huntington, *Political Order in Changing Societies* (New Haven: Yale University Press, 1968), Chap. 2.

[6] *Gitlow* v. *N.Y.*, 268 U.S. 652 (1925).

[7] See Daniel Bell, ed., *The End of Ideology* (Glencoe, Ill.: Free Press, 1960), and Everett Ladd, *Ideology in America* (Ithaca, N.Y.: Cornell University Press, 1969).

[8] Alexis de Tocqueville, *Democracy in America,* ed. Phillips Bradley (New York: Vintage, 1954), I, 185.

[9] Eugene Burdick, "Political Theory and the Voting Studies," in Burdick and Arthur Brodbeck, *American Voting Behavior* (New York: The Free Press, 1959), p. 139 f.

[10] Angus Campbell, Philip Converse, Warren Miller, and Donald Stokes, *The American Voter* (New York: Wiley, 1960), p. 91, and Sidney Verba and Norman Nie, *Participation in America* (New York: Harper and Row, 1972), Chap. 4.

[11] Bernard Berelson, Paul Lazarsfeld, and William McPhee, *Voting* (Chicago: Chicago University Press, 1954), p. 227.

[12] *The American Voter,* p. 182, and see Chap. 8 below.

[13] *Ibid.*, pp. 227-234.

[14] Philip Converse, "The Nature of Belief Systems in Mass Publics," in David Apter, ed., *Ideology and Discontent* (New York: The Free Press, 1964), pp. 219-223.

[15] Paul Lazarsfeld, Bernard Berelson, and Helen Gaudet, *The People's Choice,* 2nd ed. (New York: Columbia University Press, 1948), p. 27.

[16] *Voting,* p. 321.

[17] *Ibid.*, p. 309.

[18] Peter B. Natchez, "Images of Voting: The Social Psychologists," *Public Policy,* XVIII (Summer, 1970), 564. While Natchez attacks this view, it is supported by Lee Benson, *The Concept of Jacksonian Democracy* (Princeton: Princeton University Press, 1961), p. 281.

[19]*The American Voter,* p. 135.

[20]David Wallace, *First Tuesday* (Garden City: Doubleday, 1964), p. 272.

[21]See Herbert McClosky, "Conservatism and Personality," *American Political Science Review,* LII (March, 1958), 45; V. O. Key, *Public Opinion and American Democracy* (New York: Knopf, 1961), Chaps. 2, 3; McClosky, "Issue Conflict and Consensus among Party Leaders and Followers," *American Political Science Review,* LIV (June, 1960), 406-427.

[22]*The American Voter,* pp. 253, 543.

[23]Natchez, p. 577; cf. *The American Voter,* pp. 543-548.

[24]See Peter Bachrach, *The Theory of Democratic Elitism* (Boston: Little, Brown, 1967), and Jack Walker, "A Critique of the Elitist Theory of Democracy," *American Political Science Review,* LX (June, 1966), 285-295.

[25]Supportive data have been drawn from Samuel Stouffer, *Communism, Conformity and Civil Liberties* (Garden City: Doubleday, 1955), and Herbert McClosky, "Consensus and Ideology in American Politics," *American Political Science Review,* LVIII (June, 1964), 361-382.

[26]Talcott Parsons, " 'Voting' and the Equilibrium of the American Political System," in Burdick and Brodbeck (above, n. 9), Chap. 4.

[27]Burdick, "Political Theory and the Voting Studies," p. 145.

[28]C. Wright Mills, *The Power Elite* (New York: Oxford University Press, 1956), p. 322.

[29]Herbert Marcuse, *One-Dimensional Man* (Boston: Beacon Press, 1964), pp. 117, 40.

[30]The connection can be seen in Murray Levin, *The Compleat Politician* (Indianapolis: Bobbs-Merrill, 1962), and in Joe McGinniss, *The Selling of the President* (New York: Trident Press, 1968).

[31]V. O. Key, Jr., with the assistance of Milton C. Cummings, Jr., *The Responsible Electorate* (Cambridge: Harvard University Press, 1966), p. 2 f.

[32]David Kovenock, Philip Beardsley, and James Prothro, "Status, Party, Ideology, Issues, and Candidate Choice: A Preliminary Theory—Relevant Analysis of the 1968 American Presidential Election," a paper prepared for the Congress of the International Political Science Association (Munich, 1970), p. 24.

[33]V. O. Key and Frank Munger, "Social Determinism and Electoral Decision: The Case of Indiana," in Burdick and Brodbeck (above, n. 9), p. 297 f.; cf. Morris Janowitz and Warren Miller, "The Index of Political Predisposition in the 1948 Election," *Journal of Politics,* XIV (November, 1952), 710-727.

[34]H. Daudt, *Floating Voters and the Floating Vote* (Leiden: Stenfert Kroese, 1961), p. 94.

[35]Richard M. Merelman, "Electoral Instability and the American Party System," *Journal of Politics,* XXXII (February, 1970) 116.

[36]Anthony Downs, *An Economic Theory of Democracy* (New York: Harper, 1957), Chaps. 12 and 13.

[37]Arthur Goldberg, "Social Determinism and Rationality as Bases of Party Identification," *American Political Science Review,* LXIII (March, 1969), 5-25.

[38]*Ibid.,* p. 21.

[39]Everett Ladd, Jr., and Charles Hadley, *Political Parties and Political Issues: Patterns in Differentiation Since the New Deal* (Beverly Hills: Sage Professional Papers in American Politics, 1973), Part III. See also Chap. 8 below.

[40]John Plamenatz, "Electoral Studies and Democratic Theory: A British View," *Political Studies,* VI (February, 1958), 9.

[41]See Robert Axelrod, "The Structure of Public Opinion on Policy Issues," *Public Opinion Quarterly,* XXXI (Spring, 1967), 51-60, and Norman Luttbeg, "The Structure of Beliefs Among Leaders and the Public," *Public Opinion Quarterly,* XXXII (Fall, 1968), 398-409.

[42]Robert Lane, *Political Ideology* (New York: The Free Press of Glencoe, 1962), and "The Fear of Equality," *American Political Science Review,* LIII (March, 1959), 35-51.

[43]J. O. Field and R. E. Anderson, "Ideology in the Public's Conceptualization of the 1964 Election," *Public Opinion Quarterly,* XXXIII (Fall, 1969), 386.

[44]*The Responsible Electorate,* p. 7 f.

[45]Kovenock, p. 9 f; cf. Gerald Finch, "Policy and Candidate Choice in the 1968 American Presidential Election," Ph.D. dissertation (University of Minnesota, 1973).

[46]David RePass, "Issue Salience and Party Choice," *American Political Science Review,* LXV (June, 1971), 389-400.

[47]Richard Boyd, "Popular Control of Public Policy: A Normal Vote Analysis of the 1968 Election," *American Political Science Review,* LXVI (June, 1972), 429-449; Finch, pp. 70-79.

[48]Kovenock, p. 21.

[49]Arthur Miller, Warren Miller, Alden Raine, and Thad Brown, "A Majority Party in Disarray: Policy Polarization in the 1972 Election," a paper presented to the annual meetings of the American Political Science Association (1973), p. 5, and forthcoming, in part, in the *American Political Science Review* (1975).

[50]V. O. Key, "A Theory of Critical Elections," as cited in this context by John K. Wildgen, "The Detection of Critical Elections in the Absence of Two-Party Competition," *Journal of Politics,* XXXVI (May, 1974), 467.

[51]Donald Stokes, "Some Dynamic Elements of Contests for the Presidency," *American Political Science Review,* LX (March, 1966), 19.

[52]John Pierce, "Party Identification and the Changing Role of Ideology in American Politics," *Midwest Journal of Political Science,* XIV (February, 1970), 25-42.

[53]Norman Nie, with Kristi Andersen, "Mass Belief Systems Revisited: Political Change and Attitude Structure," *Journal of Politics,* XXXVI (August, 1974), 547-554. Also see Chap. 8 below.

[54]Ladd and Hadley, p. 18.

[55]Philip Converse, "Information Flow and the Stability of Partisan Attitudes," in Angus Campbell, Philip Converse, Warren Miller, and Donald Stokes, *Elections and the Political Order* (New York: Wiley, 1966), Chap. 8.

[56]See Philip Converse, "Public Opinion and Voting Behavior," in Fred Greenstein, ed., *The Handbook of Political Science* (Redding: Addison-Wesley, forthcoming).

[57]As in Seymour Lipset, *The First New Nation* (New York: Basic Books, 1963).

[58]Huntington, p. 129.

[59]See David C. Schwartz, *Political Alienation and Political Behavior* (Chicago: Aldine, 1973), Chap. 14.

[60]Tocqueville, I, 185 f.

CHAPTER 2 / PARTY LOYALTY AND PARTY CHOICE

[1]John P. Roche, "The Founding Fathers: A Reform Caucus in Action," *American Political Science Review,* LV (December, 1961), 799.

[2]William H. Flanigan, *Political Behavior of the American Electorate,* 2nd ed. (Boston: Allyn and Bacon, 1972), p. 37.

[3]Philip Converse, "The Concept of a Normal Vote," in Angus Campbell, Philip Converse, Warren Miller, and Donald Stokes, *Elections and the Political Order* (New York: Wiley, 1966), p. 18.

[4]*Ibid.,* p. 12.

[5]A 1974 Gallup poll shows distributions virtually identical to those pictured for 1972—42 percent Democratic, 35 percent Independent, and 24 percent Republican. The proportions for the two major parties are the lowest recorded by Gallup since 1940. See *The New York Times,* February 10, 1974. Later that year, the distribution changed slightly to 44 percent Democratic, 33 percent Independent, and 23 percent Republican. *The New York Times,* July 18, 1974.

[6]A panel study, reinterviewing the same persons over a period of years, was conducted by the Survey Research Center from 1956 to 1960. In explaining this data, Dreyer found changes in partisanship to be essentially random. See Edward Dreyer, "Change and Stability in Party Identifications," *Journal of Politics,* XXXV (August, 1973), 712-722.

[7]The proportion of constant loyalists in 1972 is 50.4 percent, but an additional 5.3 percent previously were Independents. In previous years, data were not collected on changes in this

direction, so a true comparison to past years should include this group with the constant partisans. We may hypothesize that such changes were less common in the past, since there was a smaller base of Independents from which the major parties could draw. There is no convincing way to test this hypothesis.

[8]Converse finds parallel changes in the constancy of the vote. See his "Change in the American Electorate," in Angus Campbell and Philip Converse, *The Human Meaning of Social Change* (New York: Russell Sage Foundation, 1972), pp. 317-322.

[9]See Robert Lane, "Fathers and Sons: Foundations of Political Belief," *American Sociological Review*, XXIV (August, 1959), 502-511.

[10]Angus Campbell, Philip Converse, Warren Miller, and Donald Stokes, *The American Voter* (New York: Wiley, 1960), p. 147.

[11]$G=.71$ in 1958 and .58 in 1972. M. Kent Jennings and Richard Niemi present data that further suggest the fragility of intergenerational transmission of partisanship; cf. "The Transmission of Political Values from Parent to Child," *American Political Science Review*, LXII (March, 1968), 169-184.

[12]If both parents were equally interested in politics, male chauvinism and academic research both lead us to select the father as the more important influence; cf. Kenneth Langton, *Political Socialization* (New York: Oxford University Press, 1969), Chap. 3. The problems of recall are particularly severe when respondents are asked to remember, not their own political history, but that of their parents. A strain toward consistency leads respondents to find greater continuity between the generations than probably exists in fact. However, these problems are probably constant across generations, so that conclusions can still be drawn about the relative distributions.

[13]V. O. Key, Jr., with the assistance of Milton C. Cummings, *The Responsible Electorate* (Cambridge: Harvard University Press, 1966), p. 5.

[14]Among many works, see Richard Hamilton, *Class and Politics in the United States* (New York: Wiley, 1972); Mark Levy and Michael Kramer, *The Ethnic Factor* (New York: Simon and Schuster, 1972); Charles Bullock III and Harrell Rodgers, Jr., *Black Political Attitudes* (Chicago: Markham, 1972); Kirsten Amundsen, *The Silenced Majority* (Englewood Cliffs: Prentice-Hall, 1971); Fred Dutton, *Changing Sources of Power* (New York: McGraw-Hill, 1971). These factors are explained separately in Chaps. 3-6 below.

[15]Dewey Grantham, *The Democratic South* (New York: Norton, 1963), Chap. 2.

[16]Samuel Lubell, *The Future of American Politics* (Garden City: Doubleday Anchor, 1956), Chap. 3.

[17]Louis Harris, *Is There a Republican Majority?* (New York: Harper, 1954).

[18]Everett Ladd, Charles Hadley, and Lauriston King, "A New Political Realignment?" *The Public Interest*, XXIII (Spring, 1971), 46-63.

[19]For a general comprehensive examination of the effect of religion on voting and political attitudes, see Kathleen A. Frankovic, "The Effect of Religion on Political Attitudes," Ph.D. thesis (Rutgers University, 1974).

[20]When partisanship is included in a stepwise regression, it provides 89 percent of the total explained variance. Even if it is excluded until all other variables have been entered, this factor still provides 69 percent of the total R^2.

[21]See Richard Childs, *Civic Victories* (New York: Harper, 1952).

[22]Bernard Berelson, Paul Lazarsfeld, and William McPhee, *Voting* (Chicago: University of Chicago Press, 1954), p. 316.

[23]*The American Voter*, p. 143.

[24]Walter Dean Burnham, *Critical Elections and the Mainsprings of American Politics* (New York: Norton, 1970), p. 130 f. Flanigan, pp. 45-48, also agrees that "the case against the independents has been overstated."

[25]*The Responsible Electorate*, p. 104. Cf. Walter DeVries and V. Lance Tarrance, *The Ticket-Splitter* (Grand Rapids: Eerdmans, 1972).

[26]Sidney Verba and Norman Nie, *Participation in America* (New York: Harper and Row, 1972), Chap. 12, provide further data.

[27]Burnham, p. 127.

[28]Cf. David Kovenock, Philip Beardsley, and James Prothro, "Status, Party, Ideology, Issues, and Candidate Choice: A Preliminary Theory—Relevant Analysis of the 1968 American Presidential Election," a paper prepared for the Congress of the International Political Science Association (Munich, 1970), p. 24.

[29]Such action meets the standards of rationality established by Anthony Downs, *An Economic Theory of Democracy* (New York: Harper, 1957), Chaps. 9, 11, 13.

[30]Cf. Harold Weisberg and Jerrold Rusk, "Perceptions of Presidential Candidates: Implications for Electoral Change," *Midwest Journal of Political Science*, XVI (August, 1972), 388-410, and their "Dimensions of Candidate Evaluation," *American Political Science Review*, LXIV (December, 1970), 1167-1185.

[31]Philip Converse, "Information Flow and the Stability of Partisan Attitudes," in *Elections and the Political Order*, Chap. 8.

[32]*Voting*, pp. 218-222.

[33]Arthur Miller, Warren Miller, Alden Raine, and Thad Brown, "A Majority Party in Disarray: Policy Polarization in the 1972 Election," a paper presented to the annual meeting of the American Political Science Association (1973), p. 14, and forthcoming, in part, in the *American Political Science Review* (1975).

[34]See Donald Stokes, "Some Dynamic Elements of Contests for the Presidency," *American Political Science Review*, LX (March, 1966), 19-28, and Chap. 7 below.

[35]Treatment of the Wallace vote in 1968 complicates the analysis. If it is included, with the candidates ordered Humphrey-Nixon-Wallace, G=.56. If it is entirely excluded, G=.85. It seems unreasonable to exclude a large vote, or to include it with that for Humphrey, since the Wallace vote was a large protest vote, based on Democratic defections. In this analysis, the vote of each partisan group is dichotomized as for or against the party of self-identification. The vote of Independents for Wallace is divided in proportion to the vote of Independents for Humphrey and Nixon.

[36]*The American Voter*, p. 155.

[37]"A Majority Party in Disarray," p. 89 f; Converse, "Change in the American Electorate" (above, n. 8), pp. 319 ff.

[38]Kevin P. Phillips, *The Emerging Republican Majority* (New York: Arlington House, 1969), p. 470 and *passim*.

[39]No Republican gains independent of social characteristics are found in the suburbs by Frederick Wirt, *On the City's Rim* (Lexington, Mass.: Heath, 1972). Criticisms of the Phillips thesis are also made by Ladd, et al.; Nelson Polsby, "An Emerging Republican Majority?" *The Public Interest*, XVII (Fall, 1969), 119-126; and Andrew Hacker, "Is There a New Republican Majority?" *Commentary*, XLVIII (November, 1969), 65-70.

[40]See Robert Axelrod, "Where the Votes Come From: An Analysis of Electoral Coalitions, 1952-1968," *American Political Science Review*, LXVI (March, 1972), 11-20. "A Majority Party in Disarray," p. 88 f., also shows an increase in black Independents in 1972.

CHAPTER 3 / THE IMPACT OF SOCIAL CLASS

[1]See August B. Hollingshead, *Social Class and Mental Illness* (New York: Wiley, 1958), and Arthur Kornhauser, *Mental Health of the Industrial Worker* (New York: Wiley, 1965).

[2]James Madison, *The Federalist*, No. 10 (New York: Modern Library, 1941), p. 56.

[3]*Ibid.*

[4]See Angus Campbell, Philip Converse, Warren Miller, and Donald Stokes, *The American Voter* (New York: Wiley, 1960), Chap. 10.

[5]See Louis Hartz, *The Liberal Tradition in America* (New York: Harcourt, Brace, and World, 1955), and David Potter, *People of Plenty* (Chicago: University of Chicago Press, 1954).

[6]See C. Wright Mills, *The Power Elite* (New York: Oxford University Press, 1956), Chap. 13; Herbert Marcuse, *One-Dimensional Man* (Boston: Beacon Press, 1964).

[7]Richard Hamilton, *Class and Politics in the United States* (New York: Wiley, 1972), p. 191.

[8]The metaphor is obviously borrowed from Warren Miller and Donald Stokes, "Constituency Influence in Congress," *American Political Science Review*, LVII (March, 1963), 45-56.

[9]Karl Marx and Frederich Engels, *The Communist Manifesto*, I (1848).

[10]V. I. Lenin, *What Is To Be Done?* (1905).

[11]In the analyses of occuption the work of the head of the household is employed in all cases. The alternative, using respondent occupation, makes it impossible to classify the large number of housewives. Persons in farm occupations are eliminated from these studies, as are retired or similarly unclassifiable groups. Nonmanual workers include professionals, managers, proprietors, sales and clerical employees; manual workers include craftsmen, factory operatives, protective and domestic workers.

[12]The few respondents who consider themselves "upper class" or "lower class" are included, respectively, with the middle and working classes.

[13]Tau-b is the correlation coefficient used in this chapter, because frequent comparisons are made to the findings of *The American Voter*, which relied on this measure. The gamma coefficients, used elsewhere in this book, are approximately double in magnitude.

[14]*The American Voter*, pp. 346-350.

[15]Robert Alford, *Party and Society* (Chicago: Rand McNally, 1963), Chap. 8.

[16]Also see *The American Voter*, p. 343.

[17]In 1968, the Wallace and Nixon votes are combined. The degree of class voting is higher if the Wallace ballots are omitted or combined with those for Humphrey. However, these procedures seem less valid, since the Wallace candidacy did draw substantial support and was an expression of opposition to the Democratic party.

[18]Donald Stokes, "Some Dynamic Elements of Contests for the Presidency," *American Political Science Review*, LX (March, 1966), 19-28. Also see Chap. 7 below.

[19]Lewis Chester, Godfrey Hodgson, and Bruce Page, *An American Melodrama* (New York: Dell, 1969), p. 312.

[20]James Barber, Jr., *Social Mobility and Voting Behavior* (Chicago: Rand McNally, 1970), Chap. 6.

[21]See Erich Fromm, *Escape from Freedom* (New York: Farrar and Rinehart, 1941); Seymour Lipset and Earl Raab, *The Politics of Unreason* (New York: Harper and Row, 1970).

[22]Bernard Berelson, Paul Lazarsfeld, and William McPhee, *Voting* (Chicago: University of Chicago Press, 1954), p. 333.

[23]*The American Voter*, p. 357.

[24]This generation includes those born from 1897 to 1906, aged 23 to 32 in 1929, the year of the stock market crash. It is the group isolated in Figure 13-5, p. 357 of *The American Voter*, aged 50-59 in 1956.

[25]See *The American Voter*, p. 358 f. Because the time periods used in the earlier study are not consistent among elections, I have recalculated the coefficients presented there to increase comparability.

[26]See Samuel Lubell, *The Future of American Politics* (Garden City: Doubleday Anchor, 1956), Chaps. 3, 4; Paul Kleppner, *The Cross of Culture* (New York: The Free Press, 1970); Harold Gosnell, *Machine Politics: Chicago Model* (Chicago: University of Chicago Press, 1937); Samuel Warner, *The Private City* (Philadelphia: University of Pennsylvania Press, 1968).

[27]Norval D. Glenn, "Class and Party Support in the United States: Recent and Emerging Trends," *Public Opinion Quarterly*, XXXVII (Spring, 1973), 1-20.

[28]Paul Abramson, in a similar analysis, emphasizes the differences in generational behavior. His methods differ from those employed here in excluding blacks, using different generational boundaries, and using a different correlation coefficient. However, his results still show the aging effects and the changes in class voting associated with particular elections. Cf. "Generational Change in American Electoral Behavior," *American Political Science Review*, LXVIII (March, 1974), 93-105.

[29]In all analyses, South includes both the Confederate and border states; North, all other states.

[30]Paul Lewinson, *Race, Class and Party* (New York: Grosset and Dunlap, 1932, 1959); V. O. Key, Jr., *Southern Politics* (New York: Knopf, 1949), especially Chaps. 14, 30.

[31]Philip Converse, "On the Possibility of Major Political Realignment in the South," in Angus Campbell, Philip Converse, Warren Miller, and Donald Stokes, *Elections and the Political Order* (New York: Wiley, 1966), p. 221. Cf. Alexander Heard, *A Two-Party South?* (Chapel Hill: University of North Carolina Press, 1952).

[32]As suggested by Judson James, *American Political Parties in Transition* (New York: Harper and Row, 1974), Chap. 2, and James Sundquist, *The Dynamics of the Party System* (Washington: The Brookings Institution, 1973), Chap. 12.

[33]Analyses of such Democratic liberals are found in Vicki Semel, *At the Grass Roots in the Garden State* (Cranbury, N.J.: Associated University Presses, 1975), and James Q. Wilson, *The Amateur Democrat* (Chicago: University of Chicago Press, 1962).

[34]Walter Dean Burnham, *Critical Elections and the Mainsprings of American Politics* (New York: Norton, 1970), p. 140.

[35]*The American Voter*, p. 367.

[36]*Ibid.*, p. 367 f.

[37]The importance of the context of the times is evidenced by one additional set of data—the association of class voting with individual involvement in the campaign. In the past, through 1964, those who cared more about the outcome of an election also showed more class influence in their ballots (*The American Voter*, p. 364). Since the parties emphasized class factors, those who cared which party won also cast ballots along class lines. In 1968, however, class voting is particularly evident among those with only moderate involvement, while in 1972 the only discernible influence of class is among those who have little declared interest in the outcome. These relationships reflect the changing emphases of the campaigns.

[38]Glenn, *op. cit.*

[39]Theodore Lowi, "American Business, Public Policy, Case-Studies, and Political Theory," *World Politics*, XVI (July, 1964), 677-715.

[40]Although distributions varied, in all years at least a fifth of the total sample each took the liberal or conservative position on at least two issues, and the remainder evidenced other combinations. Support of the liberal position was rated 1; an ambiguous position or no opinion was rated 2; and opposition to the program was rated 3. For most purposes, the resulting seven-point scale is collapsed into three relatively equal categories.

[41]A perception of the Democrats as favoring a particular result was rated as 1; the lack of party difference or no opinion was rated as 2; and a Republican perception was rated as 3. The resulting nine-point scale is generally collapsed into two or three relatively equal categories.

[42]From 1960 to 1972, respectively, the tau correlations are: .42, .26, .39, .22.

[43]To analyze these total effects, the technique of causal path analysis is employed in Chapter 9.

[44]To deal with the problem, Arthur Goldberg suggests the use of dynamic models. See "Discerning a Causal Pattern Among Data on Voting Behavior," *American Political Science Review*, LX (December, 1966), 913-922.

[45]See C. Vann Woodward, *Tom Watson* (New York: The Macmillan Company, 1938).

[46]Hamilton, p. 291, and his analysis of the Wallace vote in 1968, pp. 461-467.

[47]Daniel Bell, "Controversy: Is There a Post-Industrial Society?" *Transaction/Society*, XI (May/June, 1974), 24. See also *The Coming of Post-Industrial Society* (New York: Basic Books, 1973).

[48]Frederich Engels, *Anti-Dühring*, as quoted in V. I. Lenin, *The State and Revolution* (New York: International Publishers, 1932), p. 16.

[49]Norman Birnbaum, *The Crisis of Industrial Society* (New York: Oxford University Press, 1969), p. 37.

[50]*Ibid.*

[51]Hamilton, p. 218.

[52]Sidney Verba and Norman Nie, *Participation in America* (New York: Harper and Row, 1972), pp. 339 ff.

[53]Hamilton, pp. 527 ff.

[54]See U.S. Department of Health, Education, and Welfare, *Work in America* (1973), and the essays collected in Louise Howe, ed., *The White Majority* (New York: Vintage, 1970).

CHAPTER 4 / SEX, VOTING, AND WAR

[1]Gabriel A. Almond and Sidney Verba, *The Civic Culture*, abridged ed. (Boston: Little, Brown, 1965), p. 325.

[2]Martin Gruberg, *Women in Politics* (Oshkosh: Academia Press, 1968), p. 7.

[3]Alfred Hero, "Public Reaction to Government Policies," in John P. Robinson et al., *Measures of Political Attitudes* (Ann Arbor: Institute for Social Research, 1968), p. 52.

[4]Angus Campbell, Philip Converse, Warren Miller, and Donald Stokes, *The American Voter* (New York: Wiley, 1960), p. 493.

[5]Hazel Erskine, "The Polls: Women's Role," *Public Opinion Quarterly*, XXXV (Summer, 1971), 278 f; Louis Harris and Associates, *The 1972 Virginia Slims American Women's Public Opinion Poll* (1972), p. 35.

[6]Bernard Berelson, Paul Lazarsfeld, and William McPhee, *Voting* (Chicago: University of Chicago Press, 1954), p. 74.

[7]Marjorie Lansing, "Women: The New Political Class," a paper presented at the annual meeting of the American Political Science Association (1971), p. 5.

[8]The pioneering study is Herbert Tingsten, *Political Behavior* (Totowa: Bedminister Press, 1963), pp. 10-36. This book was first published in 1937.

[9]Charles E. Merriam and Harold F. Gosnell, *Non-Voting* (Chicago: University of Chicago Press, 1924), p. 7.

[10]*The American Voter*, p. 484.

[11]Merriam and Gosnell, pp. 37, 114.

[12]*Voting*, pp. 25-28; Robert E. Lane, *Political Life* (New York: The Free Press, 1959), pp. 211-213; Angus Campbell, Gerald Gurin, and Warren Miller, *The Voter Decides* (Evanston: Row, Peterson, 1954), pp. 191, 197.

[13]Erskine, p. 277 ff.

[14]Merriam and Gosnell, p. 44; Lansing, pp. 9-19.

[15]U.S. Bureau of the Census, "Voter Participation in November 1972," *Current Population Reports*, P-20, No. 244 (December, 1972).

[16]The census figures are likely to be more accurate than those of the University of Michigan study, since they are based on a larger sample and are factually closer to the actual turnout. However, the Michigan figures are only slightly less accurate and can be employed confidently for the examination of subgroups. For analysis of the sources of error, see Aage R. Clausen, "Response Validity: Vote Report," *Public Opinion Quarterly*, XXXII (Winter, 1968-69), 588-606, and U.S. Bureau of the Census, "Voting and Registration in the Election of November 1970," *Current Population Reports*, P-20, No. 228 (October, 1971), p. 6.

[17]Table 4.1 is a deliberate replication of the analysis of 1952-56 data as reported in *The American Voter*, p. 486.

[18]Similarly, no sex difference in turnout was found in two northern presidential primaries in 1968—Austin Ranney, "Turnout and Representation in Presidential Primary Elections," *American Political Science Review*, LXVI (March, 1972), 26. Greater activity among black women compared to black men is found by John C. Pierce et al., "Sex Differences in Black Political Beliefs and Behavior," *American Journal of Political Science*, XVII (May, 1973), 422-430.

[19]This disparity may be unique to the 1972 election. In 1968, college-educated southern women voted 12 percent less than men, while the disparity in the North was an insignificant 1.6 percent. All other results in 1968 evidenced the same pattern as in 1972. However, even in 1952-56, college-educated southerners were distinctive in their sexual equality.

[20]*The American Voter*, p. 487. Tingsten first noted this areal affect in *Political Behavior*, p. 14 ff.

[21]In 1968, the regional difference was even greater. In the North, women actually outvoted men by a small margin in the outlying areas. In the outlying areas in the South, however, 41 percent of women did not vote, compared to only a quarter of the men.

[22]Merriam and Gosnell, pp. 37, 44, 76.

[23]The 1972 data could not be analyzed on this point because no question was asked on the age of children in the home. The only relevant question asked if there were any school-age (5-18) children in the household. Even these poor data do show some slight sex difference. Men are not affected at all in turnout by the presence or absence of children. Women without school-age children are more likely to vote.

[24]*Virginia Slims Poll*, p. 18.

[25]Similarly, a study twenty years ago found southerners and women less tolerant of nonconformity, and a control for churchgoing could explain neither the sex nor the regional difference. See Samuel A. Stouffer et al., *Communism, Conformity and Civil Liberties* (Garden City: Doubleday, 1955), pp. 140-149. Another indication of the particularly strong influence of southern religion is found in the 1960 presidential election. See Angus Campbell, Philip Converse, Warren Miller, and Donald Stokes, *Elections and the Political Order* (New York: Wiley, 1966), pp. 88-93, 112-122.

[26]W. J. Cash, *The Mind of the South* (New York: Knopf, 1941; reprinted by Doubleday Anchor), p. 97.

[27]*Ibid.*, p. 137.

[28]The latter group includes those who have moved only within the South, and therefore have not experienced other cultural influences directly. By including intraregional migrants within our "mobile" group, we make it even more difficult to establish our hypothesis.

[29]Separate regressions were performed for men and women. The relevant beta weights in 1968 are: education, .33 for males, .26 for women; region, .01 for males, .21 for females; age of children, −.10 for men and .09 for females. In 1972 they are: education, .28 for males .33 for females; region, .10 for males and .13 for females; age of children, .05 for both sexes. Other variables included in the regression are age, residential area, race, and geographical mobility. Only for age is there a significant beta weight.

[30]Tingsten, pp. 42-47.

[31]As in Almond and Verba's summary, p. 325.

[32]Tingsten, p. 72, found higher Republican votes in Illinois, where ballots were separated, in 1916 and 1920; but class and race bias can explain these results. Cf. Robert Lane, *Political Life* (New York: The Free Press, 1959), p. 214.

[33]*The Voter Decides*, pp. 71, 75. On 1948, see *Voting*, p. 319 f.

[34]This finding contradicts Lansing, p. 7, who does not support her assertion that "women voted in greater percentages for Senator Humphrey than for Nixon."

[35]Frederick G. Dutton, *Changing Sources of Power* (New York: McGraw-Hill, 1971), Chaps. 2, 3.

[36]David Halberstam, *The Best and the Brightest* (New York: Random House, 1972), p. 532.

[37]An independent study conducted in March, 1967, found "men were almost twice as likely as women to be hawkish on the war in Vietnam, and they were about twice as likely to be active *vis-à-vis* the war"—Sidney Verba and Norman Nie, *Participation in America* (New York: Harper and Row, 1972), p. 287.

[38]The gamma correlation of opinion and sex decreases from .25 to .12 from 1968 to 1972.

[39]*Virginia Slims Poll*, pp. 68, 74.

[40]James G. March, "Husband-Wife Interaction over Political Issues," *Public Opinion Quarterly*, XVII (Winter, 1953-54), 461-470. Other differences between the sexes are summarized in *The American Voter*, pp. 489-493, and Kirsten Amundsen, *The Silenced Majority* (Englewood Cliffs: Prentice-Hall, 1971), pp. 134-138.

[41]Tingsten, pp. 12-24, 72.

[42]Alan Grimes, *The Puritan Ethic and Woman Suffrage* (New York: Oxford University

Press, 1967), and Peter Odegard, *Pressure Politcs* (New York: Columbia University Press, 1928).

[43]Merriam and Gosnell, p. 113.

[44]Gabriel A. Almond, *The American People and Foreign Policy* (New York: Harcourt, Brace, 1950), p. 121.

[45]Hero, p. 53.

[46]John E. Mueller, *War, Presidents and Public Opinion* (New York: Wiley, 1973), p. 146. The finding is confirmed by Louis Harris, *Is There a Republican Majority?* (New York: Harper, 1954), p. 111.

[47]The Gallup poll, reported in *The New York Times*, November 18, 1973.

[48]*Virginia Slims Poll*, p. 93.

[49]$G = .20$ in 1968, $.18$ in 1972.

[50]Cf. Gerald Finch, "Policy and Candidate Choice in the 1968 American Presidential Election," Ph.D. dissertation (University of Minnesota, 1971), and Arthur Miller, Warren Miller, Alden Raine, and Thad Brown, "A Majority Party in Disarray," a paper presented to the annual meeting of the American Political Science Association (1973), p. 14.

[51]*Virginia Slims Poll*, p. 79.

[52]Although not explicitly argued in these terms, suggestions along these lines may be found in Robert Ardrey, *The Territorial Imperative* (New York: Atheneum, 1966); Lionel Tiger, *Men in Groups* (New York: Random House, 1969); and Robin Fox, "The Evolution of Human Sexual Behavior," *The New York Times Magazine* (March 24, 1968), p. 32 ff.

[53]Geoffrey Gorer, *The American People* (New York: Norton, 1949), p. 94.

[54]See Naomi Weisstein, " 'Kinder, Küche, Kirche' as Scientific Law: Psychology Constructs the Female," in Robin Morgan, ed., *Sisterhood is Powerful* (New York: Random House, 1970), pp. 205-220.

[55]For a review of sex stereotyping, see Amundsen (above, n. 40), Chap. 6.

[56]See Fred I. Greenstein, *Children and Politics* (New Haven: Yale University Press, 1965), Chap. 6; David Easton and Jack Dennis, *Children in the Political System* (New York: McGraw-Hill, 1969, pp. 335-343; Almond and Verba, pp. 332-335; M. Kent Jennings and Kenneth P. Langton, "Mothers Versus Fathers: The Formation of Political Orientations among Young Americans," *Journal of Politics*, XXXI (May, 1969), 329-358; Robert D. Hess and Judith V. Torney, *The Development of Political Attitudes in Children* (Chicago: Aldine, 1967).

[57]On the transmission of partisanship, see Donald D. Searing et al., "The Structuring Principle: Political Socialization and Belief Systems," *American Political Science Review*, LXVII (June, 1973), 415-432. For recent research showing the absence of sex differences in children's political attitudes, see Anthony M. Orun et al., "Sex, Socialization and Politics," *American Sociological Review*, XXXIX (April, 1974), 197-209, and the references cited there.

[58]Amundsen (above, n. 40), p. 142.

[59]This tentative conclusion follows from a survey taken during the Korean War, in which women with more liberal sexual attitudes were found to be more willing to use atomic weapons than their traditional sisters. Cf. Mueller, p. 147.

CHAPTER 5 / THE NEW POLITICAL GENERATIONS

[1]*As You Like It*, II: 7, 150-156.

[2]Norman Ryder, "The Cohort as a Concept in the Study of Social Change," *American Sociological Review*, XXX (December, 1965), 848.

[3]Fred Dutton, *Changing Sources of Power* (New York: McGraw-Hill, 1971), p. 16 f.

[4]*Ibid.*, p. 49.

[5]For example, Kevin Phillips, "How Nixon Will Win," *New York Times Magazine* (August 6, 1972), p. 8 ff.

[6]The voters aged 25-35 in 1972 are employed in this chapter both as the "middle-aged" voters and as the "generation of the 1960s". In Chapter 2, when political generation is

emphasized, the "generation of the 1960s" is defined as those 25-36 in 1972. The difference of one year has no effect on the conclusions reached here.

[7]In a classic study, college experience was found to increase the liberalism of youth. After twenty-five years, however, the acquired attitudes continued to be held by many of the persons involved, long after their undergraduate days. See Theodore Newcomb, *Personality and Social Change* (New York: Dryden Press, 1943) and *Persistence and Change; Bennington Students After 25 Years* (New York: Wiley, 1967).

[8]See Matilda Riley, "Aging and Cohort Succession: Interpretations and Misinterpretations," *Public Opinion Quarterly*, XXXVII (Spring, 1973), 37-49.

[9]Ryder, p. 845.

[10]John Crittenden, "Aging and Party Affiliation," *Public Opinion Quarterly*, XXVI (Winter, 1962), 648-657.

[11]Neal Cutler, "Generation, Maturation and Party Affiliation: A Cohort Analysis," *Public Opinion Quarterly*, XXXIII (Winter, 1969-70), 583-592.

[12]Norval Glenn and Ted Hefner, "Further Evidence on Aging and Party Identification," *Public Opinion Quarterly*, XXXVI (Spring, 1972), 31-47; cf. William Klecka, "Applying Political Generations to the Study of Political Behavior: A Cohort Analysis," *Public Opinion Quarterly*, XXXV (Fall, 1971), 358-373.

[13]See Erik Erikson, *Childhood and Society* (New York: Norton, 1950), Chaps. 7, 8, and "Identity and the Life Cycle," *Psychological Issues*, I, Monograph 1 (1959), 58-94.

[14]Kenneth Keniston sees youth as a distinct stage. See *Young Radicals* (New York: Harcourt, Brace, and World, 1968), pp. 264-272.

[15]Erik Erikson, *Identity, Youth and Crisis* (New York: Norton, 1968), p. 184.

[16]*Ibid.*, p. 190.

[17]*Ibid.*, p. 246.

[18]Richard Merelman, "The Development of Policy Thinking in Adolescence," *American Political Science Review*, LXV (December, 1971), 1033-1047.

[19]Kenneth Keniston, "Social Change and Youth in America," in Erik Erikson, ed., *Youth: Change and Challenge* (New York: Basic Books, 1963), p. 169. Cf. S. N. Eisenstadt, "Archetypal Patterns of Youth," *ibid.*, p. 39.

[20]Merelman, p. 1047.

[21]Kenneth Keniston is most notable. See his *Young Radicals* and *The Uncommitted: Alienated Youth in American Society* (New York: Harcourt, Brace, and World, 1965).

[22]The combined effect of age and education on political knowledge is evident when the middle-aged cohort is examined in 1968. In that year, college-educated persons were about as informed as their elders. After four years, in 1972, the former group is slightly more knowledgeable. A gap does exist among the noncollege group in both 1968 and 1972. On the other hand, age appears dominant in affecting electoral involvement, as further indicated by the behavior of the middle-aged group in 1968. When it was four years younger, the gap between it and older persons was greater. As it has grown in years, its political involvement more nearly resembles that of its elders.

[23]The only differences discussed are those in which there are at least five percentage points between the age groups in the proportions holding an opinion or knowing the candidates' positions. It is possible that the young are not more knowledgeable, but only less willing to admit disinterest. However, they do not appear shy in admitting relative disinterest in electoral politics.

[24]Murray Edelman, *The Symbolic Uses of Politics* (Urbana: University of Illinois Press, 1964), and *Politics as Symbolic Action* (Chicago: Markham Publishing Co., 1971).

[25]Philip E. Converse, "Change in the American Electorate," in Angus Campbell and Philip E. Converse, eds., *The Human Meaning of Social Change* (New York: Russell Sage Foundation, 1972), p. 328 f.

[26]Converse, p. 334. A similar distinction, between "efficacy" and "trust," is made by William A. Gamson, *Power and Discontent* (Homewood, Ill.: Dorsey Press, 1968), pp. 39-48.

[27]For persons without college experience, the percentages are:

	1964	1968	1972
New Voters, 1972			
Supporters	—	—	25.1
Cynics	—	—	27.9
Trustful	—	—	19.0
Oppressed	—	—	27.9
Age 25-35 in 1972			
Supporters	65.5	41.8	30.2
Cynics	15.1	21.6	24.7
Trustful	13.7	17.0	14.2
Oppressed	5.8	19.6	30.9
Age Over 35 in 1972			
Supporters	47.8	30.6	24.2
Cynics	17.5	20.0	29.6
Trustful	19.3	22.4	12.9
Oppressed	15.4	27.0	33.3

[28]These data are from a poll by Daniel Yankelovich, reported in *The New York Times*, May 22, 1974.

[29]"Liberal" is used here, loosely but conventionally, to mean support of aid to minorities, government job guarantees, provision of medical care, more progressive taxation, relaxation of antimarijuana laws, restraint in the use of force in campus or urban protests, permitting abortion, favoring women's equality, fostering school busing, protecting rights of the criminally accused, and favoring withdrawal from Vietnam. Most of the questions are asked as 7-point scales, with positions 1-3 considered here as the liberal opinion.

[30]Philip Converse and Howard Schuman, " 'Silent Majorities' and the Vietnam War," *Scientific American*, CCXXII (June, 1970), 17 ff.

[31]Different operational conceptions of liberalism may be found in Gerhard Lenski, *The Religious Factor* (Garden City: Doubleday, 1961), pp. 208-210; Seymour Lipset, *Political Man* (Garden City: Doubleday, 1960), pp. 87-115; and Lloyd Free and Hadley Cantril, *The Political Beliefs of Americans* (New Brunswick, N.J.: Rutgers University Press, 1967), Chaps. 2, 3.

[32]Arthur Miller, Warren Miller, Alden Raine, and Thad Brown, "A Majority Party in Disarray: Policy Polarization in the 1972 Election," a paper presented to the annual meeting of the American Political Science Association (1973), p. 38.

[33]Compare Ronald Ingelhart, "The Silent Revolution in Europe: Intergenerational Change in Post-Industrial Societies," *American Political Science Review*, LXV (December, 1971), 991-1017.

[34]A basic priority ordering of human needs from survival to self-actualization has been conceptualized by Abraham H. Maslow, "A Theory of Human Motivation," *Psychological Review*, L (1943), 370-396, and later used by James Davies, *Human Nature in Politics* (New York: Wiley, 1963), and many others.

[35]Milton Rokeach, "Change and Stability in American Value Systems, 1968-1971," *Public Opinion Quarterly*, XXXVIII (Summer, 1974), 237.

[36]See John Stuart Mill, *On Liberty* and *Considerations on Representative Government;* T. H. Green, *Lectures on the Principles of Political Obligation* (Ann Arbor: University of Michigan Press, 1967); and John Dewey, *Democracy and Education* (New York: The Free Press, 1944).

[37]Ronald D. Rotunda, "The 'Liberal' Label: Roosevelt's Capture of a Symbol," *Public Policy*, XVII (1968), 377-408.

[38]The conflict in the Democratic party is discussed by Dennis G. Sullivan et al., *The Politics of Representation* (New York: St. Martin's Press, 1974), p. 33, and Aaron Wildavsky, "The Meaning of 'Youth' in the Struggle for Control of the Democratic Party," in *The Revolt Against the Masses* (New York: Basic Books, 1971), pp. 270-287.

[39]The four sets of issues are adapted from "A Majority Party in Disarray," p. 29.

[40]Benjamin Page and Richard Brody, "Policy Voting and The Electoral Process: The Vietnam War Issue," *American Political Science Review,* LXVI (September, 1972), 979-995. Gerald Finch believes Vietnam affected the presidential vote significantly in 1968, but agrees that there was no clear direction to the vote. Cf. "Policy and Candidate Choice in the 1968 American Presidential Election," Ph.D. dissertation (University of Minnesota, 1973), pp. 70-86. Also see Chap. 9, below.

[41]Education was included in separate regressions by age groups, but had little effect on the vote. The beta weights are .05, .08, .02, for increasing age. The largest impact was clearly among the 25-35 group.

[42]Keniston, "Social Change and Youth in America," p. 181.

[43]Lewis Coser, *The Functions of Social Conflict* (New York: Free Press, 1956), p. 154.

[44]Norman Nie, Dale Bent, and C. Hadlai Hull, *SPSS: Statistical Package for the Social Sciences* (New York: McGraw-Hill, 1970), p. 209. Cf. R. J. Rummel, "Understanding Factor Analysis," *Journal of Conflict Resolution,* XI (December, 1967), 444-480.

[45]The technique of varimax rotation is used. Only nine issues could be employed, since all of the issues included in Table 5.4 were not raised with all respondents. Factor score coefficients are used for the correlation with liberalism.

CHAPTER 6 / BLACK AND WHITE ASUNDER

[1]Alexis de Tocqueville, *Democracy in America,* ed. Phillips Bradley (New York: Vintage, 1954), I, 370, 394.

[2]*The Autobiography of Malcolm X* (New York: Grove Press, 1965), p. 246. Italics omitted.

[3]U.S. Senate Permanent Subcommittee on Investigations of the Committee on Government Operations, *Staff Studies of Major Riots and Civic Disorders,* 90th Congress, 2nd session (1968).

[4]Supplementary samples of blacks were drawn in 1964 and 1968 to enlarge the number of cases for detailed analysis. If simply added to the national sample, the racial proportions would be inaccurate. In this chapter, all analyses are done separately for blacks and whites, and no national biracial cross section is needed. Therefore, the supplementary sample of blacks is included in all instances. Other races are excluded from this analysis.

[5]See Reg Murphy and Hal Gulliver, *The Southern Strategy* (New York: Scribner, 1971); Lewis Chester, Godfrey Hodgson, and Bruce Page, *An American Melodrama* (New York: Dell, 1969), Chaps. 9, 11.

[6]Philip Converse, "Change in the American Electorate," in Angus Campbell and Philip Converse, *The Human Meaning of Social Change* (New York: Russell Sage Foundation, 1972), pp. 263-337.

[7]Donald Matthews and James Prothro, *Negroes and the New Southern Politics* (New York: Harcourt, Brace and World, 1966), pp. 95-98.

[8]Sidney Verba and Norman Nie, *Participation in America* (New York: Harper and Row, 1972), p. 157.

[9]*Ibid.,* p. 160.

[10]Table 6.1 is based on responses to the Survey Research Center's voter surveys. The more accurate data of the U.S. Census Bureau may be found in "Voter Participation in November 1968," *Current Population Reports,* P-20, No. 177 (December 27, 1968), and "Voter Participation in November 1972," *Current Population Reports,* P-20, No. 244 (December, 1972).

[11]Pat Watters and Reese Cleghorn, *Climbing Jacob's Ladder* (New York: Harcourt, Brace and World, 1967), p. 8.

[12]U.S. Commission on Civil Rights, *Political Participation* (1968), p. 222.

[13]Verba and Nie, p. 254.

[14]This structure of public opinion is elaborated by Donald Devine, *The Attentive Public: Polyarchy and Democracy* (Chicago: Rand McNally, 1970).

[15]David Easton and Jack Dennis, *Children in the Political System* (New York: McGraw-Hill, 1969), p. 63.

[16]The decline in political support had largely occurred even by 1970, according to Arthur Miller, Thad Brown, and Alden Raine, "Social Conflict and Political Estrangement: 1958-1972," a paper delivered to the annual meeting of the Midwest Political Science Association (1973).

[17]Harrel P. Rodgers, Jr., "Toward Explanation of the Political Efficacy and Political Cynicism of Black Adolescents: An Exploratory Study," *American Journal of Political Science,* XVIII (May, 1974), 257-282.

[18]Peter Eisinger, "Racial Differences in Protest Participation," *American Political Science Review,* LXVIII (June, 1974), 592-606.

[19]Joel D. Aberbach and Jack L. Walker, *Race in the City* (Boston: Little, Brown, 1973), p. 208.

[20]William A. Gamson, *Power and Discontent* (Homewood, Ill.: Dorsey Press, 1968), p. 83.

[21]Aberbach and Walker, p. 208.

[22]Robert Conot, *Rivers of Blood, Years of Darkness* (New York: Bantam Books, 1967), p. 109.

[23]U.S. Commission on Civil Disorders, *Report,* p. 1.

[24]Angus Campbell, Philip Converse, Warren Miller, and Donald Stokes, *The American Voter* (New York: Wiley, 1960), pp. 303-306.

[25]Philip Converse, Warren Miller, Jerrold Rusk, and Arthur Wolfe, "Continuity and Change in American Politics: Parties and Issues in the 1968 Election," *American Political Science Review,* LXIII, (December, 1969), 1085.

[26]Robert Axelrod, "Where the Votes Come From: An Analysis of Electoral Coalitions, 1952-1968," *American Political Science Review,* LXVI (March, 1972), 15-17.

[27]Austin Ranney and Willmoore Kendall, *Democracy and the American Party System* (New York: Harcourt, Brace, 1956), p. 509.

[28]In factor analysis of opinions on racial issues, J. Michael Ross finds five underlying dimensions of attitudes. Opinions on civil rights and activity of government are closely related. J. Michael Ross, "Race Issues and American Electoral Politics," a paper presented to the annual meeting of the American Political Science Association (1973).

[29]Only those answers that unreservedly support the integrationist alternatives are considered pro-integration opinions.

[30]In 1960, respondents were given only one option: they could either agree or disagree that "the government in Washington should stay out of the question of whether white and colored children go to the same school." In later years, they could choose between two options: "the government in Washington should see to it that white and Negro children are allowed to go to the same schools," or "this is not the government's business."

[31]Andrew Greeley and Paul Sheatsley, "Attitudes Toward Racial Integration," *Scientific American,* CCXXV (December, 1971), 15-17. Similar changes in the 1967-71 period are found by Aberbach and Walker in Detroit.

[32]Illustratively, 60 percent of Greeley and Sheatsley's 1970 national sample support the goal of school integration, while only 45 percent of the Survey Research Center's 1972 national sample support federal government action to accomplish this objective.

[33]Jerome H. Skolnick, *The Politics of Protest* (New York: Ballantine Books, 1969), p. 186.

[34]Matthews and Prothro, p. 334.

[35]See Stokely Carmichael and Charles Hamilton, *Black Power* (New York: Random House, 1967), and Hamilton, "An Advocate of Black Power Defines It," *New York Times Magazine* (April 14, 1968), pp. 79-83.

[36]James Baldwin, *The Fire Next Time* (New York: The Dial Press, 1963), p. 108.

[37]The indexes of class and race differences are adopted from Robert Alford, *Party and Society* (Chicago: Rand McNally, 1963).

[38]"The Troubled American: A Special Report on the White Majority," *Newsweek,* LXXIV (October 6, 1969), 32.

[39]See Thomas J. Pavlak, "Social Class, Ethnicity and Racial Prejudice," *Public Opinion*

Quarterly, XXXVII (Summer, 1975), 225-231; Seymour Lipset, *Political Man* (Garden City: Doubleday, 1960), Chap. 4.

[40]Ross (above, n. 28), p. 12.

[41]Gamma correlations are .40 in 1964, .43 combining the Nixon and Wallace votes in 1968, and .42 in 1972.

[42]Cf. Richard Boyd, "Popular Control of Public Policy: A Normal Vote Analysis of the 1968 Election," *American Political Science Review*, LXVI (June, 1972), 429-449.

[43]Ross (above, n. 28), pp. 53-65, minimizes the unique impact of race issues in 1968.

[44]See Harold Weisberg and Jerrold Rusk, "Perceptions of Presidential Candidates: Implications for Electoral Change," *Midwest Journal of Political Science*, XVI (August, 1972), 388-410.

[45]These distinctions are basic to the work of Richard Hamilton, *Class and Politics in the United States* (New York: Wiley, 1972).

[46]Chalmers Johnson, *Revolutionary Change* (Boston: Little, Brown, 1966), p. 32.

[47]*Ibid.*, p. 87.

[48]*Ibid.*, p. 166.

[49]Greeley and Sheatsley, p. 19.

CHAPTER 7 / THE CONCERNS OF VOTERS

[1]V. O. Key, Jr., with the assistance of Milton C. Cummings, Jr., *The Responsible Electorate* (Cambridge: Harvard University Press, 1966), p. 150.

[2]Albert Cantril and Charles Roll, Jr., *Hopes and Fears of the American People* (New York: Universe Books, 1971), p. 31.

[3]The Gallup poll, *The New York Times,* October 20, 1974.

[4]Key, pp. 78, 129-134.

[5]The concept is developed in Donald Matthews and James Prothro, "The Concept of Party Image and its Importance for the Southern Electorate," in M. Kent Jennings and Harmon Ziegler, eds., *The Electoral Process* (Englewood Cliffs: Prentice-Hall, 1966), Chap. 8, and *Negroes and the New Southern Politics* (New York: Harcourt, Brace and World, 1966), pp. 377-388. It is elaborated by Richard J. Trilling, "Party Image and Partisan Change, 1952-1972," a paper presented to the annual meeting of the American Political Science Association (1974).

[6]The table combines up to three comments for each respondent. Five opportunities for comments were offered in 1960 and 1968, but only the first three are included in order to provide a more direct comparison with 1972 answers. Few persons actually gave a fourth or a fifth response.

[7]This finding is predicted in Angus Campbell, Philip Converse, Warren Miller, and Donald Stokes, *The American Voter* (New York: Wiley, 1960), p. 61.

[8]*Ibid.*, p. 87.

[9]These dimensions were developed by the authors of *The American Voter* and are employed in that work and in Donald E. Stokes, Angus Campbell, and Warren E. Miller, "Components of Electoral Decision," *American Political Science Review*, LII (June, 1958), 367-387. The present work modifies the original formulation in two important ways. First, new scales are added to measure the impact of the social issue, Vietnam, and general philosophy. In the earlier work, these items were included in the domestic policy, foreign policy, and group scales. Second, these dimensions have been constructed from the individual items and do not correspond to the particular classifications of the Survey Research Center. Illustratively, comments about the candidates as party leaders are included here in the evaluations of the candidates themselves. In the previous work, these comments were included in the evaluations of party performance. A full coding description will be mailed to readers on request.

[10]These scores are developed from a scale with possible maximum scores of -12 and $+12$.

For example, a −12 score would result on the domestic policy scale if a voter always referred to domestic policy when asked what he liked about the Democratic party and candidate, gave the same response when asked what he disliked about the Republican party and candidate, and never found anything in the arena of domestic policy which he liked about the Republicans or their candidate or which he disliked about the Democratic party or candidate. The maximum positive score, +12, would result from the opposite evaluations. Only the first three responses to the open-ended questions are included. The scores were constructed through use of the COUNT procedure, as described in Norman Nie and C. Hadlai Hull, *SPSS: Statistical Package for the Social Sciences, Update Manual* (Chicago: National Opinion Research Center, 1972), pp. A012-076-01 or A-012-076-03.

[11]Cf. Gerald Pomper, *Elections in America* (New York: Dodd, Mead, 1968), Chap. 7; David Mayhew, *Party Loyalty Among Congressmen* (Cambridge: Harvard University Press, 1966).

[12]Richard Scammon and Ben Wattenberg, *The Real Majority* (New York: Coward-McCann, 1970), pp. 41, 97.

[13]For an attempt to explain the 1969 election while saving the book's thesis, see *ibid.*, pp. 233-238.

[14]See Richard Boyd, "Popular Control of Public Policy: A Normal Vote Analysis of the 1968 Election," *American Political Science Review*, LXVI (June, 1972), 435-448.

[15]*Newsweek*, LXXXIV (August 19, 1974), 15.

[16]See Leon Festinger, *A Theory of Cognitive Dissonance* (Stanford: Stanford University Press, 1968).

[17]Compare these results to those reported on p. 36 above.

[18]Stanley Kelley, Jr., and Thad Mirer, "The Simple Act of Voting," *American Political Science Review*, LXVIII (June, 1974), 588.

[19]Key, p. 61.

[20]The method used to derive Figure 7.1 is adapted from *The American Voter*, p. 129. As in that work, the mean position of each partisan group on the dimensions is divided by its standard deviation, to lessen differences in the means that result simply from the number of responses. In the earlier work, all of the lines are consistently parallel.

[21]The method replicates that of Donald Stokes, as explained in the Appendix to "Some Dynamic Elements in Contests for the Presidency," *American Political Science Review*, LX (March, 1966), 27 f. Recodings of the original variables have produced some differences from the results reported there for 1960 and 1964. For example, mentions of the candidates in evaluations of the parties are coded here as personal references. In 1964, this change substantially increases the effect of the "Democratic candidate" dimension on the vote.

[22]See the text of the televised debates by the candidates, in Sidney Kraus, ed., *The Great Debates* (Bloomington: Indiana University Press, 1962), pp. 348-430.

[23]Theodore White, *The Making of the President 1964* (New York: Atheneum Publishers, 1965), Chap. 12.

[24]Philip Converse, Aage Clausen, and Warren Miller, "Electoral Myth and Reality: The 1964 Election," *American Political Science Review*, XLIX (June, 1965), 332.

[25]See Walter Dean Burnham, "Election 1968: The Abortive Landslide," *Transaction*, VI (December, 1968), 18-24; Philip Converse, Warren Miller, Jerrold Rusk, and Arthur Wolfe, "Continuity and Change in American Polities: Parties and Issues in the 1968 Election," *American Political Science Review*, LXIII (December, 1969), 1083-1105. Using different methods, Boyd (above, n. 14), pp. 429-449, finds that the major influences on the 1968 vote were the Vietnam war, Johnson's record, and some elements of the civil rights issue.

[26]Stokes, "Some Dynamic Elements in Contests for the Presidency," p. 20.

[27]Richard Trilling, "Party Image, Party Identification and Partisan Realignment" (mimeo, 1974), pp. 25-28.

[28]Barbara Hinckley, Richard Hofstetter, and John Kessel, "Information and the Vote: A Comparative Election Study," *American Politics Quarterly*, II (April, 1974), 142.

[29]Donald Stokes, "Spatial Models of Party Competition," in Angus Campbell, Philip

Converse, Warren Miller, and Donald Stokes, *Elections and the Political Order* (New York: Wiley, 1966), pp. 170-174.

[30]Trilling, "Party Image and Partisan Change," p. 14 ff.

[31]Compare these results to those achieved through ordinal correlation in Chapter 2. See p. 36 f. above and Table 2.6.

[32]Cf. Arthur Miller, Warren Miller, Alden Raine, and Thad Brown, "A Majority Party in Disarray: Policy Polarization in the 1972 Election," a paper presented to the annual meeting of the American Political Science Association (1973), p. 67.

CHAPTER 8 / FROM CONFUSION TO CLARITY

[1]Edmund Burke, *Thoughts on the Cause of the Present Discontents* (1770), in *The Works of Burke* (London: Oxford University Press, 1906), II, 82.

[2]This conception of political parties is developed by Anthony Downs, *An Economic Theory of Democracy* (New York: Harper, 1957), Chap. 2; Joseph Schumpeter, *Capitalism, Socialism and Democracy* (New York: Harper, 1942), Chap. 22; and Judson James, *American Political Parties in Transition* (New York: Harper and Row, 1974), Chap. 1.

[3]The differences in wording consist largely of changes in form. In 1956 and 1960, the questions were asked as statements with which the respondent could agree or disagree (and also indicate the intensity of his opinion), for example, "if cities and towns around the country need help to build more schools, the government in Washington ought to give them the money they need." In 1964 and 1968, the respondent was offered a choice between two policies, each of which was advocated by "some people," for example, "the government in Washington should help towns and cities provide education," or "this should be handled by the states and local communities." There are two differences in wording of possible substance. In 1956 and 1960, the question dealing with full employment asks whether or not "the government in Washington ought to see to it that everybody who wants to work has a job and a good standard of living," while the later alternative does not include "who wants to work." In the earlier surveys, the question on racial equality asks whether, "If Negroes are not getting fair treatment in jobs and housing, the government should see to it that they do," while in later years the question is more narrowly presented as dealing with jobs alone. The differences in 1972 questions are discussed further in the text.

[4]The substantive content of these programs has often been tied to the procedural emphasis on federal government action. As John Kessel suggests, this may complicate analysis. See his "Comments: The Issues in Issue Voting," *American Political Science Review*, LXVI (June, 1972), 459-465.

[5]Angus Campbell, Philip Converse, Warren Miller, and Donald Stokes, *The American Voter* (New York: Wiley, 1960), Chap. 9.

[6]To increase comparability, answers to these items were divided into three groups, with positions 1-3 grouped as "liberal," positions 5-7 grouped as "conservative," and position 4 disregarded as purely neutral.

[7]The answers of 1956 respondents can be found in Table 8.3 of *The American Voter*, p. 182. It might be argued that 1956 voters were far more issue-conscious than the data reveal, but that they were thinking about different issues from those raised by the parties or the survey. This argument seems hardly plausible, since it would require a degree of ideological originality for which there is no evidence among any mass public.

[8]*Ibid*, p. 182.

[9]The perceptions of party are asked in different ways in the four surveys, so the data must be handled differently. In 1956, respondents were asked which party "is closer to what you want." To locate those who believe the Democrats are liberal on federal aid to education, for example, one must combine those who favor the policy and think the Democrats are closer to their own position, with those who oppose the policy and think the Republicans are closer. In 1960, 1964, and 1968, the question was asked in a straightforward manner, "which party is

244 / VOTERS' CHOICE

likely to favor federal aid to education?" The 1972 survey, using proximity measures, is discussed below.

[10]The method is computationally simple. The location of the Republican party on the particular issue was subtracted from the location attributed to the Democratic party. Any nonzero result, whether positive or negative, meant that the respondent saw a party difference on that issue. A negative result meant that the respondent viewed the Democratic party as more liberal; a positive result, that he believed the Republicans more liberal.

[11]Cf. p. 58 f. and Table 3.6.

[12]The Vietnam war issue will be separately considered in the next chapter.

[13]On the method of cohort analysis, see Neal E. Cutler, "Generation, Maturation and Party Affiliation: A Cohort Analysis," *Public Opinion Quarterly*, XXXIII (Winter, 1969-70), 583-592, and Chap. 5 above

[14]See Bernard Cosman, "Republicanism in the South," *Southwestern Social Science Quarterly*, XLVIII (June, 1967), 13-23; Philip Converse, Warren Miller, Jerrold Rusk, and Arthur Wolfe, "Continuity and Change in American Politics: Parties and Issues in the 1968 Election," *American Political Science Review*, LXIII (December, 1969), esp. 1095-1101; Kevin Phillips, *The Emerging Republican Majority* (Garden City: Doubleday Anchor, 1970), Part III. The Wallace campaign in 1968 did not substantially affect the perceptions of the major parties' positions on civil rights. In noting the parties' stands, a respondent could answer that there was no difference between the major parties, but Wallace did represent a distinctive position. Few respondents chose this option; those who did were included in this analysis with the "no difference" group.

[15]Cf. Chap. 6 above.

[16]Kirk Porter and Donald Johnson, *National Party Platforms*, 3rd ed. (Urbana: University of Illinois Press, 1966), pp. 590-614.

[17]On the development of medicare, civil rights, and other programs in this period, see James Sundquist, *Politics and Policy* (Washington: Brookings Institution, 1968).

[18]Also see Lloyd Free and Hadley Cantril, *The Political Beliefs of Americans* (New Brunswick: Rutgers University Press, 1967), Chap. 3.

[19]Cf. Daniel Bell, *The End of Ideology* (New York: The Free Press, 1960); Herbert Agar, *The Price of Union* (Boston: Houghton Mifflin, 1950); Austin Ranney and Willmoore Kendall, *Democracy and the American Party System* (New York: Harcourt, Brace, 1956), Part VI.

[20]*The American Voter*, p. 232, and Chap. 10.

[21]David Repass has conducted a similar, unpublished analysis of responses of 1964 voters. See "Levels of Rationality Among the American Electorate," a paper presented at the annual meeting of the American Political Science Association (1974).

[22]Philip Converse, "The Nature of Belief Systems in Mass Publics," in David Apter, ed., *Ideology and Discontent* (New York: The Free Press, 1964), Chap. 6. These findings have been directly attacked by John Pierce and Douglas Rose, "Nonattitudes and American Public Opinion: The Examination of a Thesis," *American Political Science Review*, LXVIII (June, 1974), 626-649; 661-666. They have been sharply defended by Converse in his "Comment," *ibid.*, pp. 650-660.

[23]Jack Walker, "A Critique of the Elitist Theory of Democracy," *American Political Science Review*, LX (June, 1966), 285-295.

[24]Norman Nie, with Kristi Andersen, "Mass Belief Systems Revisited: Political Change and Attitude Structure," *Journal of Politics*, XXXVI (August, 1974), 540-591. The cited coefficients are on p. 558.

[25]*Ibid.*, pp. 566-571. Aside from domestic issues, however, there is a decline in consistency among these persons in 1972.

[26]*Ibid.*, p. 571. Similarly high levels of issue constraint are found by Arthur Miller, Warren Miller, Alden Raine, and Thad Brown, "A Majority Party in Disarray: Policy Polarization in the 1972 Election," a paper presented to the annual meeting of the American Political Science Association (1973), pp. 31-37, and by Stephen Bennett, "Consistency Among the

Public's Social Welfare Policy Attitudes in the 1960's," *American Journal of Political Science,* XVII (August, 1973), 544-570.

[27]As in the case of the issue questions, direct comparisons are asked in 1960 and 1968, while a seven-point scale is used in 1972.

[28]This system was most forcefully advocated by the American Political Science Association, Committee on Political Parties, "Toward a More Responsible Two-Party System," *American Political Science Review,* XLIV (September, 1950), Supplement.

[29]Everett Ladd, Jr., and Charles Hadley, *Political Parties and Political Issues: Patterns in Differentiation Since the New Deal* (Beverly Hills: Sage Professional Papers in American Politics, 1973), p. 22 f. Also see Samuel Kirkpatrick and Melvin Jones, "Vote Direction and Issue Change in 1968," *Social Science Quarterly,* LI (December, 1970), 689-705.

[30]Nie, p. 584; cf. Chap. 1 above.

[31]For further supporting argument, see Richard Trilling, "Party Image, Party Identification and Partisan Realignment (mimeo, 1973), pp. 7-12; Nie, pp. 585-587; Walter Dean Burnham, *Critical Elections and the Mainsprings of American Politics* (New York: Norton, 1970), Chap. 5.

[32]Samuel Kirkpatrick, William Lyons, and Michael Fitzgerald, "Candidates, Parties and Issues in the American Electorate: Two Decades of Change (mimeo, 1974), p. 28, forthcoming in *American Politics Quarterly.*

CHAPTER 9 / VARIABILITY IN ELECTORAL BEHAVIOR

[1]This point is emphasized in Philip E. Converse, "The Nature of Belief Systems in Mass Publics," in David Apter, ed., *Ideology and Discontent* (New York: The Free Press, 1964), Chap. 6.

[2]V. O. Key, Jr., with the assistance of Milton C. Cummings, *The Responsible Electorate* (Cambridge: Harvard University Press, 1966); Richard Boyd, "Popular Control of Public Policy: A Normal Vote Analysis of the 1968 Election," *American Political Science Review,* LXVI (June, 1972), 429-449; Norman Nie, with Kristi Andersen, "Mass Belief Systems Revisited: Political Change and Attitude Structure," *Journal of Politics,* XXXVI (August, 1974), 540-591.

[3]Matilda White Riley and Edward E. Nelson, "Research on Stability and Change in Social Systems," in B. Barber and A. Inkeles, eds., *Stability and Social Change* (Boston: Little, Brown, 1971), p. 408.

[4]Richard Merelman, "Electoral Instability and the American Party System," *Journal of Politics,* XXXII (February, 1970), 115-139.

[5]Angus Campbell, Philip Converse, Warren Miller, and Donald Stokes, *The American Voter* (New York: Wiley, 1960), p. 135.

[6]Donald Stokes, "Some Dynamic Elements in Contests for the Presidency," *American Political Science Review,* LX (March, 1966), 19.

[7]Key, p. 6.

[8]David RePass, "Issue Salience and Party Choice," *American Political Science Review,* LXV (June, 1971), 389-400.

[9]Jerrold Rusk and Harold Weisberg, "Perceptions of Presidential Candidates: Implications for Electoral Change," *Midwest Journal of Political Science,* XVI (August, 1972), 388-410.

[10]William R. Shaffer, *Computer Simulations of Voting Behavior* (New York: Oxford University Press, 1972); Ronald Weber et al., "Computer Simulations of State Electorates," *Public Opinion Quarterly,* XXXVI (Winter, 1972-73), 549-565.

[11]Gerald Finch, "Policy and Candidate Choice in the 1968 American Presidential Election," Ph.D. dissertation (University of Minnesota, 1973); David Kovenock, Philip Beardsley, and James Prothro, "Status, Party, Ideology, Issues and Candidate Choice: A Preliminary, Theory-Relevant Analysis of the 1968 American Presidential Election," a paper prepared for the meeting of the International Political Science Association (Munich, 1970).

[12]See John Kessel, "Comment: The Issues in Issue Voting," *American Political Science Review*, LXVI (June, 1972), 459-465.

[13]Benjamin Page and Richard Brody, "Policy Voting and the Electoral Process: The Vietnam War Issue," *American Political Science Review*, LXVI (September, 1972), 985.

[14]*Congressional Quarterly Weekly Report*, XXX (July 15 and August 26, 1972), 1743, 2153.

[15]Cf. Finch, p. 169.

[16]Page and Brody, p. 986.

[17]The amount and direction of difference is the arithmetic difference between the scores given the two candidates on the Vietnam Action Scale. The 1968 figures, and the method, are those of Page and Brody, p. 976.

[18]Page and Brody, p. 983; Finch, p. 75.

[19]These problems are discussed by Richard Brody and Benjamin Page, "Comment: The Assessment of Policy Voting," *American Political Science Review*, LXVI (June, 1972), 450-58.

[20]Kovenock et al., p. 10. Italics omitted.

[21]Finch, pp. 70, 79.

[22]*Ibid.*, p. 118.

[23]The correlation (Pearson r) is .46 between policy position and the vote, and .54 between relative proximity and the vote.

[24]In a multiple regression including standard demographic variables, the beta weight of partisanship declined from .43 to .40, while that for opinion on Vietnam rose from .14 to .25.

[25]For extended explanations and examples, see Hubert Blalock, Jr., *Social Statistics* (New York: McGraw-Hill, 1970), pp. 337-343; *Causal Inferences in Non-Experimental Research* (Chapel Hill: University of North Carolina Press, 1964); and his edited collection, *Causal Models in the Social Sciences* (Chicago: Aldine-Atherton, 1971), See also Donald Stokes, "Compound Paths: An Expository Note," *American Journal of Political Science*, XVIII (February, 1974), 191-214.

[26]Blalock, *Causal Inferences*, p. 8.

[27]See Hugh Forbes and Edward Tufte, "A Note of Caution in Causal Modelling," *American Political Science Review*, LXII (December, 1968), 1258-1264.

[28]Arthur Goldberg, "Discerning a Causal Pattern Among Data on Voting Behavior," *American Political Science Review*, LX (December, 1966), 913-922.

[29]Four important modifications have been made in Goldberg's analysis: (1) mothers, as well as fathers, are included in family characteristics; (2) Independent voters are included; (3) the voters' evaluations of candidates and policy questions have been separated; (4) a separate issue index has been constructed.

[30]A similar measure is used by Stanley Kelley, Jr., and Thad Mirer, "The Simple Act of Voting," *American Political Science Review*, LXVIII (June, 1974), 572-591.

[31]More technically, the first and third variables are derived from a dummy variable regression analysis on five demographic variables of the party identification of the parent or respondent, while the issue index is derived from a dummy variable regression analysis of the vote on the five issues. Party identification is scored as 1 for Republicans, 0 for Democrats, and 0.5 for Independents. Vote—the dependent variable—is scored 1 for Republican, 0 for Democrats.

[32]V. O. Key, Jr., and Frank Munger, "Social Determinism and Electoral Decision: The Case of Indiana," in Eugene Burdick and Arthur Brodbeck, eds., *American Voting Behavior* (New York: The Free Press, 1959), pp. 281-299.

[33]In 1964 and 1972, a comparison of the responses to the "salient issue" and "like-dislike" questions show high correspondence in the issues selected. The salient issue question was not asked in 1956. This high correspondence further indicates the salience of the issues employed. Cf. Repass, "Issue Salience and Party Choice." In 1972, only half of the respondents were asked these questions; only they therefore could be analyzed.

[34]In contrast, see the emphasis on subjective rationality through the use of proximity indexes by Michael Shapiro, "Rational Political Man: A Synthesis of Economic and Social-

Psychological Perspectives," *American Political Science Review,* LXIII (December, 1969), 1106-1119, and Arthur B. Miller, et al., " Majority Party in Disarray: Policy Polarization in the 1972 Election," a paper presented at the annual meeting of the American Political Science Association (1973), pp. 3-38.

[35]*The American Voter,* Chap. 7; Fred Greenstein, *Children and Politics* (New Haven: Yale University Press, 1965), Chap. 4.

[36]Stokes, "Some Dynamic Elements," pp. 20-22.

[37]For techniques that permit assumptions of two-way causation, see Blalock, *Causal Models in the Social Sciences,* Part III.

[38]The significant paths (p<.001) were the same in each of the three-elections, with the exception in 1972 of FSPP/RSPP. This path is retained as a dashed line in the 1972 diagram solely for comparability.

[39]Reliance on the 1956 data is evident in both *The American Voter* and in a later book by the same authors, *Elections and the Political Order* (New York: Wiley, 1966). The influence of these works is also evident in such subsequent research as William H. Flanigan, *Political Behavior of the Electorate* (Boston: Allyn and Bacon, 1968, 1972).

[40]Walter Dean Burnham, "American Voting Behavior and the 1964 Election," *Midwest Journal of Political Science,* XII (February, 1968), 1-40.

[41]V. O. Key, Jr., "A Theory of Critical Elections," *Journal of Politics,* XVII (February, 1955), 3-18; Walter Dean Burnham, *Critical Elections and the Mainsprings of American Politics* (New York: Norton, 1970).

[42]Goldberg, p. 919.

[43]In this case, the indirect path is obtained by multiplying the following: ISSI/CE $\bullet$ CE/RV.

[44]With RPI as the dependent variable, the following compound path coefficients result:

	FSPP/RSPP/RPI	FSSP/FPI/RPI
1956	.251	.155
1964	.152	.121
1972	.005	.131

For explanation of these coefficients, see the text.

[45]See Warren E. Miller and Donald E. Stokes, "Constituency Influence in Congress," in *Elections and the Political Order,* Chap. 16, for another use of compound path coefficients. For general discussion, see Blalock, *Causal Models in the Social Sciences,* Part II.

[46]Note the argument of H. Daudt, *Floating Voters and the Floating Vote* (Leiden: Stenfert Kroese, 1961), p. 94.

[47]This conclusion is in keeping with new findings in developmental psychology, where many heretofore hypothesized "maturational" differences, such as cognitive abilities and intelligence levels, are now viewed as products of "generational" differences. See K. Warner Schaie and C. R. Crother, "A Cross-Sectional Study of Age Changes in Cognitive Behavior," *Psychological Bulletin,* LXX, No. 6 (1968), 671-680.

[48]See Blalock, *Social Statistics,* Chap. 20.

[49]The correlation ratio is .770 for 1956-64 and .784 for 1956-72, with the election years considered as the columns in the analysis of variance. The ratio is a stark zero for the comparison of 1964-72, indicating the great similarity of results within age cohorts in this pair.

[50]Stanley Kelley, Jr., *Political Campaigning* (Washington: The Brookings Institution, 1960), p. 52.

[51]*Ibid.*

[52]Key, *The Responsible Electorate,* p. 7.

[53]For contrasting views of 1964, see Philip Converse, Aage Clausen, and Warren Miller, "Electoral Myth and Reality: The 1964 Election," *American Political Science Review,* LIX (June, 1965), 330-335, and David Segal, "Partisan Realignment in the United States: The Lesson of the 1964 Election," *Public Opinion Quarterly,* XXXII (Fall, 1968), 441-444.

[54]Walter Bagehot, "Introduction to the Second Edition" (1872), *The English Constitution* (Garden City: Doubleday Dolphin), p. 18.

[55]Key, *The Responsible Electorate,* p. 7.

CHAPTER 10 / THE NEW AMERICAN POLITICS

[1]Rowland Evans, Jr., and Robert D. Novak, "Jerry Ford: The Eisenhower of the Seventies?" *Atlantic,* CCXXXIV (August, 1974), 25-32.

[2]The secretary of defense took precautions against unauthorized military action, but none was even contemplated. What does *not* happen is often most revealing of the character of a nation's politics. See *The New York Times,* August 25, 1974.

[3]Sidney Verba and Norman Nie, *Participation in America* (New York: Harper and Row, 1972), pp. 157-160.

[4]See James Rosenau, *Citizenship Between Elections* (New York: The Free Press, 1974).

[5]Peter Eisinger, "Racial Differences in Protest Participation," *American Political Science Review,* LXVIII (June, 1974), 600.

[6]*Congressional Quarterly Weekly Report,* XXXI (December 8, 1973), p. 3214 f.

[7]For a different emphasis, see Daniel Elazar, *American Federalism: A View From the States,* 2nd ed. (New York: Thomas Y. Crowell, 1972).

[8]Joel Aberbach and Jack Walker, "The Meanings of Black Power," *American Political Science Review,* LXIV (June, 1970), 367-388.

[9]This is the classic picture of James Madison, *The Federalist,* No. 10, and David B. Truman, *The Governmental Process* (New York: Knopf, 1951).

[10]Norman Nie, with Kristi Andersen, "Mass Belief Systems Revisited: Political Change and Attitude Structure," *Journal of Politics,* XXXVI (August, 1974), 540-591.

[11]Samuel Huntington, *Political Order in Changing Societies* (New Haven: Yale University Press, 1968), p. 24.

[12]Arthur Kornhauser, *The Politics of Mass Society* (New York: The Free Press, 1959), p. 32.

[13]*Congressional Quarterly Weekly Report,* XXXII (February 23, 1974), 440. In 158 districts, Nixon won while the Republican candidate lost. In an additional 35 districts, Nixon won but there was no Republican candidate.

[14]See Donald Robinson, "Presidents and Party Leadership," a paper presented to the annual meeting of the American Political Science Association (1974).

[15]Testimony of Gordon Strachan, on July 23, 1973, in the *Hearings* before the Select Committee on Presidential Campaign Activities, U.S. Senate, 93rd Congress, First Session, Book VI, pp. 2483-2485.

[16]Walter Dean Burnham, "Rejoinder," *American Political Science Review,* LXVIII (September, 1974), 1057.

[17]George Reedy, "On the Isolation of Presidents," in Rexford Tugwell and Thomas Cronin, *The Presidency Reappraised* (New York: Praeger, 1974), p. 123. Cf. Reedy, *The Twilight of the Presidency* (New York: World, 1970), Chap. 9.

[18]Reedy, "On the Isolation of Presidents," p. 123.

[19]For extended discussion of the press, see Emmet Hughes, *The Living Presidency* (New York: Coward, McCann, and Geoghegan, 1973), pp. 156-166.

[20]John Mitchell's Watergate defense can be read in this way. See U.S. Senate, Select Committee on Presidential Campaign Activities, 93rd Congress, First Session, July 10, 1973-July 12, 1973: Book IV, pp. 1601-1681, and Book V, pp. 1816-1938.

[21]Bernard Bailyn, *The Origins of American Politics* (New York: Vintage, 1970), pp. 28-30. Also see Lewis Namier, *The Structure of Politics at the Accession of George III* (London: MacMillan, 1929), 2 vols.

[22]Edmund Burke, *Thoughts on the Cause of the Present Discontents* (1770), in *The Works of Burke* (London: Oxford University Press, 1906), II, 79.

[23]Richard Hofstadter, *The Idea of a Party System* (Berkeley: University of California Press, 1970), p. 6. Italics omitted.

[24]See Vicki Semel, *At the Grass Roots in the Garden State* (Cranbery, N.J.: Associated University Presses, 1975).

[25]See John Kenneth Galbraith, *The Modern Industrial State* (Boston: Houghton Mifflin, 1967), Chaps. 26, 27.

[26]President Gerald Ford's remarks at his inauguration, *Congressional Quarterly Weekly Report*, XXXII (August 17, 1974), 2211.

[27]Albert Hadley Cantril and Charles Roll, *Hopes and Fears of the American People* (New York: Universe Books, 1971), p. 53.

[28]U.S. House of Representatives, Committee on the Judiciary, Report No. 93-1305, *Impeachment of Richard M. Nixon, President of the United States* (1974), pp. 1-4.

[29]James Madison, *The Federalist*, No. 51 (New York: Modern Library, 1941), p. 337.

[30]Timothy A. Tilton, "The Social Origins of Liberal Democracy: The Swedish Case," *American Political Science Review*, LXVIII (June, 1974), 561-571.

[31]*The New York Times Co.* vs. *U.S.*, 29 L. Ed. 2d. 822 (1971).

[32]*Nixon* vs. *U.S.*, 41 L. Ed. 2d. 1039 (1974).

[33]For provisions of the budget reform, see *Congressional Quarterly Weekly Report*, XXXII (June 15, 1974), 1591-1593.

[34]*Congressional Quarterly Weekly Report*, XXXII (October 12, 1974), 2896 f.

[35]Huntington, p. 91.

[36]For changes by the House Democrats, see *Congressional Quarterly Weekly Report*, XXXII (December 7, 1974), 3247.

[37]For provisions of the new federal law, see Congressional Quarterly Weekly Report, XXXII (October 5, 1974), 2691. For recent state legislation, see *ibid.* (August 31, 1974), 2360-2365.

[38]For further discussion, see David Broder, *The Party's Over* (New York: Harper and Row, 1972), Chap. 10. Also see John Saloma and Frederick Sontag, *Parties* (New York: Knopf, 1972).

[39]American Political Science Association, Committee on Political Parties, "Toward a More Responsible Two-Party System," *American Political Science Review*, XLIV (September, 1950), Supplement, pp. 91-96.

[40]Walter Dean Burnham, *Critical Elections and the Mainsprings of American Politics* (New York: Norton, 1970), Chap. 5.

[41]See Arthur Miller, Warren Miller, Alden Raine, and Thad Brown, "A Majority Party in Disarray: Policy Polarization in the 1972 Election," a paper presented to the annual meeting of the American Political Science Association (1973), p. 75 f.

[42]See Everett Ladd, "The Dynamic of Contemporary American Electoral Politics" (mimeo, 1974).

[43]James Sundquist, *Dynamics of the Party System* (Washington: The Brookings Institution, 1973), p. 373.

AUTHOR INDEX

SUBJECT INDEX

DATE DUE

PRINTED IN U.S.A.